The
BIBLE
COOKBOOK

The
BIBLE
COOKBOOK

By MARIAN MAEVE O'BRIEN

Illustrated by DORIS HALLAS

THE BETHANY PRESS, St. Louis

MY FAITH

For I am sure
that neither death, nor life,
nor angels, nor principalities,
nor things present, nor things to come,
nor powers, nor height, nor depth,
nor anything else in all creation,
will be able to separate us
from the love of God. . . .

—Romans 8:38-39

Someone has said that there is always one person, other than the author, without whom a book would never have been written. In the case of this book, there are three: Darrell Wolfe, who first broached the idea to me and who has been so kind about developing it since; Estelle Hess, whose cheerfulness and helpfulness in research can never be measured; and Tom O'Brien, the husband without whose patience and understanding none of my ventures would come to fruition.

M.M.O'B.

7

CONTENTS

GENESIS

TWO THINGS, our faith and our food, are more closely
bound up with our daily living than any others. And since this
book was conceived, I have marveled over and over at the
strength of the link between food for the body and food for the
soul. How much of joy, of sorrow, of love, of memory is marked
by feasting and fasting, and has been since time began! And
how wonderful it is to find, as we turn to the Bible for comfort,
for courage, for inspiration, and for fortitude, that even in this
greatest of all Messages, a great deal of concern is expressed
for our daily food and drink!

Food was an important facet of biblical life; important
enough that we read that following the resurrection while Jesus
was at table at Emmaus, "He took the bread and blessed, and
broke it, and gave it to them. And their eyes were opened and
. . . he was known to them in the breaking of the bread."
(Luke 24:30, 35.)

Then, when his followers refused to believe that he had re-
turned even in his actual presence and when he had shown
them the wounds, he convinced them by the act of eating. He
said, "Have you here anything to eat?" And they offered him
a piece of broiled fish and he ate it before them.

Later when Peter and the other fishermen failed to catch anything, the risen Christ told them where to cast the nets and
when they brought them ashore full to breaking, he said to
them, "Come and have breakfast." And with these homely
words, they knew him as the Lord. (John 21:4-12.)

He was recognized in the eating of food. What better way
to bring us closer to Christ, then, than to feel that, even at
table, we are trying to live as he did?

True, it is a far cry from the dark-skinned woman of biblical days, kneeling beside her footworn sill to grind her grain between two flat stones, to you and me in our beautiful modern kitchens, glowing with color and crowded with delicacies from all the corners of the world.

But are we, after all, so different? All through this book you will be reminded that the housewives of biblical days turned to food to mark the great days of their lives, enshrined their love and hopes in their homes as they used their crude tools just as today's homemaker thinks of her family's pleasure as she opens the package of biscuit mix to produce a new treat for them.

In our hearts we are the same, and I hope that the likeness will become real to you, too, as you go through these pages.

Marian Maeve O'Brien
Kirkwood, Missouri

August 1st, 1957

He took bread, and giving thanks to
God in the presence of all he broke
it and began to eat.—Acts 27:35

CHAPTER ONE

HEAR OUR GRACE

Be present at our table, Lord;
Be here and everywhere adored.
These creatures bless, and grant that
   we
May feast in Paradise with thee.
   Amen.
                              John Wesley

As the body apart from the spirit is dead, so faith apart from works is dead.—James 2:26

FROM EARLIEST times, the faithful have gathered together to thank God for their blessings; in an old manuscript of a speech given in the first century we find a grace before the meal in the bare statement, "We invoke the gods."

In our own hurried times, grace before meals is even more satisfying since mealtime is often the only moment when the homemaker can bring the whole family together. Here is her life, her existence, complete for once in the day. And as one of the voices is raised to ask God for his blessing on the food and the family, she adds her own whispered thanks for God's goodness in giving her the opportunity to serve.

In this chapter you will find a number of small and, to me, charming graces which I have gathered over the years, and perhaps one of them will appeal to you. Many families have their traditional prayers for the custom and you may, perhaps, have your own. I know of one family in which each of the children asks the blessing on a certain night; another in which each one is expected to compose the grace he says. This brings a very personal effort to the prayer and saves it from becoming a cold ritual—a mere repeating of meaningless words.

DO bring your children into the charmed circle by making this THEIR tradition; it will be something that will stay with them in all the years to come.

Our heavenly Father, thou hast provided us with all good things, so fill our hearts with thy love and grace that we may use every gift to thy glory. Amen.

Thou hast given so much to us, give one thing more—a grateful heart. Amen.

George Herbert
(1593-1633)

Thank you, God, for all our blessings and especially for sending me the one I asked you for this morning.

From a three-year-old in Dallas, Texas

Dear God, bless those who bear the hardship of famine in humility and share fullness and plenty with their neighbors. Wrap beneath the fold of thy mantle of protection those borne to us out of the fullness of trusting hearts, and care for those who wander from home in anger.

From an ancient Hawaiian Food Prayer

Blessing and glory and wisdom and thanksgiving and honor and power and might be to our God for ever and ever!

Revelation 7:12

First, I thank my God through Jesus Christ for all of you, because your faith is proclaimed in all the world.

Romans 1:8

Master of life, make our table companionship a revelation of thy presence, and turn our daily bread into the bread of Life. Amen.

O God, we give thanks for our family. Help us learn to live and work and play in our home as followers of our Lord, Jesus Christ.

From Grace Church, Kirkwood, Missouri

O Lord, I pray thee to bless all that I do this day. Accept it as an act of worship and give me grace to find thee in every task and duty, however dull and small it may be. Amen.

O God, bless, reward, and keep all mothers in your loving care. Amen.

We thank thee, our heavenly Father, for thy care over us, and pray that thou wilt bless this food to our use. Amen.

It is good to give thanks to the LORD,
   to sing praises to thy name, O Most High. Amen.

            Psalm 92:1

O loving Father, make us all thy true and happy children, and fill this house with the gladness of thy presence. Amen.

We thank thee, Father, for the love that has kept us together during another day and for granting us the full measure of happiness that comes from the knowledge that you are with us.

> Let all of us, in full accord,
> Give grateful thanks unto the Lord;
> A very kind and gracious Lord
> Who gives us more than our reward.
>
>   From an old New England schoolbook

> We thank thee, then, O Father,
> For all things bright and good,
> The seed-time and the harvest,
> Our life, our health, our food.
>
>   Matthias Claudius

> Father, we thank Thee for love.
> We thank Thee for food.
> We thank Thee for work.
> We thank Thee for understanding.
> Keep our hearts humble, please,
> That we may never forget
> From whence all this comes.

Father of all Mercies, we would lift our hearts unto Thee in Thanksgiving, for Thy abundant goodness to us. Amen.

> It is very nice to think
> The world is full of meat and drink,
> With little children saying grace
> In every Christian kind of place.
>   Robert Louis Stevenson

> By Thy hand must all be fed;
> We thank Thee, Lord,
> For daily bread. Amen.
>   Anonymous

> Dear Father, bless the circle around this table.
> Keep it alive with love,
> Strong with faith,
> And grateful for the
> Blessings which enrich it.

> For all the glory of the Way,
> For Thy protection night and day,
> For rooftree, fire and bed and board,
> For friends and home, we thank Thee, Lord.
>   Canon Riley

We thank thee, O Father, for the food on our table, for the mother who prepared it with love, for the father who serves it with faith, for the children who, by your grace, eat it with love and gratitude. Amen.

Dear God, all this day is thine. Help me to plan it so that every task will be completed with love and faith, so that I may serve thee in the small things as well as the large.

Morning prayer from a girl in Little Rock, Arkansas

Dear God, our Father, we thank thee for the meat and drink and for Mommy and Daddy who you put here to watch over us for you. We thank thee for our teachers, too, and may you make them more kind and understanding.

From a ten-year-old in Phoenix, Arizona

Dear Father, I thank thee for my family, gathered round this table once again in health and happiness; for the health to work to earn the food that we need; for the privilege of serving them and, through them, thee.

From a housewife in Chicago, Illinois

May the blessed One . . . bless us.

Anonymous

Dear Father, I thank thee for giving me the strength I needed to complete this day. Give me, please, the serenity needed for tomorrow, and the knowledge of your presence that will make even the dull tasks glisten.

From a mother of five in Springfield, Illinois

Dear God, our Father, this was a happy day. Bless me, please, as I sleep, and help me to understanding of all those around me, so that tomorrow will be a happy day, too.

Evening prayer from a family in New Haven, Connecticut

How precious is thy steadfast love,
O God!
The children of men take refuge
in the shadow of thy wings.

Psalm 36:7

Some have meat but cannot eat;
Some could eat but have no meat;
We have meat and can all eat;
Blest, therefore, be God for our meat.

The author of this little prayer, known as the "Selkirk Grace," is unknown; it is from a manuscript of about 1650.

Behold, I stand at the door and knock; if any one hears my voice and opens the door, I will come in to him and eat with him.—Revelation 3:20

CHAPTER TWO

MEALS

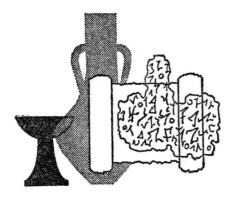

When Jesus lived on earth, he loved to come into people's homes to share a meal and to bless the family. Let's prepare every meal, today, as though he were to be our guest.

Whatever your task, work heartily, as serving the Lord, and not men.—Colossians 3:23

YOU AND I in our shining kitchens planning three meals a day to keep our families healthy and happy are not so very far removed from the woman who gave Jesus a bit of food as he paused in his travels through the countryside. Then, the character of the work being done determined the time of meals; the small morning meal taken by boys at cockcrow before they went out into the fields was a kind of pancake, spread with honey and cheese and then rolled up for easy eating.

The natural pause during the noonday heat suggested that break in the day as a convenient dining hour when the meal served was simple and frugal as well as unceremonious—probably nothing more than pieces of bread dipped in a bowl of vinegar and a handful of parched corn. In the cities this meal varied from a piece of bread to quite an elaborate spread: either hot or cold fish, fowl, butcher's meat, vegetables, fruit, and so forth.

The evening meal was the main one of the day. In the country, the housewife simply spread the board with such foods as cheese, milk, honey, pickled olives, fresh figs, and grapes. She may have added a few vegetables cooked in oil or water, perhaps with a bit of mutton.

In the city the evening meal, or Cena, consisted of much greater variety. The first course was very similar to our appetizer course. Then came the meal proper: roasted meats, fish in many separate dishes, and a wide variety of fruits and vegetables. After the Cena was finished a grace after meals was said, and after the grace came the dessert—various pastries and fresh and dried fruits.

Actually our taking of food hasn't changed basically since people supped with Christ. Let us try to prepare every single meal today with love and tenderness and understanding, so that if he were to sit down with us, he would feel welcome.

Ten Commandments for Planning Good Meals

1. Plan every meal so that you have time to cook and serve it properly, without fuss.

2. Make sure daily meals are adequate by including one from each of the "basic seven" foods which are so widely publicized.

3. Shop thriftily to take advantage of seasonal foods, price specials, and government-designated "plentifuls."

4. Resolve not to stick too closely to old meal patterns; the main course at dinner doesn't always have to be meat and potatoes, you know.

5. Plan meals with an eye to color; white cauliflower on a plate next to white fish will look dead, whereas sunny carrots would have made the whole serving a joy to behold.

6. Plan ahead. A dinner planned on the way home from a guild meeting or before the open refrigerator will taste like what it is—an afterthought.

7. Avoid monotony as you would the plague.

8. Keep an index of favorite recipes; planning meals can be an adventure if you have a stock of ideas available.

9. Save time and money by planning on cooking double quantities for use in future meals.

10. Serve meals gaily with a smile on your lips. Beef stew served with love tastes better than Boeuf Bordelaise served in a temper.

There they made him a supper; Martha served.
—John 12:2

Some records of actual meals served in biblical times have been preserved for us. The following menu gives us a perfect picture of the midday meal of a middle-class family in Jerusalem in the first century:

Fish from the Lake
Locusts Baked in Flour or Honey
Onions
Butcher's Meat
Beverages
For Dessert
the Cheapest of Fruit—Probably
Grapes or Figs

In contrast, the menu of a priestly inauguration which took place between 73 and 63 B.C. is so elaborate as to be almost unbelievable. The first course is written as:

Sea Urchins
Plain Oysters *ad libitum*
Two Sorts of Mussels
Thrush on Asparagus
A Fatted Hen
A Ragout of Oysters and Mussels
Black and White Chestnuts

The second course consisted of:

Udders of Sows
A Pig Head
Fricassee of Fish and Sow's Udders
Two Kinds of Ducks, Boiled
Hares, a Meal Pudding
Pecentine Bread

The record of the sweet served to finish this meal has apparently been lost. This was truly a festival of some sort; a banquet celebrating some great occasion at which Caesar himself probably presided, otherwise a writer of four or five centuries later would hardly have troubled to record it.

I am going to suggest here some simple meals which have always been favorites in our house; you will find them as classic as biblical meals, and as modern as tomorrow. I have tried to use every modern innovation in food that I know in order to make preparation easier for you, but you will find all the tried and true favorites included, even though I have rechristened them with biblical names!

> * Meals marked with one asterisk will take a little extra time in the kitchen—but they are worth it.

> ** Meals marked with two asterisks will take less than an hour—and be delicious.

> *** Meals marked with three asterisks will be on the table in less than thirty minutes—and be so good that the family will be cheering!

You will notice that I have divided the meals in this book into three seasons—Seed Time, Harvest Time, and Cold. It is a natural division of seasons. Recipes are on pages indicated in parentheses.

> *Do not boast about tomorrow,*
> *for you do not know what a day may bring*
> *forth.—Proverbs 27:1*

Seed Time

Israeli Herb Soup (43) ***	Cheesed Veal Cutlet (72) ***
Meat and Potato Cakes (66)	Eggplant Casserole (136)
Braised Carrots (127)	Perfection Salad (170)
Broccoli Salad (165)	Oatmeal Nut Bread (218)
Fruit Custard (202)	Black Devil's Food (249)

Peppered Pig (79) **
Gnocchi (189)
Lettuce Salad (164)
Coffee Creme (201)

Lamb with Rice (74)	Supper Salad (91) ***
Lettuce au Gratin (142)	Onion Pancakes (232)
Sweet-sour Beets (120)	Herbed Carrots (128)
Golden Crescents (225)	Relishes
Sweetmeat Cake (245)	Baked Bananas (276)

Dried Beef Curry ***
on Rice (142)
Buttered Peas (148)
Cauliflower Salad (129)
Fruit Ribbons (279)

Pickled Chicken (90)*	Veal Rolls (70) **
Spicy Lentils (204)	Barley Kasha (188)
Asparagus with Cream (117)	Cheesed Chard (121)
Apple Pudding (277)	Lemon Custard (108)

*Genesis 8:22 is the earliest mention of a knowledge of
the seasons in the Bible.*

Lamb Kabobs (75) ***   Veal Croquettes (71) ***
Rice with Mushrooms (100)   Sweet-sour Beets (120)
Cauliflower Crisp (129)   Beans with Gravy (118)
Wilted Greens (164)   Corn-Nut Muffins (230)
Raisin Cream Pie (262)   Rhubarb Custard Pie (262)

Noodle-Cheese Casserole (97) **
Cauliflower Fritters (130)
Blueberry Cheese Salad (166)
Cherry Relish (269)
Pudding with Sugar Shapes (252)

Chicken Loaf (92)   Rice Ring (198) **
Olive Sauce (92)   with Crab Flakes
Sweet-sour Cabbage (125)   Stuffed Cucumbers (134)
Garden Salad (170)   Carolina Salad (167)
Cocoanut Torte (275)   Fruit Charlotte (273)

Hearty Chowder (46) ***
Chunks of Challah (211)
with Minute Preserves (268)
Relish Platter
Wheat Sweet (280)

Hot Crab Salad (171) **   Barley Consommé (187) **
Beets with Cream (120)   Garden Spinach (138)
Light Biscuits (224)   Curried Cheese Salad (163)
Herbed Peas (148)   Scones (228)
Blueberry Crisp (276)   Fruit Ice with Carrot Cookies
(251)

In all your ways acknowledge him, and he will make straight your paths.—Proverbs 3:6

Harvest Time

Rich Beef Stew (67) *
Buttered Noodles
Broccoli with Soy Sauce (122)
Garden Salad (170)
Melon Peach Compote

Curried Pork Chops
with Pineapple (80) **
Spiced Spinach (139)
Polenta (206)
Apple Pudding (277)

Potted Beef (69) ***
Braised Celery (130)
Lettuce Ripple (162)
Rich Egg Bread (214)
Plum Pudding (200)

Lamb with Red Noodles (77) *
Coleslaw with Cheese (100)
Rye Crackers
Fruit Coffeecake (222)

Herbed Fricassee (90) **
Vegetables with Pasta (193)
Wilted Greens (164)
Beans with Gravy (118)
Fruit Pudding (271)

Veal Loaf Supreme (72)*
with Sauce Allemande (178)
Waffled Fritters (136)
Perfection Salad (170)
Buttermilk Sherbet (278)

Barbecued Brisket (65) *
with Carrot Relish (128)
Eggplant Casserole (136)
Fruit Salad (170)
Custard Pudding (106)

Broiled Haddock (59) ***
Herbed Scramble (119)
Polenta (206)
Curried Cheese Salad (163)
Plum Pudding (200)

"Go into all the world and preach the gospel to the whole creation."—Mark 16:15

Kettle Meal (88) *** Best-ever Meat Loaf (106) **
Mixed Green Salad (311) Stuffed Zucchini (150)
Rich Egg Bread (214) Johnny Cake (229)
Sundae Cake (240) Soufflé Salad (166-167)
Parish Cake (241)

Cheese-stuffed Peppers (98) **
Cabbage and Bacon (126)
Holiday Salad (166)
Corn-Nut Muffins (230)
Upside-down Cake with Topping (105)

Quick Bologna Supper (143) *** Sweet and Sour (54) ***
Baked Acorn Squash (149) Luncheon Ring (123)
Brown Bread (220) Carolina Salad (167)
Waldorf Salad (166) Fruit Puffs (225)
Date-Nut Candy (274) Raisin Pudding (196)

Savory Liver (194) **
Field Greens with Garlic
and Onion
Corn-Nut Muffins (230)
Layered Pie (260)

Spiced Chicken (89) * Cabbage-Beef Rolls (124)*
Rice Egg and Lemon Sauce (124)
Stewed Celery (131) Cauliflower Salad (129)
Cottage Cheese Molds (170) Citrus Bowl
Maple Nut Chiffon Cake (243) Nut Cream Cake (247)

*God is love, and he who abides in love abides in God,
and God abides in him.—1 John 4:16*

Cold

Lentil Stew (66) *
Braised Lettuce (141)
Citrus Bowl with French
Dressing (157)
Brown Bread (220)
Lemon Pudding with
Almond Spice Cookies (253)

Flank Steak Broil (65)
Rice Ring (198)
Spiced Spinach (139)·
Green Onions Vinaigrette (158)
Applesauce Cake (246)

Fruited Pot Roast (68)
Vegetable Casserole (140)
Cabbage Slaw with Cooked Dressing (161)
Simnel Cake with Hard Sauce (248)

Veal Stew with
Parsleyed Dumplings (70) *
Curried Cabbage (126)
Perfection Salad (170)
Pumpkin Puddin' Pie (261)

Veal Pot Roast (73) *
Braised Root Vegetables (144)
Herbed Scramble (119)
Wheat Egg Bread (217)
Cherry Cobbler (312)

Pasta Supper (191) ***
Apple Muffins (227)
Green Salad with
Vinegar and Oil
Fruit Ribbons (279)

Sweet-sour Dinner (78) **
Rice Ring (198)
Young Beets
Grapefruit and Orange Salad
(302)
Spice Torte (251)

Tuna Patties (60) ***
Garlic Sauce (179)
Spiced Spinach (139)
Stuffed Date Salad
Ice Cream—Hot Fruit Sauce
(182)

"If you have faith, . . . nothing will be impossible to you."—Matthew 17:20

Cheese Fondue (99) **
with Creamed Salmon
Quick Green Beans (118)
Savory Squash (149)
Canned Figs with Shortbread
(252)

Cabbage-Beef Rolls (124) *
Braised Cucumbers (133)
Rye Bread
Carrot and Raisin Salad
Cherry Upside-Down Cake
(105)

Lamb Pilaf (76) **
Carolina Salad (167)
Bran Buttermilk Biscuits (226)
Honey—Preserves

Cheese Balls (38) ***
Salmon Loaf (56)
Cucumber and Onion Salad
Peas with Tomato (148)
Wheat Sweet (280)

Chicken Salad Supper (169) **
Spoon Bread (228)
Relish Platter (314)
with Cottage Cheese
Sundae Cake (240)

Stuffed Fillets **
with Spinach Stuffing (52)
Tomato Sauce
Rice Squares (202)
Coffee Ice (278)

Onions with Sausage (146)
Herbed Peas (148)
Beet Top Greens (119)
Molded Vegetable Salad (169)
Honey Rice Custard (273)

Shrimp-Stuffed Peppers (56)
Tomato Sauce
Eggplant Stacks (135)
Sliced Cucumbers
Cocoanut Pudding with Coffee
Cookies (254)

It is God's gift to man that every one should eat and drink and take pleasure in all his toil.—Ecclesiastes 3:13

And at mealtime Boaz said to her,
"Come here, and eat some bread,
and dip your morsel in the wine."—
Ruth 2:14

CHAPTER THREE

BEGINNINGS

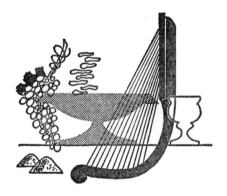

From earliest times, salt has sym-
bolized hospitality, and highly seasoned foods have been a part of the
ceremony of breaking bread with
one's friends.

Let every man be quick to hear, slow to speak, slow to anger.—James 1:19

APPETIZERS, almost exactly as we know them, were an integral part of biblical meals, especially in the cities. In Old Testament times, especially in Rome, a large table was spread with salted dishes to whet the appetite and increase the thirst. This custom persisted into the time of the New Testament when, even in the farm lands where Jesus was teaching, the housewife offered a bowl of vinegar and a piece of bread for dipping, while the guest waited for the table to be laid.

The vinegar that Jesus knew was not of the sort that we use for salads and sauces, but one called *posca,* or *sera,* that the housewife of his time used for making the sharp relishes which she used for appetizers. The caperberry, much resembling the capers which we use in salads today, was preserved in oil and vinegar and eaten before meals as an appetizer. Half-grown grapes, too, were eaten with salt, as were olives, preserved by salting and drying.

The drink which accompanied these small appetizers was handed to each guest in separate bowls or cups, a very different service from that of the food, which was placed on the table in a common dish.

Along the road where Jesus stopped for a bite to eat and a moment of rest from his journeyings, there must have been much gaiety while these small tidbits were being enjoyed and, truly, appetites must have been whetted while the meal proper was made ready.

Cups of oil—a common emblem for gladness and grace of every kind—were passed, and often these contained bits of meat and cracknels (see page 228), crumbled pieces of crisp bread, much as the dips on our party tables do.

"There is nothing better for a man than that he should eat and drink," we read in Ecclesiastes 2:24. And that he should eat and drink with his friends, as Jesus loved to do, is the very essence of enjoyment.

Ten Commandments for Successful Beginnings

1. Remember that appetites are meant to be whetted by appetizers, not satisfied by them.

2. Remember that a canapé or hors d'oeuvre is supposed to be a bite, to be eaten out of hand and easily.

3. Keep first courses a bit on the salty side, for thirst, too, whets the appetite.

4. Remember that soup was a fine first course long before we Americans ever wrestled with a potato chip dipped in cheese.

5. Make a canapé just before serving; food on a piece of limp and soggy toast is an abomination.

6. Avoid repetition as you would sin; a food included in the first course loses all appeal if encountered again later in the meal.

7. As with all food, serve hot ones hot and cold ones cold. Flavors, like love, are disappointing when lukewarm.

8. Use your imagination; scorn a food idea copied from a friend as firmly as you would a copied dress or hat.

9. Hors d'oeuvres, like any other foods, should have a certain balance. Some should be cold, some hot; some bland, some spicy; some crisp, some soft.

10. As always, put some life in it. Lavish care on garnishing, and serve with pride. After all, love and gaiety are the best sauces for appetite.

Let your speech always be gracious, seasoned with salt, so that you may know how you ought to answer every one.
—Colossians 4:6

Hors d'Oeuvres

Olive Bowl
Antipasto Bowl

This is a quick and truly delicious appetizer that I love to serve because it seems to me that this is the very manner in which the housewife of Bible times must have served her first course. I have passed the recipe on to so many guests that it may not be new to you!

1 can tomato paste	½ cup olive oil
1 teaspoon orégano	1 7-ounce jar pickled onions
1 4-ounce can button mushrooms	½ cup tiny whole green beans
1 4-ounce jar stuffed olives, drained	1 7-ounce jar sweet gherkins
	1 can solid pack tuna
	1 can sardines in tomato sauce

Drain the stuffed olives, pickled onions, and sweet gherkins. Combine all the ingredients except the tuna and sardines in a 2-quart bowl. Mix gently. Chill thoroughly. At the same time, chill the tuna and the sardines in the cans. When ready to serve, give the Antipasto one last mix, then add the tuna with its oil, broken into bite-sized pieces, and the sardines with their sauce. Use these mostly for garnish for the top, since they break up easily. Serve very cold, with small plates and one or two pickle forks so that guests may help themselves. Pass a tray of toast or crackers, or even tiny dollar-sized pancakes, which would be the biblical way.

In the beginning was the Word, and the Word was with God, and the Word was God. He was in the beginning with God; all things were made through him, and without him was not anything made that was made.—John 1:1-3

Baruch Puffs
Deviled Puffs

1 8-ounce package cream cheese	1/2 teaspoon baking powder
1 teaspoon onion juice	1 egg yolk
	24 small bread rounds

2 2 1/4-ounce cans deviled ham

Blend together the cheese, onion juice, baking powder, egg yolk and salt to taste. Toast the bread rounds on one side. Spread the untoasted sides with deviled ham, then cover each with a mound of the cheese mixture. Place on a cookie sheet and bake at 375° for 10-12 minutes, or until puffed and brown. Serve hot.

Zayith Stuff
Braunschweiger Roll

This is another little trick which is easier done than described; it will be very popular on your relish tray. Simply place a stuffed olive in the palm of the hand, add about a tablespoonful of braunschweiger, and work the sausage around the olive until it is covered entirely. Roll in minced parsley to give an attractive green color and prevent discoloration of the sausage.

Obededom Nugget
Cheese Balls

1/2 cup grated natural Swiss cheese	1/2 teaspoon prepared mustard
1/2 cup minced ham	1 egg yolk
	1/4 teaspoon salt

1/4 teaspoon pepper

Blend all ingredients thoroughly, rubbing until smooth. Shape into small balls and roll in chopped parsley. Chill and serve on toothpicks.

Salim
Cheese Roll

1 8-ounce package Old English cheese

2 tablespoons chopped onion

3 tablespoons chopped green pepper

3 stuffed olives, chopped

2 tablespoons chopped sour pickle

1 tablespoon pimento, chopped

1 hard-cooked egg, chopped

½ cup cracker crumbs

¼ cup mayonnaise

½ teaspoon salt

Grind or shred the cheese very fine. Add remaining ingredients and rub together until thoroughly blended. Turn out onto a sheet of waxed paper and shape into a roll about 3 inches in diameter. Wrap tightly in the waxed paper and chill overnight. Serve on a cheese board bordered by dark green grape leaves. Pass crackers.

Jordan Squares
Limed Fish

This delicious appetizer employs a method of preparation which has come down to us from Old Testament times. The fish is actually raw but it doesn't taste raw, and you'll find it popular with everyone.

Thaw one package of frozen fillets of haddock or halibut, and cut into neat one-inch squares. Arrange in a Pyrex baking dish or pie plate, and cover with lime or lemon juice. Refrigerate for 2 hours, then rinse well in cold water, drain, and store in the refrigerator. This may be prepared the day before serving; the fish becomes firm and white, as though cooked, and deliciously flavored.

"And" is the word used most in the Bible; it appears 46,227 times.

Burning Bush
Dried Beef Bits

Dried Beef   **8 ounces cream cheese**

Chop the dried beef very fine. Divide the cream cheese into
32 small cubes, then carefully shape each cube into a round.
Toss each ball in the chopped beef until entirely coated. Put
a toothpick through each ball and stick into a grapefruit or a
large apple. Chill until ready to use.

Dips

Artaxerxes Dip
Celery with Anchovy

This is another very ancient appetizer; it draws its distinction from the contrast of very hot sauce with very cold celery.
You can make it in less time than it takes to tell it.

Prepare celery ahead of time by taking off the coarse outer
pieces and splitting the stalks lengthwise into about 6 pieces.
Each piece must have a part of the center, or heart. Chill stone
cold in a pitcher with ice cubes.

To make the sauce, place in a small saucepan a tin of flat
anchovy fillets which have been rinsed in warm water, 1 tablespoon olive oil, and 2 tablespoons herb vinegar. Cook gently,
mashing with a fork, until a smooth sauce results. All this may
be done ahead of time. At serving time put the sauce in a small
dish—a butter warmer over a candle is fine.

Wipe the celery dry and serve separately on a cold platter.
The guests are to dip the cold celery into the hot sauce and
gobble it down. This amount should be sufficient for 4, but it
never is. And since it is so delicious and different and so inexpensive, I make it in large quantities and use it often.

Be doers of the word, and not hearers only.—James 1:22

Taberah Dip
Clam Rarebit

3 tablespoons butter or margarine	¼ pound sharp cheese, cut into small pieces
1 small onion, chopped	4 tablespoons catsup
½ green pepper, chopped	1 tablespoon Worcestershire sauce
1 10½-ounce can minced clams	
1 tablespoon milk	

Drain the clams. Melt the butter in the top of a double boiler, then add the remaining ingredients and cook over hot water, stirring frequently, until the cheese has melted. Check the seasoning. To serve, place in a small casserole or heat-proof dish over a candle warmer and serve hot with rye toast. Serves about 4. This may be made ahead of time.

Sakkuth
Sardine Dip

Combine 1 can boneless, skinless sardines, with the oil; 4 ounces Roquefort or blue cheese; 2 small packages cream cheese; ¼ cup diced green pepper; 1 tablespoon cut chives, and 1 teaspoon prepared mustard. Blend until creamy.

Cracknel Spread
Bacon Spread

Into a small bowl, crumble 8 or 10 strips of bacon which have been cooked crisp and drained. Add ¼ cup cream, ½ pound cream cheese, a thin slice from a small onion, 3 sections Brie or Camembert cheese, a tablespoon of lemon juice, and a dash of cayenne pepper. Rub together until smooth; if you have an electric blender, simply turn everything into the bowl and whirl until smooth. Be sure to use ripe (soft) cheeses. Makes nearly 2 cups.

Jokdeam Spread
Blue Cheese Spread

Blend thoroughly, 2½ ounces blue cheese with ½ pound creamed cottage cheese, 1 tablespoon grated onion, and 6 tablespoons sour cream. Flavor with about a tablespoon of Worcestershire sauce.

Bukki Spread
Clam Spread

One 7-ounce can clams with ¼ cup of the liquor, two 3-ounce packages cream cheese, 2 teaspoons chives or green onion tops, chopped, ¼ teaspoon salt, a teaspoon of Worcestershire sauce, 3 drops Tabasco, a tablespoon lemon juice, and about 3 tablespoons chopped parsley. Makes about 1½ cups. Again, simply put everything into a bowl and blend until smooth.

Soups

Soup is the song of the hearth and the home and, although the word in this form is not found in the Bible, we know that this delicious product of the kettle and the fire was a mainstay of the meals of the time. Try experimenting with some soup ideas of your own, using just what is on hand, as the biblical housewife did; you'll find it inspiring and rewarding.

Jehoash Stew
Haddock Stew

3 pounds fish	1 clove garlic, chopped
salt and pepper	1 carrot, diced
juice of 1 lemon	1 cup chopped celery with
½ teaspoon thyme	leaves
2 medium onions, chopped	2 tablespoons flour

Either fillets or a whole fish may be used; if using the whole fish, stew head and all. Cut fish into five or six pieces. Sprinkle with salt and pepper, lemon juice and thyme, and set aside. Measure about 3 tablespoons oil into a kettle; heat, then add onions, garlic, carrot, and celery and cook, stirring, until golden and tender—about 10 minutes. Put in the fish and cook about 20 minutes more over low heat, adding a bit of water (not more than ½ cup) as it cooks. When the fish is cooked, remove to a serving dish. If the pan juice is quite thin, thicken it with the flour, rubbed smooth in a little cold water. Serve this juice over the fish, with the vegetables.

The Greeks often served this soup as a whole meal; you might add a hearty salad and use it, with crisp bread, for a delicious adventure in eating for your family. Haddock is an excellent choice as the fish, but any fish may be used. Serves 4 or 5.

For a typical Israeli herb soup, strain 2 cups vegetable soup, add ¼ cup herbs and a teaspoon lemon juice, and heat for 5 minutes. Dill, parsley, thyme, marjoram are all good.

Corinth Lentil Soup
Lentil Soup

1 cup dried lentils	¼ teaspoon pepper
2 cups chopped onion	2 cups chopped raw spinach or
2 quarts water	Swiss chard
1 tablespoon salt	1 tablespoon oil
3 tablespoons lemon juice	

Soak the lentils overnight as the package label directs. Rinse several times in cold water. Cook onions and lentils in the water with salt and pepper until the lentils are tender—about 1½ hours. Add the remaining ingredients and cook 20 minutes longer, or until the spinach is tender. Serves 8.

Kanah Soup
Chick-Pea Soup

This pottage, made with chick-peas and a few slivers of whatever green herb the housewife had on hand, was probably the mainstay of many a meal in biblical times. It is delicious and nourishing and a good substitute for meat. I hope you'll try it.

2 pounds chick-peas	3 carrots, diced
1 teaspoon salt	1 tablespoon oil
3 medium onions, chopped	leftover meat

Soak the peas overnight in lukewarm water with the salt. Drain, cover with a soft tea towel, and rub to remove the hulls. Wash off the remaining hulls by running water into the pan; the hulls will rise to the top and may be drained off. Turn the peas into a deep kettle with water to cover. Add a little salt—perhaps another teaspoonful—and set over low heat. When the peas come to a boil, add the remaining ingredients and simmer slowly about 2 hours, or until the peas are soft. Then add the oil and the meat cut into slivers, stir and serve.

Beroea Pottage
Egg Drop Soup

This is the classic Greek "Egg Drop" soup; Paul must have known it well.

6 cups chicken broth from a stewing chicken	6 tablespoons grated Parmesan cheese
½ cup uncooked rice	2 tablespoons chopped parsley
6 egg yolks	6 slices lemon

Heat the chicken broth to boiling, adding salt and pepper to taste. Sprinkle the rice slowly into the boiling broth, and continue cooking about 20 minutes or until the rice is tender. Beat the egg yolks slightly; stir in the Parmesan cheese. Preheat a soup tureen or large bowl by filling with hot water and then draining; place the egg-cheese mixture in the tureen and gradually add the hot soup, stirring constantly. Sprinkle with parsley and serve with a lemon slice in each bowl. Serves 6.

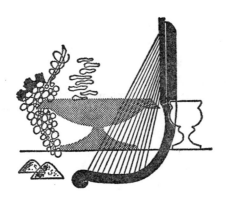

Arnon Cream
Quick Potato Soup

½ bunch green onions
1 tablespoon butter or margarine
1 cup canned or fresh peas

1½ cups water
2 frozen potato patties
2 cups milk
salt and pepper

Chop green onions and tops. Melt the butter in a heavy pan, add the onions and sauté until very lightly browned. Add the water, peas, and potato patties (1 medium potato, grated or chopped, may be substituted for the patties). Bring to a rolling boil. Cook, stirring constantly, about 5 minutes. Add the milk, salt and pepper to taste, and ½ teaspoon savory if you like herbs. Bring to the boiling point, but don't boil. Serves 4.

Jacob's Bowl
Hearty Chowder

1 10½-ounce can minced clams	1 8-ounce can tiny onions
1 16-ounce can corned beef hash	3 cups milk
	2 tablespoons butter

1 16-ounce can cream style corn

Use the clams with their juice; drain the onions. Cut the corned beef hash into 1-inch cubes and the onions into quarters. Combine all ingredients in a saucepan, mix well, and heat, stirring frequently, until just below the boiling point. Serves 6—this is a hearty and delicious chowder, made in minutes.

Let us not love in word or speech but in deed and in truth.—1 John 3:18

They gave him a piece of broiled fish.
—Luke 24:42

CHAPTER FOUR

FISHES OF THE SEA

From the beginning of time, the
sea has been man's magic larder;
with the coming of Christ, the fish
became the symbol of Christianity.

Fight the good fight of the faith; take hold of the eternal life. . . . —1 Timothy 6:12

IT SHOULD be a source of great pleasure to any good cook to read and reread the quotation from Luke which appears on the title page of this chapter. Broiling in biblical times, it is true, may have been different from broiling as we know it, but even so, it is good to be reminded that there are other ways of preparing fish than frying.

Fish was one of the food staples of biblical times; there was a regular industry on the shores of the Sea of Galilee for salting down fish and packing them into barrels, and the products were sold not only in Palestine, but as far west as Rome. At one time the pious fishermen of Tiberias are said to have entered into an agreement not to fish on ANY of the days of the Feasts of Tabernacles and of the Passover, instead of on some of them. The result was a serious shortage of fresh fish, never very plentiful inland at the best of times, so that the public had to fall back on salt fish, or go without altogether.

Today, with frozen food perfected to the point that it is, we can enjoy fish delicacies that the ancients never dreamed of, remembering that we are told, in the dietary laws set out in Deuteronomy, that "Of all that are in the waters you may eat these: whatever has fins and scales you may eat." (Deuteronomy 14:9)

Ten Commandments for Fish Cookery

1. Promise yourself that you will never join the army of sinners who overcook fish. It should be cooked to develop flavor, not to make it tender.

2. Discard with a firm hand that recipe which says "boil the fish." A fish must never be boiled; only poached.

3. If buying fresh fish, look to the eyes. Fish, like young girls, must have bright, clear eyes to be acceptable, and the fish's must bulge.

4. Resolve that no method of cooking will remain unknown to you; once you know broiled fish, you'll wonder why you enjoyed it fried, or if you did.

5. Get acquainted with the whole fish family, now that they're all available everywhere. The next new one you taste may be your favorite.

6. A bay leaf or two adds appeal to any fish. So do rosemary, thyme, and savory. Why neglect any of God's gifts?

7. Give every fish a brisk rubdown with lemon or lime before cooking. This makes him sparkle on the tongue.

8. Remember all the good canned fishes and their endearing qualities, one of which is economy. Use them often.

9. Reserve not fish for Friday alone; the variety of flavors and textures are delicious any day of the week.

10. Above all, approach fish with an open mind; a myriad of new flavors and combinations will reward you.

Did you know that at least four of Jesus' disciples were fishermen?

Abel-maim Mold
Luncheon Mold

1½ tablespoons unflavored gelatin	⅛ teaspoon sugar
1¾ cups cold water	1 teaspoon prepared horse-radish
1 can condensed tomato soup	3 tablespoons lemon juice
1 teaspoon salt	1½ cups cooked or canned fish, flaked
¼ teaspoon pepper	

Soften the gelatin in ½ cup water. Combine the remaining water with the tomato soup and heat to boiling; add the gelatin and stir until dissolved. Add remaining ingredients, except the fish, and chill until slightly thickened—about the consistency of a heavy syrup. Now stir in the flaked fish, pour into a 5-cup mold that has been rinsed in cold water, and chill until set—at least 4 hours. Serves 4.

This is a delightful dish for club or committee meetings, because it may be made ahead of time. It may be varied by changing the flavors; by adding chopped ripe olives, or nuts; or by serving with a dressing of mayonnaise which has been flavored with a teaspoon of curry powder. Or it may be made a bit heartier by adding 1 cup chopped celery or 1 cup chopped, drained cucumbers. Try chilling it in individual molds and serving with broccoli and cheese sauce and hot cornbread, for a pretty and tasty luncheon.

The central message of early Christianity is in Paul's words, "For I delivered to you as of first importance what I also received, that Christ died for our sins in accordance with the scriptures, that he was buried, that he was raised on the third day in accordance with the scriptures."
—1 Corinthians 14:3-4

Fillets Jaffa
Baked Fillets

1 to 1½ pounds fish fillets or steaks	⅛ teaspoon pepper
1 tablespoon salad oil	1¼ cups milk
a pinch of salt	1 or 2 egg yolks
2 tablespoons cornstarch	3 tablespoons lemon juice
¾ teaspoon salt	¼ cup salad oil
	1 can asparagus tips

Thaw the fillets, if frozen. Brush with the salad oil, sprinkle lightly with the salt, then arrange in a buttered shallow baking pan. Bake at 425° for 20 minutes. While the fish is baking, make the sauce. Mix the cornstarch, salt, and pepper in about ¼ cup of the milk until smooth. Turn the remaining milk into a saucepan and place over low heat; stir in the dissolved cornstarch and cook over low heat, stirring constantly, until the sauce thickens and boils. Boil 1 minute, stirring constantly. Remove from the heat; add 1 or 2 tablespoons of hot sauce to the egg yolks, stir until blended, then stir the egg yolk mixture into the remainder of the sauce. Cook about 2 minutes, stirring constantly. Remove from the heat and beat in the lemon juice and salad oil, beating until smooth. Arrange the asparagus around the fish, top with the sauce, and place under the broiler for a moment until lightly browned. Serve at once. Serves 4.

Fillets Koheleth
Stuffed Fillets

2 medium onions, chopped	1 pound fresh spinach or 1 package frozen, cooked and drained
1 tablespoon butter or margarine	
2 pounds fillets, thawed	1 can meatless spaghetti sauce

Cook the onion in the butter until tender but not brown. Spread each fillet with cooked spinach, sprinkle with the onion, roll up, and place in a shallow, buttered baking dish.

Top with the spaghetti sauce. Bake at 400° for about 20-30 minutes or until the fish is flaky when tested with a fork. A nice finish is a dusting of grated cheese over the top, with a minute or two under the broiler to melt it a bit. Serves 4.

Trout Hagar
Trout Kabob

4 fresh or frozen trout	½ teaspoon pepper
lime or lemon juice	24 small bay leaves
1 teaspoon salt	butter or olive oil

Carefully split the trout and take out back and side bones; if this is done carefully, the bones will come out in one piece.

Cut the fish into 1-inch squares, leaving skin on one side of each square. Arrange in a shallow, glass baking pan, cover with lemon or lime juice and place in the refrigerator for an hour or two. The fish will get very firm, as though cooked. Now, drain and arrange on skewers, 8 to 10 pieces on each with a bit of bay leaf between the chunks. Lay the skewers on a shallow broiling pan, brush with butter or oil, and broil, turning several times, about 5 minutes on each side. When cooked, brush with more butter or oil and garnish with chopped parsley. These skewers may be cooked on the outdoor grill. Biblical and ancient Roman cooks served grilled fish with laurel (bay) leaves, lighted and smoking, around the edge of the dish; why not try this yourself?

Daniel 4:37 contains every letter of the alphabet except "M" and "Q." Your children will enjoy looking it up and checking it.

Trout Sisera
Poached Trout

I use a great many of the fine little trout which are in the frozen-food counters, packed two to a carton. Their flavor is excellent and their texture, if carefully cooked, unmatched. One trout makes a nice serving. Any of these recipes may be used with fresh trout of your own catching.

4 fresh or frozen trout	½ cup mild vinegar
water to cover the fish	½ cup butter, melted
2 teaspoons salt	¼ cup minced parsley
¼ teaspoon pepper	

Thaw the trout and remove the heads. If fresh, clean and wash. Arrange the fish in a large skillet that will hold them in one layer (if cooking a large number, use a long flat pan, heated on two burners). Add boiling water to come just to the top of the fish; add salt and vinegar, bring to a gentle simmer, cover and simmer very gently for 12 minutes. Remove trout with a pancake turner, place on a heated platter, and add the melted butter, parsley, and pepper mixed to a sauce. This is a classic, simple dish that everyone will enjoy.

Solomon's Largesse
Sweet and Sour

3 pounds trout or whiting	¼ cup seedless raisins
3 cups water	½ cup brown sugar
1 cup vinegar	4 gingersnaps, crushed
1 onion, sliced	3 tablespoons chopped parsley
1 lemon, sliced	

Wash the fish; soak in lightly salted water (1 tablespoon to a quart of water) for an hour. Remove from the water and rinse thoroughly. In a 2-quart enamel or glass pan, combine the water, vinegar, onion, and raisins and cook until the onion is tender—about 10 minutes. Add the sugar and the crushed gingersnaps and blend thoroughly. Add the fish and barely simmer until the fish is tender—about 12-15 minutes. Remove the fish to a warm platter and serve garnished with parsley and lemon. Serve the sauce from the pan in a separate bowl. Serves 6.

Kishon Salmon
Salmon Mousse

1 tablespoon butter or margarine
1½ tablespoons flour
½ cup milk
1 No. 2 can salmon
1 small can sliced mushrooms
2 tablespoons chopped celery
1 small onion, chopped

2 tablespoons chopped parsley
1 tablespoon dry mustard
3 tablespoons cream
1 teaspoon salt
¼ teaspoon pepper
2 eggs, separated
¼ cup fine bread crumbs

Melt the butter or margarine in a small saucepan, stir in the flour until smooth, then add the milk gradually and stir over low heat until thick. Drain the salmon, remove bones and skin, and flake with a fork. Add cream sauce, mushrooms, celery, onions, parsley, mustard, cream, and salt, and pepper. Separate the eggs and stir the unbeaten yolks into the fish mixture, then beat the whites stiff and fold in gently. Turn into a buttered 1½-quart baking dish and sprinkle with the bread crumbs. Set in a pan containing 2 inches of hot water and bake at 350° for about 40 minutes. Serves 4 or 5. This is a beautiful soufflélike dish, ideal for a main luncheon dish when accompanied by a hot bread and a green salad.

When they got out on land, they saw a charcoal fire there, with fish lying on it, and bread.—John 21:9

Eshcol Loaf
Salmon Loaf

1 pound can red salmon	2 eggs
milk, added to salmon liquid to make one cup	½ teaspoon salt
	¼ teaspoon sage
2 cups cooked fine noodles	

Drain the salmon, reserving the liquid; add milk to the liquid to make 1 cup. Beat the eggs and add to this liquid. Flake the salmon, add the other ingredients and mix thoroughly. Line a greased loaf pan with aluminum foil, turn in salmon mixture, and bake at 350° for 1¼ hours. Turn out on a platter, garnish with stuffed tomatoes, and serve hot. This is also delicious cold; bake a day ahead of time, turn out, chill, and serve with Sauce Egyptian (page 179).

Bethany Peppers
Shrimp Stuffed Peppers

4 large green peppers	¼ cup fine bread crumbs
1 onion, chopped	1 teaspoon salt
1 clove garlic, minced	¼ teaspoon pepper
1 teaspoon minced parsley	1 egg, beaten
1 No. 2 can tomatoes	1 cup canned shrimp, chopped

Split and seed the peppers and parboil for 5 minutes in salted water to cover. Drain. Melt about 2 tablespoons butter or margarine in a saucepan and cook the onion in it until soft and golden. Add garlic, parsley, tomatoes, and bread crumbs and cook, stirring, until soft and well mixed. Season with the salt, a bit of freshly ground pepper, and then stir in the beaten egg and the shrimp. Stuff the peppers with this mixture, top with a sprinkling of bread crumbs and a few dots of butter, and bake at 350° for about 20 minutes. Serves 6.

Shrimp Zebedee
Buttered Shrimp

This is a real classic which you'll find easy to make and a real conversation piece at the table. It is a bit expensive because of the butter, but well worth it!

1 small clove garlic	Tabasco sauce
½ teaspoon salt	½ cup fine bread crumbs
6 tablespoons butter or mar-	1 tablespoon lemon juice
garine	3 tablespoons cream

1 can shrimp, drained

Clean the shrimp if they are not already cleaned. Now rub the salt and garlic together with the back of a spoon—this is an easy job since the salt liquefies the garlic and makes a paste of it—and then blend in the other ingredients, except the shrimp. Have ready two little casseroles that can come from the oven to the table. Arrange layers of bread crumb mixture and shrimp alternately, ending with crumbs. Top with a bit of chopped parsley and a dab of butter. Bake at 400° for about 20 minutes. This may be prepared ahead of time and baked when ready to serve.

Shammah Casserole
Scalloped Fish

¼ cup butter or margarine	1 cup milk
½ teaspoon salt	1 teaspoon Worcestershire
2 tablespoons minced green	sauce
pepper	1½ cups flaked, cooked or
1 tablespoon minced onion	canned fish
2 tablespoons flour	⅓ cup grated Cheddar cheese

½ cup bread crumbs

Melt butter in a saucepan over very low heat. Add salt, pepper, and onion and cook a minute or so, until tender. Stir in the flour, then stir the milk in slowly, cooking until smooth and slightly thickened. Add the Worcestershire sauce and cook again until thick. Check the seasoning. Grease a 1-quart casserole or individual baking dishes, then arrange alternate layers of fish and sauce. Top with the cheese mixed with the crumbs. Bake at 400° about 20 minutes, or until bubbly and browned. Serves 4. This may be made ahead of time and heated just before serving.

Shellfish, a combination of fish and hard-cooked eggs, or any canned fish may be used for the fish in this recipe.

Fillets Bethsaida
Fillets Almondine

2 packages haddock fillets par-	2 teaspoons flour
tially thawed	½ teaspoon salt
4 tablespoons butter	dash of pepper
⅓ cup sliced, blanched almonds	1 cup light cream

Cut the fish in serving pieces and fry in the butter in a heavy skillet for 10 to 15 minutes, browning both sides. Remove to a platter and keep hot. Add the almonds to the butter left in the skillet, and sauté to a golden brown. Add flour, salt, and pepper. Blend thoroughly, then stir in the top milk or cream. Cook, stirring constantly, until the sauce is smooth and thick. Pour over the fish, touch up with a dash of paprika, and serve to 4.

Any fish fillet may be used in this recipe.

Haddock Galilee
Broiled Haddock

1 pound haddock or other fillets	1½ tablespoons lemon juice
	dash of paprika
1 tablespoon melted butter	2 teaspoons minced parsley
¾ teaspoon salt	2 teaspoons chopped onion
⅛ teaspoon pepper	½ teaspoon basil
4 tablespoons butter or margarine	

Butter or grease a shallow, oven-glass baking dish, then arrange the fish on it. Brush each fillet with some of the melted butter and sprinkle with the salt and pepper. Broil about 2 inches from the heat until lightly browned and flaky. (Never turn fish while broiling.) Meanwhile, cream the 4 tablespoons butter, then blend in the remaining ingredients. When the fish is done, remove from the broiler, spread with the herb butter, and run under the broiler again for a moment or so. Any fish may be cooked in this manner; experiment with other herbs in the butter topping, so that you have a variety of flavors.

Add buttered string beans, mashed potatoes, hot rolls, and a black cherry gelatin whip for a good and easy dinner.

Luke, too, loved supper tables and the companionable breaking of bread. Notice how many of his scenes are set in homes at mealtimes.

Hassenaah
Tuna Spread

3 large potatoes	¼ teaspoon salt
1 cup milk	¼ teaspoon pepper
2 cans grated tuna fish	1 cup mayonnaise

Boil the potatoes in the skins until tender, peel, then mash. Add the milk and beat until smooth. Now add tuna, salt, and pepper and mix well. Mold in a fish shape or in any form you particularly like, and serve very cold with a dressing of the mayonnaise. Serves 4. I sometimes add ½ cup pickle relish and ½ cup chopped nuts, and use this as a dip for an appetizer, serving it with rye melba toast. Here is another version of the same idea:

Patties Mordecai
Tuna Patties

2 cans grated tuna fish	1 clove garlic, minced fine
2 cups mashed potatoes	½ teaspoon salt
¼ cup grated Parmesan cheese	¼ teaspoon pepper
3 eggs, well beaten	½ cup bread crumbs
4 tablespoons chopped parsley	½ cup oil

Mash the tuna thoroughly and mix to a smooth paste with the potatoes, cheese, eggs, parsley, garlic, and seasoning. Shape into flat cakes about a half-inch thick and 2 inches in diameter. Dip in the bread crumbs and sauté in the hot oil until golden. Serve hot or cold; hot with tomato sauce, and cold with mayonnaise (page 158). Serves 6.

"Bring me a heifer . . . , a she-goat . . . , a ram . . . , a turtledove, and a young pigeon."—Genesis 15:9

"And prepare for me savory food, such as I love, and bring it to me that I may eat."—Genesis 27:4

CHAPTER FIVE

SAVORY MEAT

From the time that man first used fire, meat has been an important part of his diet. Both Old and New Testaments are replete with instructions for its cookery and use.

"We must work the works of him who sent me, while it is day; night comes, when no one can work."—John 9:4

MEAT is a necessary part of today's diet; the modern cook plans her family's meals with a conscious striving to include the proper proportion of meat (protein) to other foods.

In biblical times, however, meat was a secondary food; grains, vegetables, and fruit were far more important. In Old Testament days the word didn't even mean flesh as we know it today, but rather all food (Proverbs 6:8), food for the mind, or wisdom (Psalm 145:15).

Our sister homemakers knew meat, and valued it, and used it gratefully whenever it was available to them. When they had the flesh of a sheep or a goat, they usually roasted or boiled it.

Roasting was much in vogue in biblical days, as it always is among simple people, for this is the oldest method of preparing meat. The Passover lamb (Exodus 12:8) was roasted in an oven, spitted on a rod of pomegranate laid across the top of the oven. Most of the ceremonial meats for feasts were prepared in the same way, but for the simple people of the middle classes meat was boiled, from Jacob boiling his pottage (Genesis 25:29) to the priest's servant reaching into the pot "while the meat was boiling," to take out for the priest "all that a three-pronged fork brought up." (1 Samuel 2:14)

When meat formed part of the daily food, it was usually served as a mark of distinction and wealth (Deuteronomy 12:20) and was restricted to the flesh of sheep or goat, so it is reasonable to assume that the housewife in Bible lands, setting out the midday meal of radishes, rice, and fruit, managed once in a while to save a few precious slivers of the cooked flesh to make a treat for the men who came in from the work of the fields.

All of us do the same thing today; we are plagued by the vision of a dish of this and a saucer of that in the refrigerator, and are constantly on the lookout for a way to put the morsels to good and tasty use.

Ten Commandments for Meat Cookery

1. Always buy meat of first quality for the use you intend to make of it; U.S. graded choice beef is not necessary for a stew, but it is for a steak.

2. Always refrigerate the meat loosely covered, at the earliest possible moment, and use as soon as possible.

3. All meat is more tender and juicy if cooked at low instead of high temperature. This is true for fine roasts as well as for hamburgers.

4. If you haven't time to cook a certain cut of meat right, buy a cut that can be cooked properly in the time you have.

5. Never, never put a good roast into a cold oven.

6. Suit the method of cookery to the meat: dry heat for roasting and for cuts suited to oven-broiling, pan-broiling, and pan-frying; and moist heat for cuts suited to braising, stewing, and other cooking in water.

7. Figure on one pound of boneless meat for 4 servings; one pound with a small amount of bone for 3 servings; one pound with a great deal of bone for 2 servings.

8. Early salting brings the juices to the surface of the meat; use it only for soups and stews, where the juice will go into the broth or gravy. Allow ¾ teaspoon salt to 1 pound ground meat, 1 teaspoon to 1 pound meat with bone.

9. Time the cooking of meat accurately. If you don't have a meat thermometer, prick the meat with a skewer or fork. If the juice runs red, it is rare; if pink, medium rare; if colorless, done. Except for pork and fowl, meat at this stage is over-done in most cooks' opinions.

10. Have serving platter hot enough to sizzle, garnish with a bit of green or fruit to point up the luscious brown crust.

Beef

Brisket Zillah
Barbecued Brisket

4 pounds brisket of beef	1 tablespoon prepared mustard
½ cup sharp barbecue sauce	1 tablespoon lemon juice
2 cups catsup	3 bay leaves
⅓ cup wine vinegar	1 clove garlic crushed
¼ cup Worcestershire sauce	6 whole peppercorns

2 tablespoons liquid smoke (optional)

Wipe the meat with a damp cloth, trim off any excess fat, and rub lightly with a little salt. Prepare the sauce by combining the remaining ingredients in a bowl. Lay the meat in a heavy shallow roasting pan and cook at 350 degrees for about 2 hours, with the sauce spread over the top of the meat. Turn the meat every half hour and baste with more of the sauce. If the sauce becomes too thick, thin it with a little bouillon. This is absolutely delicious with potato pancakes, and even better reheated. Serves 6.

Steak Adah
Flank Steak Broil

1 pound flank steak	1 cup canned tomatoes
½ cup sliced onion	1 cup water
¼ cup chopped green pepper	2 teaspoons salt
1 cup diced celery	¼ teaspoon pepper
1 cup diced carrots	1 cup uncooked rice

Cut the steak in thin strips crosswise and brown in a small amount of fat in a heavy skillet. Add onion and green pepper and brown again. Stir in other ingredients except rice, cover, and simmer 1 hour, or until tender. Meanwhile cook rice. When meat is tender, serve over a mound of rice. Serves 4.

A cheerful heart has a continual feast.—Proverbs 15:15

Sinai Cakes
Meat and Potato Cakes

2½ cups leftover roast, ground
1½ cups mashed potatoes,
　　seasoned
½ teaspoon salt

pinch of pepper
1 teaspoon A-1 sauce
2 teaspoons minced onion
flour
2 tablespoons drippings

Combine all ingredients except the flour and drippings, shape into 6 patties or cakes. Roll very lightly in the flour and sauté in drippings until nicely browned. These are delicious served with tomato sauce (page 180), canned beef gravy, or one of the canned steak sauces that are so economically priced.

Lentils and Beef Moriah
Lentil Stew

This dish combines so many foods of biblical times that it might well be one of the very foods served to the men of the Bible. You'll find it both delicious and economical.

1 cup lentils
3 cups water
1 pound boneless beef plate
1 medium onion, chopped
2 cloves garlic, minced

4 carrots, sliced
2 teaspoons salt
¼ teaspoon pepper
½ teaspoon pickling spice
3 cardamon seeds (optional)
2 slices lemon

Wash the lentils; place in a saucepan, add the water, bring to a boil, and boil 2 minutes. Remove from the heat and set aside to soak for an hour. Meanwhile, cut the beef into serving size chunks and brown in a heavy skillet without adding any fat; you will have to watch this carefully at first, until the fat in the meat begins to cook out. Add onion and garlic, and brown lightly, then add the remaining ingredients (better tie the spice, cardamon, and lemon slices in a little bag) and cook for 35 minutes, or until the lentils are tender. Remove the spice bag before serving. Serves 4.

Unless you are sure that you like cardamon, don't use it; it has a very definite flavor that some people dislike.

Jabal's Stew
Rich Beef Stew

3 pounds lean chuck or flank steak	3 tablespoons catsup
1 chunk fat from the meat	1 teaspoon Worcestershire sauce
1 quart boiling water	1 teaspoon sugar
1 clove garlic	½ teaspoon paprika
1 bay leaf	4 medium onions, sliced
1 tablespoon salt	½ cup diced celery
½ teaspoon pepper	parsley sprigs
	5 potatoes

This looks like a formidable list of ingredients, but please notice that most of them are seasonings which are already on your pantry shelf. Cut the meat into 1½-inch cubes. Cut the fat into small pieces, and cook it in a heavy heated Dutch oven until it is crisp and brown. Now add the meat and brown it thoroughly, on all sides. Add the remaining ingredients except the potatoes, cover tightly, and let simmer for about 1½ hours or longer, if you have time. Then add the potatoes and simmer gently for about another hour. Some people add carrots to stew, but I think it's an insult to the flavor. To serve, lift out the meat and potatoes and thicken by stirring into the juice, 2 tablespoons flour blended with 3 tablespoons water for each cup of liquid in the pan. You may need a little Kitchen Bouquet to deepen the color. Serves 6.

And be kind to one another, tenderhearted, forgiving one another.—Ephesians 4:32

Aaron's Roast
Fruited Pot Roast

3 to 5 pounds chuck or rump
    roast
2 tablespoons fat
1 teaspoon thyme

2 cups water
3 tablespoons mixed pickling
    spice
1 cup dried apricots

Brown the roast in the heated fat, in a heavy kettle. Add the water and spices and apricots, cover tightly, and simmer gently until fork-tender, about 3 to 3½ hours. Long cooking such as this leaves you free to do other things; do more of it.

Amorite Roasts
Individual Pot Roasts

2 pounds boneless chuck
¼ cup flour
1½ teaspoons salt
¼ teaspoon pepper
1 bay leaf, crumbled

½ teaspoon orégano
½ cup chopped onion
¼ cup water
2 tablespoons flour
½ cup cold water

Have the butcher cut the chuck into 6 individual servings. Mix together the flour, salt, and pepper, and rub this well into each piece of meat. Melt about a tablespoon of lard or drippings in a heavy kettle or Dutch oven, and brown the meat on all sides. Add the bay leaf, orégano, onion, and water, cover tightly, and simmer for 1½ to 2 hours, or until the meat is tender. Remove the meat and keep warm; skim off any excess fat. For each cup of liquid, thicken with the 2 tablespoons flour stirred smooth in cold water. Stir into the liquid and cook over low heat, stirring constantly, until smooth and thick. Arrange the meat in nests of buttered noodles or rice on a chop plate and serve the gravy separately. This is a dish of real elegance, nice enough for your most important guests.

Gift of Huram
Potted Beef

2 cups cooked beef, minced	½ teaspoon soy sauce
2 medium onions, sliced	1 package Instant mashed
2 cups cooked carrots, sliced	potatoes
1 tablespoon salt	2 tablespoons heavy cream
½ teaspoon pepper	4 tablespoons bread crumbs

1 tablespoon melted butter

Cook the sliced onions in a bit of butter until just limp and tender. Now use them to line a 1½ quart baking dish, over the bottom and up the sides if you can manage it. Add a layer of beef, a layer of carrots, then repeat, seasoning each layer with salt and pepper and a few drops of the soy sauce, until all is used. Now make up the mashed potatoes according to the directions on the package (or use leftover potatoes), spread over the meat with a nice swirl, then trickle the cream over and top with the crumbs and melted butter. Bake at 400° just until heated through—about 30 minutes. Serves 4.

This is a real man's dish—the kind he comes home bragging about, after he eats it at $2.00 per portion in a restaurant.

Veal

Veal Caleb
Veal Rolls

2 veal round steaks, cut ½ inch
   thick
1 slice bacon
1 hard-cooked egg, diced
1 teaspoon minced onion

1 2-ounce can mushroom pieces
2 tablespoons drippings
Salt and pepper
1½ cups canned tomatoes
1 teaspoon basil

Cut the bacon into small squares and combine with the diced
egg, onion, and 2 tablespoons mushrooms. Pound the veal on a
floured board with the edge of a saucer until it is about ¼ inch
thick, adding flour gradually as you pound. Cut into 6 equal
pieces. Spread each piece with the bacon-and-egg mixture, roll
and fasten with a toothpick or skewer. Brown the rolls in the
drippings, season lightly with salt and pepper, then add tomatoes, basil, and remaining mushrooms with juice, cover and
simmer gently or bake at 325° for 45 minutes to 1 hour, or
until tender. Remove the rolls and thicken the tomato liquid
with a little flour stirred smooth in cold water, to make gravy.
This makes 6 servings.

Potted Calf
Veal Stew with Dumplings

2½ pounds rump or shoulder
   of veal
1½ quarts water
¼ cup chopped onion
½ bay leaf
1 teaspoon salt
1 whole clove
¼ teaspoon rosemary

1 tablespoon Worcestershire
   sauce
2 cups flour
1 teaspoon salt
3 teaspoons baking powder
1 tablespoon shortening
1 cup milk
½ cup minced parsley

Buy the veal boned, and have the butcher cut it into 2-inch pieces. Cover with the water, add the seasonings with the exception of the Worcestershire sauce, cover and simmer very gently until the meat is tender—about 1 hour. Remove the bay leaf and add the Worcestershire sauce. Check the seasoning— you may need more salt. Any of the herbs, by the way, may be omitted, but I do hope that you'll try them in this dish. Now mix the dumplings by sifting flour, salt, and baking powder together. Cut the shortening in with a fork, then turn in the milk all at once. With as few strokes as possible, mix in the parsley. Bring the stew to a boil, drop the dumplings onto the surface by teaspoonfuls, cover tightly, and cook exactly 15 minutes without lifting the lid. Lift out onto a hot platter with 2 forks, add the meat, thicken the gravy with a little flour stirred smooth in cold water, and serve hot. Serves 6.

Croquettes Poratha
Veal Croquettes

2 cups ground cooked veal	2 teaspoons grated onion
1 cup mashed cooked peas	½ cup fine dry bread crumbs
½ teaspoon salt	1 egg, slightly beaten
¼ teaspoon pepper	fat for frying

I enjoy these croquettes because this method does away with the tedious making of white sauce. Simply combine veal, peas, salt, pepper, and onion. Shape into croquettes, roll in crumbs, dip in egg and roll again in crumbs, then fry in deep fat heated to 360° for about 2 minutes, or until brown. Drain and serve with tomato sauce. Serves 6.

"The Lord *gives you in the evening flesh to eat and in the morning bread to the full."—Exodus 16:8*

Loaves Abijah
Veal Loaf Supreme

1 pound ground veal	1 egg
1 pound ground pork	2 teaspoons salt
1 can chicken soup	1/4 teaspoon pepper
1 cup quick-cooking oatmeal	1 tablespoon onion juice
1/2 teaspoon rosemary	paprika

Combine these ingredients in the order given. Shape into 8 individual loaves and pack on edge in an oiled loaf pan, making a solid loaf. Sprinkle with paprika. Bake at 350° for 1½ hours, then serve with Sauce Allemande (page 178). Serves 6.

Bethaven
Cheesed Cutlet

1 pound veal culet	1 clove garlic
1/2 teaspoon salt	1/4 cup salad oil
1/4 teaspoon pepper	1 can condensed cream of
1 egg, beaten	tomato soup, undiluted
2 tablespoons grated Parmesan	1/4 teaspoon dried basil
or other goat's cheese	1/2 teaspoon salt
1/2 cup fine bread crumbs	1/4 teaspoon pepper
1/4 cup salad oil	1 teaspoon cider vinegar
1 cup sliced onion	1/2 cup grated Swiss cheese

Heat the oven to 350°. Cut the veal into 4 pieces and pound thin with the edge of a saucer. Add salt and pepper to beaten egg. Mix Parmesan cheese with bread crumbs. Dip the cutlets in egg, then in bread crumbs. Heat the salad oil in a skillet and sauté the cutlets until a golden brown. Remove to a shallow baking pan. Now, using the same skillet, sauté the onion and garlic in the second 1/4 cup salad oil for 5 minutes. Remove the garlic. Add remaining ingredients with the exception of the Swiss cheese and simmer, uncovered, for 10 minutes, stirring frequently. Pour over the cutlets in the baking pan. Bake at 350° for 15 minutes, then sprinkle the grated Swiss cheese over the top and bake for 15 minutes longer. Serves 4.

Omri
Veal Pot Roast

3- to 4-pound rump or shoulder	1 cup water
2 tablespoons flour	2 tablespoons vinegar
2 teaspoons salt	1 large onion, chopped
1 tablespoon sugar	¼ cup chopped parsley
2 teaspoons dry mustard	½ cup chopped celery leaves
½ teaspoon poultry seasoning	6 medium carrots
3 tablespoons drippings	6 medium potatoes

Combine the flour, salt, sugar, and spices. Rub the pot roast thoroughly with the seasoned mixture and brown in the drippings, which have been heated in a Dutch oven or deep kettle. Add water, vinegar, and chopped onion, parsley, and celery leaves; cover closely and simmer at 300° or on top the stove for 1½ hours. Add the carrots and potatoes and continue cooking about 1 hour or until the meat is tender and the vegetables done. If you want to make this a whole meal-in-a-pot, double the carrots and potatoes. Serves 6-8.

Lamb

Lamb may be used in nearly all of the recipes given for veal. Here are some favorites of my family, that I think you'll enjoy.

Lamb with Rice, Athena
Lamb with Rice

1 5-pound lamb roast	1 small head lettuce
1 cup rice	3 tablespoons butter or mar-
2 cups canned chicken broth	garine
salt and pepper	1 cup cooked green peas
¼ pound pork sausage	½ teaspoon mixed herbs

Prepare a roast leg, saddle, or shoulder of lamb in your usual manner for roasting. (Lamb, for best flavor, should be roasted in an uncovered pan for 25 to 30 minutes per pound, at 350°.) Thirty minutes before the lamb is to be finished, cook the rice in the boiling chicken broth until tender, adding more broth if it becomes too dry, but being careful not to have an excess of liquid. Season lightly with salt and pepper. While the rice cooks, fry the sausage until brown, breaking up with a fork as it cooks. Drain off fat. Push to the side of the pan. Shred the lettuce fine. Add butter and herbs to the pan containing the sausage, add the lettuce and cook slowly about 5 minutes. Gently mix the rice, lettuce, sausage, and peas, and serve very hot on the platter with the sliced lamb. Serves 6.

Syrian Lamb
Lamb Dolmades

1 large head cabbage	2 large onions, chopped
1 pound ground lamb shoulder	2 tablespoons chopped parsley
¼ cup rice	1½ teaspoons salt
juice of ½ lemon	¼ teaspoon pepper
½ cup tomato puree	2 cups boiling water

Cut the core from the cabbage head in a cone; remove 40 medium or 20 large leaves. Wash them, drop into a little boiling salted water, and cook until tender enough to roll—about 15 minutes. Blend together the remaining ingredients except the boiling water, put a spoonful of the mixture on each of the cabbage leaves, fold the sides in, then roll. Carefully place the rolls close together, in a large saucepan which has been lined with cabbage leaves to prevent scorching. Add the boiling water, lay a plate on top the rolls to keep them in place, then simmer over low heat for 1 hour. Serve hot, to 8, with a bowl of seasoned sour cream.

Gilgal
Lamb Kabobs

6 1-inch lamb steaks, cut in inch cubes	⅓ cup salad oil
1 pound salami, cut in inch cubes	3 tablespoons soy sauce
3 cloves garlic, minced fine	3 tablespoons vinegar
	1½ teaspoons sugar
	¼ teaspoon pepper

2 larged onions, sliced

Arrange the lamb and salami cubes alternately on 6 skewers. Lay the skewers in a shallow glass dish; combine the remaining ingredients with the exception of the onion slices and pour over the skewered meat. Top with the onions. Cover with a lid or with aluminum foil; let stand in the refrigerator several hours or overnight. Broil over hot coals or in the broiler of your range about 20 minutes, turning frequently. Cook the onions in the remaining sauce until golden brown and serve over the kabobs. The combination of lamb and salami flavor in this dish is almost exactly the flavor in many Syrian dishes.

The middle and shortest chapter in the Bible is Psalm 117.

Atarah Dish
Lamb Pilaf

1 cup Sower's pilaf (page 190)	1 stick butter or margarine
1 pound lean lamb, ground fine	1 pound lean and fat lamb, ground fine
2 onions, chopped	1½ teaspoons salt
½ teaspoon pepper	

Try to plan so that you have the pilaf left over; chill in the refrigerator an hour or longer. To the ground lean lamb, add half the onions and blend thoroughly. Sauté the rest of the onions in 2 tablespoons of the butter until golden. Here the biblical housewife probably added chopped nuts; ¼ cup pecans or walnuts will be good, if you have them. Stir onions and nuts into the meat mixture.

To the other pound of ground meat, add the chilled pilaf, and the salt and pepper. Blend this mixture thoroughly, using the hands if necessary. When well blended, divide in two parts; spread one half in a greased 9-inch square Pyrex cake pan. Spread the onion-and-meat mixture on this; cover with the rest of the pilaf-and-meat mixture. Pat down firmly. Now, with a thin, sharp knife, such as a paring knife, cut the mix into diamond-shaped pieces. Run the knife around the edge of the pan. Dot the top with the remaining butter. Bake at 375° for about an hour. Serve with extra pilaf to 6 or 8.

This is another dish that is wonderful for quantity serving because it may be put together ahead of time, and keeps well. You will find that serving it with extra pilaf, tomato sauce (page 180), and a green salad is easy, inexpensive, and a truly delightful biblical meal.

All the people went their way to eat and drink and to . . . make great rejoicing.—Nehemiah 8:12

Lamb Aram
Lamb with Red Noodles

1½ pounds neck or breast of lamb	1½ teaspoons salt
1 clove garlic, minced	¼ teaspoon pepper
1 6-ounce can tomato paste	a dash of cayenne
3 cups water	1 5-ounce package broad noodles
1 bay leaf	¼ cup grated cheese

Have the meat cut in stew-sized pieces. Brown slowly in a large heavy skillet without added fat. Add the garlic, tomato paste, water, and seasonings. Cover and cook slowly for an hour and 15 or 20 minutes. Now add the uncooked noodles, making sure that the red sauce covers the noodles, adding more water if necessary as the noodles cook. Cover and cook slowly for 20 minutes, or until the noodles are tender. Serve with a sprinkling of grated cheese.

You'll like the fresh, springy flavor of mint with lamb; simply combine ⅓ cup chopped mint leaves, 2 tablespoons sugar and ½ cup hot vinegar and stir until sugar dissolves.

Midian Patties
Lamb Patties

The lamb patties that your butcher sometimes features are delicious when dipped in a mixture of 2 tablespoons melted butter, 1 tablespoon Worcestershire sauce, juice of 1 lemon, 1 teaspoon prepared mustard, and 2 teaspoons salt, before broiling. Pour any extra sauce over the patties before serving.

The Old Testament took more than 2,000 years to complete. The New Testament took about 100 years.

Pork

Although the flesh of swine was forbidden as food (Leviticus 11:7; Deuteronomy 14:8), it is probable that dietetical consideration influenced the prohibition, for there is little doubt that the heathen nations of Palestine used the flesh as food. Abraham, Isaac, and Jacob, as well as Joseph and the other leaders of the Jews for the first 400 years of their recorded history, seem to have eaten hog meat freely.

Meshach Plate
Sweet-Sour Dinner

1½ pounds fresh spareribs
1 tablespoon bacon fat
2 tablespoons cornstarch
2 cups water
2 teaspoons salt
1 tablespoon sugar
1 tablespoon vinegar
3 tablespoons soy sauce
¼ cup pineapple juice
½ green pepper, cut in 1-inch squares
¾ cup uncooked rice
1½ cups boiling water
½ teaspoon salt
2 bunches young beets
2 tablespoons butter or margarine
⅛ teaspoon ground cloves

Have the butcher cut the ribs into serving-size pieces. I use the pressure cooker for this dish; you could use a kettle with a trivet and tightly fitting lid just as well. Melt the fat in the pot, brown the ribs well on both sides, and remove. Blend the cornstarch with the water, add to the fat in the pan with salt, sugar, vinegar, soy sauce, and pineapple juice. Cook and stir until the liquid is smooth and thickened. Now put the trivet into the pot; arrange the ribs on one half and sprinkle with the green pepper pieces. Put the rice into a greased No. 2 empty can, add boiling water and salt and cover tightly with aluminum foil. Set on the other half of the rack. Peel the beets, dot with butter or margarine, sprinkle with the cloves, wrap in aluminum foil in a

neat package, and set on top of the meat. Cook at 15 pounds'
pressure for 15 minutes, then reduce the pressure at once. Or,
if cooking in an ordinary kettle, cover tightly and simmer for
one hour. Serves 4.

Tattenai Bowl
Peppered Pig

2 pounds boned pork, loin or shoulder	3 tablespoons chopped onion
3 cups water	3 tablespoons flour
3 green peppers	1 teaspoon salt
3 tablespoons fat	¼ teaspoon pepper
	1 9-ounce package noodles

Cut the boned pork into neat 1-inch cubes. Bring the water
to a gentle simmer, add a few onion slices, a few leaves from
a stalk of celery, a little parsley, and a teaspoon of thyme. When
this cooks, add the pork and simmer gently until tender—about
45 minutes. This can be done ahead of time. Drain, reserving the
stock. Cut the peppers into ¼-inch strips, discarding all seeds
and white membrane. Melt the fat in a hot skillet, add the
onion, and sauté about 3 minutes. Add green pepper and sauté
another minute or two. Sprinkle the flour over all and stir in
thoroughly. Gradually stir in 2 cups of the stock obtained from
cooking the meat and cook, stirring, until thickened and smooth.
Add salt, pepper, and pork and simmer 10 minutes. Meanwhile,
cook the noodles in boiling salted water. Serve the pork over
the bed of tender noodles on a heated platter. Serves 6.

Another variation of this dish is to omit the noodles, shred
finely enough cabbage to measure 3 cupfuls, and arrange this
over the pork and sauce in the skillet. Sprinkle with salt and
pepper, cover, and cook 10 or 15 minutes more or until the
cabbage is tender. Serve in a casserole. Serves 5 or 6.

Hamutal Morsel
Curried Pork Chops

8 pork chops, ½ inch thick	2 cups milk
½ pound mushrooms	¼ cup water
4 tablespoons fat or oil	1½ teaspoon salt
½ cup minced onion	¼ teaspoon pepper
4 tablespoons flour	2 teaspoons curry powder

Mix together about ¼ cup flour, 1 teaspoon salt, ½ teaspoon thyme, and a few grains of pepper and dredge the chops well in this coating. Heat a little fat in a heavy skillet (it will probably take about 3 tablespoonfuls) and brown the chops on both sides. Place in a greased, 2-quart casserole. Cover with the mushrooms which have been washed and sliced. Heat the 4 tablespoons fat or oil in the skillet; add the onion and cook over low heat until golden brown. Stir in the flour. Add the remaining ingredients, stirring constantly, and cook, stirring, until smooth and thick. Pour over the chops, cover, and bake at 350° about 1½ hours, or until tender. Skim off the surface fat, and serve. Serves 6. This dish may be prepared completely ahead of time, ready for the final heating in the casserole.

Curried Pineapple is delicious with the curried chops. Simply melt 2 tablespoons butter or margarine, blend in a teaspoon of curry powder, add ⅔ cup crushed pineapple and cook about 5 minutes to blend the flavors. Serve as a relish with the pork.

It was Christ who laid down the revolutionary principle that purity is a matter of the heart; that what goes into a man cannot defile him. (See Mark 7:1-23; Luke 11:41.)

"You may eat all clean birds."—Deuteronomy 14:11

CHAPTER SIX

FOWL

Although domestic fowls are alluded to only once in the Old Testament, in New Testament times they were as common as they are today.

When Solomon prayed for the greatest gift he could think of, he asked for an "understanding mind."

—1 Kings 3:9

THOU didst prepare quails to eat,
       a delicacy to satisfy the desire of appetite,
we read in Wisdom of Solomon 16:2.

Birds were plentiful in Palestine; they were so easily hunted with slingshots that there is little doubt that the homemaker of Jesus' time used them frequently to supplement her scanty supply of meat. Four species of pigeon and three of dove, for instance, were found in the land where Jesus taught. These were in demand as offerings by the poor (Leviticus 5:7; Luke 2:24) and were probably much the same birds that we know under these same names today.

Geese, too, were available; we have no positive evidence that the Hebrews reared poultry before the captivity, but the "fatted fowl" of Solomon's provision for one day (1 Kings 4:23) seems to have been geese such as we know today, and it is likely that the wise one had introduced from India a variety of other domestic fowls, too, including peacocks, which we know were used for food.

Quail, of course, of the variety common to northern Africa and the Arabian peninsula (a bit different from the one we know) were common as food. Their annual migration northward in the springtime, their long flights across the arms of the Red Sea, their sudden appearance in countless numbers in the Arabian desert, where they were relished as food, all support the story of their appearance to the Hebrews in the wilderness, as it is told in Exodus 16:13, Numbers 11:31, and Psalm 105:40.

Even sparrows were used as cheap food in New Testament days (Matthew 10:29) and in the books of both Matthew and Luke we find frequent mention of both hen and cock. We read of partridge being found in Palestine, too. They were hunted just as they are today (1 Samuel 26:20), and their eggs were valued as food.

Ten Commandments for Poultry Cookery

1. Learn the different ways in which birds are sold—"dressed," "New York dressed," "ready-to-cook," and so forth.

2. Purchase the chicken that will give you the best results in the dish you have in mind; an old hen that would make a rich and luscious contribution to a chicken pie will be defiant and rebellious in the frying pan.

3. Remember that poultry has one of the most delicate of all food flavors, and should be stored so as to preserve that flavor. Keep frozen birds frozen until time to thaw for cooking. Use cooked birds within 3-4 days.

4. Test the tenderness of a chicken by bending the breast bone. If it is still flexible, the bird is young; if stiff and hard, the bird is old.

5. Beware of a dry, hard, purplish or scaly skin, or of long hairs on leg and wing tips; that bird is past its prime, though it will make a good soup.

6. Know all of the poultry family: capon, Cornish game hen, duck, turkey, guinea hen.

7. Proportion of meat to bone is an important consideration in buying poultry; get more meat for your money by buying a larger bird than you need, and planning for left-over dishes or freezing what you don't use.

8. Insist that the chickens and other poultry carry a label that tells you the packer's name and brand, as a guide to quality, and shows a U.S. inspection mark, or U.S. grade and inspection mark, denoting quality and wholesomeness.

9. Buy only from the retailer who refrigerates poultry. When you get it home, remove it from the wrapper, wrap loosely in waxed paper or foil with the ends open, and store just below the freezing unit.

10. Remember that poultry is truly a cosmopolitan food. Why limit yourself to fried chicken and roast duck, when experiences with Hens Damaris and Patmos Loaf await you?

To Roast Poultry and Game

We have discarded completely our mothers' theory that poultry must first be seared at high temperatures, then cooked covered or basted endlessly. Maintaining a temperature of 325° throughout the entire cooking period causes less shrinkage and gives us tenderer and juicier meat.

With the exception of wild duck, which should cook no longer than 10 to 12 minutes per pound for rare and 15 to 20 minutes per pound for well done, and the dainty quail, which requires a total time of about 30 minutes, you will be safe in figuring about 25 minutes per pound on small fowl and 15 to 20 minutes per pound on large birds if the meat is at room temperature. If you are putting it into the oven in a chilled state, add at least 30 minutes to the cooking time. These cooking times will produce meat that is moist and firm, not meat which "drops from the bones," as our mothers used to say in describing a particularly tasty bird. If you like fowl very well done, increase the baking time by about 30 minutes.

Place the fowl on a rack in a shallow pan, be sure that the oven is properly heated, then roast the entire time without adding water. In the case of a large bird, such as a large turkey or goose, I like to add a little water to the pan for the last hour of cooking, to prevent the delicious pan juices from getting too brown.

When cooking a turkey, roast for the first half of the cooking time with the bird placed breast down in the rack; this prevents the breast from drying out, since all the juices will drain down through it. Set upright for just the last hour or two to allow the breast to brown nicely.

Do you know which was the first missionary journey? You'll find the travelogue in Acts 13:1-5.

Hens Damaris
Roast Cornish Hens

3 teaspoons salt	2 teaspoons prepared mustard
¾ cup salad oil or fat	2 teaspoons vinegar
½ cup butter or margarine	1 teaspoon paprika

1½ cups soft bread crumbs

We know that the housewife of biblical times often encased her game (probably quail) in a bread or paste crust and roasted them in the coals. Since you may find it hard to get hot coals ready and may not even find quails at hand, this makes a fine substitute. Order one 1-pound Cornish game hen for each serving. Thaw, sprinkle with a little salt, then brown well in about ½ cup of the oil or fat in a skillet over high heat.

Meanwhile, cream together the butter, mustard, vinegar, paprika, and remaining teaspoon of salt. Spread each of the browned birds thickly with this mixture and fit them into a 2- or 3-quart casserole. Sprinkle with the crumbs which have been mixed with the remaining ¼ cup oil or fat, then cover and bake at 450° for about 40 minutes or until the birds are tender and the crumbs are brown—you may have to remove the cover for the last ten or fifteen minutes. A 3-pound fryer, cut up, is also delicious prepared in this way, as are wild quail.

Chicken Priscilla
Chicken Supreme

2 small onions, sliced	¼ cup butter or margarine
2 small carrots, diced	¼ cup flour
¼ bay leaf	½ cup heavy cream or evaporated milk
8 peppercorns	
2 sprigs parsley	2 cups diced cooked chicken
2 cups chicken broth	2 hard-cooked eggs, sliced

Add onions, carrots, bay leaf, peppercorns, and parsley to broth; simmer about 10 minutes; strain. Melt butter in saucepan; stir in the flour. Add the first mixture slowly, stirring all the while, then cook, stirring, until smooth. Add the cream, cook until thickened, then fold in the chicken and eggs. Heat thoroughly, then add salt and pepper to taste. Serve in rice ring. This is a delicious sauce in which to use leftover ham, veal, or turkey. Use it often.

Chicken Jeremiah
Roast Chicken with Whole Grain Stuffing

This delicious roast chicken might well have been a favorite dish of biblical times, since the stuffing of bulgur, a cracked wheat, was widely used. Nutlike in flavor and perfectly delicious, bulgur can be found now in more and more markets, or ordered by mail from Byrd Mill.[1]

1 4-5 lb. roasting chicken	2 stalks celery
1 cup bulgur	¼ cup oil
2 cups bouillon	¼ teaspoon herbs (orégano,
1 small onion	savory or poultry seasoning)
½ green pepper	cook giblets, chopped fine

Rinse the chicken with cold water and dry. To make the stuffing, cook the bulgur and bouillon together in a covered pan for 10 minutes, or until the liquid is absorbed. Chop onion, green pepper, and celery fine; cook in the heated oil until the onions are limp. Mix in the remaining ingredients, then salt and pepper to taste; it will take about ½ teaspoon salt and a dash of pepper. Spoon stuffing into the chicken cavity, sew or skewer the opening together, and roast at 325° in an uncovered pan about 3½ hours, or until the meat feels soft when the thick part of the drumstick is pressed between your fingers. Baste occasionally with a little melted butter. Serves 4 to 6.

---

[1]Route 5, Louisa, Virginia. Write for information.

Pasach Pottage
Kettle Meal

Except for a few changes in ingredients, this is probably one of the truest of the biblical dishes, for the two methods of cooking most generally used were roasting and boiling in a pot. It is, in addition, one of the classic dishes of all time; it is the "burgoo" of the southern United States; the *pot au feu* of the French peasant; the *stifath* of the Greeks. Its duplicate is to be found in the cookery of almost every country. Any ingredient listed may be left out or another substituted, just as the biblical housewife used whatever she had on hand, but the best flavor is obtained by using beef, pork, and chicken. With freshly baked bread, a good green salad, and a fruit dessert, you'll have a feast.

1 pound stewing beef	1 pound pork (shank or shoulder)
1 4-pound stewing chicken	4 quarts water
2 medium potatoes	2 medium onions
½ cup chopped parsley	salt, cayenne pepper
1 cup lima beans	3 carrots
1 green pepper	1 cup cabbage, chopped
1 medium can tomatoes	1 cup canned corn
1 pod red pepper	2 teaspoons Worcestershire sauce
1 bay leaf	

This can cook while you go about your tasks. Place the beef and pork in a large kettle, cover with water, and cook an hour. Add the chicken, cut in pieces, and simmer gently about one more hour, until the meat is very tender and falls from the bones. Remove from the broth. Cool, then remove the meat from the bones and dice into one-inch cubes. Peel and dice the vegetables. Return all the ingredients to the broth, season to taste, and simmer until the vegetables are tender and the mixture is thick. This will serve 8 generously, but it freezes perfectly, so, if your family is small, make it all anyway and freeze half for another day.

Canaan Pot
Spiced Chicken

1 3-pound fryer, cut up	2 tablespoons chili powder
3 cups boiling water	2 tablespoons tomato paste
juice of 1 lemon	4 tablespoons vinegar
1 teaspoon salt	½ teaspoon ginger
6 medium onions, chopped	½ teaspoon black pepper
4 tablespoons fat	6 hard-cooked eggs

Place the chicken in a deep kettle, add hot water, lemon juice, and salt and simmer, covered, for 10 minutes. Remove chicken from the liquid. In another pan such as a Dutch oven, brown the onions lightly in the fat, stirring so that they cook evenly. Add 1 cup of the liquid from the chicken, chili powder, and tomato paste. Blend well and simmer for 5 minutes. Add vinegar, ginger, pepper, and a second cup of the broth. Place chicken in this sauce and simmer until the chicken is tender, 30-40 minutes. Add the hard-cooked eggs about 3 minutes before serving, piercing each egg with a fork so that the sauce penetrates the egg. Serve over rice, with a cottage cheese salad. Makes a delicious biblical meal for 6.

Nazareth Bowl
Pickled Chicken

1 3-pound frying chicken	1/3 cup Worcestershire sauce
1/2 stick butter or margarine	2 teaspoons sugar
1/2 cup vinegar	salt and pepper
3 tablespoons water	1 onion, sliced and peeled

Wipe the chicken thoroughly with a damp cloth and disjoint it, if it is whole. Melt half the butter or margarine in a large skillet or heavy shallow pan. When hot, brown the chicken pieces lightly. In a measuring cup, mix together the vinegar, water, Worcestershire sauce, sugar, about 1/2 teaspoon salt, and 1/4 teaspoon pepper, and pour this over the chicken. Top with the sliced onion, cover, and bake at 325° for about 2 hours. If you are in a hurry, this may be baked at 375° for about an hour, but be sure that the chicken pieces are turned once or twice, so that the vinegar reaches all of them. Serves 4.

Chicken Eli
Herbed Fricassee

I like this old method of preparing chicken because it does away with the mess of actually frying the bird.

1 2½-3 pound fryer	2 tablespoons minced onion
1/2 cup salad oil	1 clove garlic, minced
2 tablespoons minced parsley	1½ teaspoons salt
2 teaspoons rosemary	3 tablespoons flour
1/2 teaspoon savory	1½ cups milk

Buy the chicken cut up. Arrange in a shallow baking pan— I like the shining brightness of Pyrex for this dish, but a pretty pottery dish that can come to the table is nice, too. Brush with some of the salad oil and bake at 450° for about 30 minutes, or until golden brown. Reduce the temperature to 325°, add the remaining ingredients except the flour and milk to the salad oil, and pour this over the chicken. Bake about 20 minutes longer, or until the chicken is tender. Now, remove the chicken to a hot platter; stir the flour into the fat left in the baking pan. Scrape into a pan that can go onto direct heat; place over medium heat, and add the milk gradually, stirring all the while. Cook, stirring, until smooth and thickened. Pour the gravy over the chicken in the baking pan and serve hot, with browned biscuits. Serves 4.

Salad Mark
Supper Salad

The only way to describe this intriguingly different supper salad is to have you taste it—you'll want it several times a week, once you try it.

½ cup mayonnaise	1 cup Swiss cheese cut in strips
1 teaspoon salt	¼ cup chopped dill pickle
dash of pepper	2 cups hot cooked rice
1 cup cooked chicken or other meat cut in strips	1 cup cooked green peas
	3 ripe tomatoes, in wedges

6 ripe olives

Prepare the rice by the basic cooking method given on page 197. Mix together salt, mayonnaise, and pepper; if you like onion, add 1 teaspoon grated onion to this mixture. Add chicken, Swiss cheese, pickle, and hot rice. It is important that the rice be hot. Add the peas and mix gently. Cover and chill about 1 hour, or for a very different flavor, serve at room temperature. Serve on salad greens garnished with tomato and olive wedges. Serves 6-7.

If I give away all I have, . . . but have not love, I gain nothing.—1 Corinthians 13:3

Patmos Loaf
Chicken Loaf

4 cups diced cooked chicken	1½ teaspoons chili powder
3 tablespoons grated onion	2 cups cracker crumbs
4 tablespoons chopped pimento	1½ cups chicken stock
1½ teaspoons salt	1½ cups milk

3 eggs, beaten

Combine all ingredients in the order given and mix thoroughly. Prepare a loaf pan by oiling thoroughly, then coating with cracker crumbs. Fill with the chicken mixture, set the pan in a pan containing about 2 inches of hot water. Bake at 350° for 1 hour, or until a knife inserted comes out clean. Serve hot with olive sauce or cold with Hollandaise sauce.

This loaf will serve 8 to 10; it is a fine dish to serve to groups because it can be prepared ahead of time. I like it particularly for church groups because there is so much biblical food in it.

Sauce Chloe
Olive Sauce

14 large green or ripe olives	½ cup shredded, toasted almonds
4 cups chicken stock	1 cup coffee cream
4 tablespoons cornstarch	2 tablespoons Worcestershire sauce
4 tablespoons cold water	

Cut the meat from the olive pits in large pieces. Rub the cornstarch smooth in the 4 tablespoons cold water. Heat the chicken stock in a saucepan, stir in the dissolved cornstarch and cook, stirring, until thickened and smooth. Add the remaining ingredients and heat thoroughly. Serve over chicken loaf.

"Take these ten cheeses to the commander of their thousand. See how your brothers fare."—1 Samuel 17:18

CHAPTER SEVEN

CURDS AND MILK

How many of God's creatures we must thank for the gift of cheese—the cow, the ewe, the goat, the camel, the mare, and many other animals which were known to people of biblical times!

The prayer of faith will save the sick man, and the Lord will raise him up.—James 5:15

No ONE knows the actual date of the appearance of the first cheese; records of the Near and Far East as ancient as 2000 B.C. mention it as a familiar staple in the diet of that time. Hippocrates, Aristotle, Caesar, and Pliny wrote about it, but historians generally believe that both cheese and butter were developed shortly after the domestication of the cow.

Arabia was probably the first country to know it, and according to tradition an Asian traveler set forth upon a desert journey carrying with him a canteen of milk to sustain him along the way. As was the custom, his canteen was made from the dried stomach of a sheep, goat, or other domestic animal. At a stopping place along the route, he took down his canteen, preparing to satisfy his thirst, but as he began to drink, only a thin colorless liquid poured out—something quite unlike the creamy milk he had poured into the skin earlier.

Disappointed, he split open the canteen. There he found settled to the bottom, a handful of snowy white curd, the world's first cheese. Hunger and curiosity moved him to taste it, and he must have found it pleasant. He must have repeated the story of the miraculous change which had taken place in the milk. Probably, he repeated the experiment over and over again, until he discovered that the change had come about because his canteen was made of an animal stomach.

In Jerusalem cheese was to be bought in the Valley of the Cheese Makers. In the early morning, the city gates were used as market places, lined with men and women offering for sale the produce of farms and gardens, much as our markets offer them today. The cheeses offered were probably of the two or three kinds which were staple in the land in Jesus' time: leben, a sort of yogurt that was one of the best-loved foods of the day, and the cheese of 2 Samuel 17:29, a preparation of dried curds which, when mixed with water, made a refreshing drink.

Ten Commandments for Cheese Cookery

1. Get acquainted with the whole family of cheeses . . . there are hundreds of varieties other than Cheddar and grated Parmesan.

2. Cook cheese, always, over low heat to prevent toughening, stringing, and separating. Use a double boiler or chafing dish when the recipe so directs.

3. Always grate cheese with a rotary-type grater with a hand-operated crank. Remember that one half pound cheese will yield about 2 cups grated.

4. Always shred cheese with a standard kitchen shredder. One half pound will yield about 2 cups shredded.

5. Always slice cheese with a wire cheese slicer for uniform, even slices.

6. Always store hard cheeses such as Cheddar and Swiss in the refrigerator, after wrapping them tightly in aluminum foil or moisture-vapor proof material to prevent drying.

7. Store soft, uncured cheeses such as cottage cheese or cream cheese in the refrigerator for no longer than 2 or 3 days. Cream cheese should be stored in its original wrapper; cottage cheese in a tightly covered container.

8. Remember that mold development on cheese during storage is a normal process. Scrape or cut the mold from the surface, discard it, and use the remainder of the cheese.

9. Never serve cheese for a dessert or a snack until it has warmed to room temperature. The single exception to this rule is cottage cheese, which must always be cold.

10. Except for Camembert and Liederkranz, freezing is an insult to cheese. Never, never resort to it.

Barzillai Casserole
Noodle-Cheese Casserole

3 quarts boiling water	2 teaspoons salt
3 teaspoons salt	few grains of pepper
3½ cups wide noodles	1 teaspoon celery seed
¼ cup minced onion	1⅓ cups milk
¼ cup minced green pepper	1 pound cottage cheese
½ stick butter or margarine	2 tablespoons lemon juice
3 tablespoons flour	

Break the noodles into 1½-inch pieces and cook in the boiling salted water until tender (about 10 minutes), stirring often. Drain thoroughly. Light the oven and set at 350°. Now, in a saucepan, sauté the onion and green pepper in the butter or margarine for about 3 minutes. Stir in the flour and seasonings, then stir in the milk gradually and cook, stirring, until the sauce is smooth and thick. Grease a 2-quart casserole; turn the sauce into it. Add noodles, cottage cheese, and lemon juice, and toss until well blended. Sprinkle with paprika. Bake, uncovered, 40 to 45 minutes. Serves 4-6. This is another one of those "basic" cheese dishes that may be varied a thousand ways with the addition of a bit of leftover meat, fish, etc.

Shobai Pancakes
Cheese-Stuffed Pancakes

½ pound soft cottage cheese	1 teaspoon salt
3 tablespoons flour	3 eggs
1 tablespoon sugar	

Force the cottage cheese through a ricer or sieve; add remaining ingredients and beat until well mixed. Drop by tablespoonfuls onto a hot greased griddle and cook until well browned. Serves 4. Just try these with strawberry jam!

Peppers Capernaum
Cheese-Stuffed Peppers

6 green peppers

1½ cups cottage cheese

2½ cups cooked rice

1 egg

salt and pepper

buttered soft crumbs

Wash the peppers, cut off about half an inch of the tops, then remove stems, seeds, and white fiber. Drop into boiling salted water and cook about 5 minutes or until barely tender. Drain. Mix the remaining ingredients, except for the bread crumbs. Taste to check the seasoning—you may need more pepper. Add the chopped pepper tops. Fill the peppers with this mixture, top with the bread crumbs, and place in a buttered baking pan. Bake at 375° for about 25 minutes. Serves 6.

> Whenever a recipe calls for buttered bread crumbs, I save time by topping with dry crumbs, dotting generously with bits of butter, and then baking. Gives the same results.

Epaphras Mousse
Rice-Cheese Mousse

1 tablespoon unflavored gelatin

¼ cup water

½ pound blue cheese

1 3-ounce package cream cheese

½ pint heavy cream, whipped

1 tablespoon Worcestershire sauce

½ teaspoon paprika

2 cups cooked rice

Soften the gelatin in the water, then place over boiling water until dissolved. (The simplest way to do this, something all books neglect to explain, is to soften the gelatin in a Pyrex measuring cup and then simply place the cup in a saucepan containing about an inch of hot water.) Press the cheeses through a coarse sieve, or break up with a fork; beat until softened, then beat in the whipped cream, seasoning, dissolved gelatin, and last of all the rice. Pour into a 6-cup ring mold or casserole which has been rinsed in cold water, and chill 3 or 4 hours.

I use this recipe for everything from an accompaniment for fruit salad, at luncheon, to a filling for green peppers for a cold summer supper.

Fondue Machir
Cheese Fondue

12 slices white bread	1 cup milk
¼ cup butter or margarine	1 teaspoon salt
1 cup grated sharp cheese	¼ teaspoon paprika
2 eggs	½ teaspoon dry mustard

Cut two of the slices of bread across in an X, making 8 small triangles. Butter lightly. Butter the remaining bread, then cut into neat cubes—you should have about 4 cups. Place a layer of bread cubes in a buttered 1½-quart casserole, sprinkle with cheese, repeat with cubes and cheese. You should have plenty for two or three layers. Now combine the remaining ingredients, beating until the eggs are well broken up, then pour this milk mixture over the bread. Let stand 20 minutes until the bread soaks up the milk mixture. (This, by the way, is one of the basic rules for a successful fondue.) Now, place the triangles of bread upright around the edge to form a crown. Bake at 350° for about 30 minutes. Serve at once to 4 people. I have never found anyone who doesn't love this dish. Just try it with creamed salmon as a sauce.

The first thought of the woman of Endor, faced with King Saul's despair at the prophecy of Samuel's spirit, was to feed him.—1 Samuel 28:24

Risotto Jesse
Rice with Mushrooms

1 pound rice	2 cups sliced mushrooms
12 bouillon cubes	(canned or fresh)
1 tablespoon tomato paste	⅛ teaspoon saffron
1 cup grated Parmesan cheese	13 cups boiling water

Measure the 13 cups of water, add the bouillon cubes and tomato paste, and stir briskly until the cubes are dissolved. Then add the rice slowly so the water does not stop boiling. Boil for 20 minutes. Add mushrooms and saffron and bring back to the boil, then stir in the cheese and cook, stirring, just long enough to heat through and melt the cheese. The saffron is merely a flavoring, and may be omitted if you do not have it on hand; the mushrooms, too, are purely optional. Any leftover meat may be added, just as Naomi might have added precious scraps of a leftover main dish; shrimp, lobster, or crabmeat, too, is a delicious variation. This is an ample dish; it will fill a 2-quart casserole and feed 8 people well. Just see how many ways you can use it!

Hattil Coleslaw
Coleslaw with Cheese

4 cups shredded cabbage	1½ cups drained cottage cheese
⅓ cup chopped parsley	⅓ cup olive or salad oil
1½ teaspoon celery seed	2 tablespoons cider vinegar
1½ teaspoon salt, divided	2 teaspoons prepared mustard

Stir together lightly the first four ingredients, using only 1 teaspoon of the salt. Sprinkle the cottage cheese over the top. Chill thoroughly. Make a dressing by beating together the remaining ingredients, with the remaining ½ teaspoon salt, until well blended. Add to the cheese and cabbage just before serving, and toss thoroughly. Serves 6. To make a fine main dish for warm weather, garnish with finger-sized strips of any left-over cold meat, or deviled eggs.

Raddai Spread
Cheese Spread

1 3-ounce package cream cheese	1 teaspoon paprika
¾ stick butter or margarine	½ teaspoon anchovy paste
1 teaspoon capers	½ teaspoon caraway seeds
1 tablespoon minced onion	

Bring all the ingredients to room temperature, then blend the butter and cheese, add the other ingredients and mix thoroughly. Pack into a little round dish or cup and chill thoroughly. Serve with thinly sliced Melba toast, both white and rye. Let the guests spread their own. This is enough for 6—a most economical first course for any dinner.

Eglah Omelette
Cheese Omelette

6 eggs	½ teaspoon salt
¼ cup grated Parmesan cheese	¼ teaspoon black pepper
¼ cup diced Swiss cheese	⅛ teaspoon nutmeg
4 tablespoons butter	

Beat the eggs very lightly in a bowl; add the remaining ingredients, except the butter. Melt the butter in a 9-inch skillet or omelet pan, letting it heat until it has a nutty fragrance, but isn't browned. Pour the egg mixture into the pan and cook over low heat until lightly browned, pulling the mixture from the sides of the pan with a fork, as it cooks. Turn and brown lightly on the other side. Serves 4.

Haggith Pudding
Cheese Mold

6 eggs, separated	few grains pepper
¼ cup flour	½ cup sour cream
¼ teaspoon salt	½ cup milk

⅓ cup grated Parmesan cheese

Beat the egg whites until stiff, then with the same beater beat the yolks until light, add dry ingredients, sour cream and milk, and beat again until smooth. Add the cheese and the stiffly beaten whites, and mix or fold gently into the batter. Butter the upper part of a 1½-quart double boiler, put in about ¼ cup fine dry bread or cracker crumbs, and turn and tip the pan until it is well coated with crumbs. Turn in the cheese batter; cover tightly and cook over gently boiling water for 50 to 60 minutes. Serves 6. This is a delicious supper dish served with additional cheese, sautéed mushrooms, or the tomato sauce given on page 180.

Phoebe's Dish
Cheese Luncheon Loaf

1 tablespoon butter	1 cup chopped walnuts
2 tablespoons minced onion	1 cup dry bread crumbs
salt and pepper	1 tablespoon lemon juice
1 cup grated cheese	½ cup milk

Sauté the onion in butter until golden. Combine all ingredients, stirring in the milk last, then add the tender onions and turn into a buttered 1-quart baking dish. Bake at 400° about 15 minutes, or brown under the broiler. Serves 4. Particularly nice to balance a cool salad menu.

If David had not been sent to the Israelite camp with the ten cheeses, he would not have been present to face Goliath. See 1 Samuel 17:17-18

Gebinah Puff
Easy Cheese Soufflé

1 can condensed cream soup   ¾ cup grated cheese
(asparagus, chicken, or cel-   4 eggs, separated
ery)

Heat the oven to 325°. Place the soup and cheese in the top of a double boiler over boiling water and cook, stirring, until the cheese melts. Stir in the egg yolks one at a time. Blend thoroughly, then cool. (This much of this dish may be prepared ahead of time.) When ready to bake, beat the egg whites stiff enough to hold soft peaks, then fold into the first mixture. Pour into a buttered 1½-quart casserole and place in a pan containing an inch of hot water. Bake at 300° for an hour and 15 minutes. Serves 4.

This recipe may be varied ad infinitum, too, by the addition of one cup leftover vegetables, finely cut meat, minced fish, and such foods. If you have never used soufflés to any extent, be sure to try it.

You will seek me and find me; when you seek me with all your heart.—Jeremiah 29:13

Leben, a sort of yogurt made from soured milk, was one of the first and best-loved foods of Bible lands. The housewives of Jesus' time added a little leben to fresh milk to make it ferment, then poured the milk into a leather bag hung on three poles in the form of a cone, and two women then shook it violently between them. This produced a sort of butter, and also a form of buttermilk which was put into little cloth sacks so that the water could be squeezed out. The cheeselike substance which remained was rolled into balls which kept indefinitely; it undoubtedly saved many a life in arid regions where potable water was unavailable. The Bedouins, too, coagulated buttermilk and ground it to a powder; it was one of their staple foods.

I think of this facet of biblical living every time I use our very modern, perfected nonfat dry milk, for this, essentially, is what the leben was. I like to ponder for a bit on how wise biblical people were in the ways of life, and how long it has taken us to come back to some of the valuable ideas they developed for us. It gives me a warm feeling of being not so different, after all, from Mary and Martha and all the other wise women of the biblical stories. I hope that you, too, will experience this feeling of kinship as you go through these pages; it will make you feel closer to God all through the day.

Nonfat dry milk, in addition to being a close relative of a favorite biblical food, is one of our most economical high-quality protein foods; all the vitamins, minerals, and protein content in fresh skim milk come to us unaltered in this product. There is a slight loss of Vitamin C which is not present in quantity in whole milk, anyway. Nonfat milk is low in calories; it has an attractive flavor; it whips easily. I want you to try some of my favorite recipes using it so that you can see what I mean.

Do all things without grumbling or questioning.
—Philippians 2:14

David's Cake
Upside-Down Cake

1 1-pound-4-ounce can sliced pineapple	1 cup brown sugar
¼ cup butter or margarine	1 17-ounce package white cake mix
¼ cup nonfat dry milk	

Drain the syrup from the pineapple; add enough water to make 1⅓ cups liquid. In a 10-inch skillet that can go into the oven, melt the butter; remove from the heat and sprinkle with the brown sugar. Arrange 8 slices of pineapple on the sugar. Let stand. Choose a white cake mix that calls for milk on the package; turn this into a 2-quart bowl and mix in the nonfat dry milk. Add ⅔ cup of the pineapple syrup; beat hard 2 minutes. Add ⅓ cup syrup and beat hard one minute. Add remaining syrup and beat again for 1 minute. Pour batter over the pineapple in the skillet; bake 45 to 50 minutes at 375° or until the cake pulls away from the sides of the pan. Remove from the oven, let the cake stand 5 minutes, then turn out. If you use an iron skillet, reduce the heat to 350° and bake from 5 to 10 minutes longer. This is a good basic recipe usable with any fruit such as peaches, pears, cherries, etc. Serve with:

Whipped Topping

½ cup instant nonfat dry milk	3 tablespoons lemon juice
½ cup ice cold water	3 tablespoons sugar

Place the nonfat dry milk in a 1-quart bowl. Add the ice water and beat with a rotary beater at high speed until the mixture stands in peaks—about 2 minutes. Add the lemon juice, beat again, and then gradually beat in the sugar. This is better if it chills for about 30 minutes. Makes about 2½ cups.

Some of the finest stories ever written are found in the Books of Ruth and Jonah and Esther.

Julia's Meat Loaf
Best-Ever Meat Loaf

1 pound ground lean beef	½ cup instant nonfat dry milk
⅓ cup uncooked rolled oats	1¼ teaspoons salt
¼ cup minced onion	⅛ teaspoon pepper
1 cup drained canned tomatoes	2 bacon slices, cut in half

Mix all ingredients thoroughly with the exception of the bacon slices. When well blended, turn into a greased, shallow baking pan and with your hands wet shape into a rounded loaf. Arrange the 4 pieces of bacon on top the loaf. Bake on the center rack of the oven about 1 hour or until brown. We like to coat the top of the loaf with catsup during the last 15 minutes of cooking. 350° is the best temperature for meat loaves to cook through without drying. Serves 4.

Galeed Pudding
Custard Pudding

⅓ cup instant nonfat dry milk	¼ teaspoon nutmeg
3 tablespoons sugar	3 slices bread ½ inch thick
pinch of salt	1½ tablespoons butter
2 eggs	⅓ cup seedless raisins
1½ cups water	2 tablespoons sugar
1 teaspoon vanilla	¼ teaspoon cinnamon

Make a custard mixture by turning the instant nonfat dry milk into a 1½-quart bowl, adding sugar, salt, eggs, and nutmeg and beating lightly. Add water and vanilla and stir. Toast the bread on both sides, then spread with the butter and cut into inch cubes. Arrange in a buttered baking dish holding about 6 cups. Sprinkle the sugar, cinnamon, and raisins over the toast. Now pour the custard mixture over the toast in the baking dish, heat the oven to 350° and bake the pudding on the center rack for 45 minutes or until a knife inserted near the edge comes out clean. Makes 4 servings. My family loves this good pudding served with sugared fruits or fruit sauces.

Sidon Sweet
Gingered Dessert

1 envelope unflavored gelatin	6 tablespoons lemon juice
6 tablespoons sugar	⅓ cup cold water
1¼ cups hot water	⅓ cup instant nonfat dry
2½ cups peach purée	milk

1 tablespoon chopped, crystallized ginger

Set the refrigerator control at the coldest point. Canned, frozen, or fresh peaches may be used; for purée; simply chop very fine or force through a food mill. In a deep bowl mix gelatin and sugar together. Add hot water; stir until gelatin is dissolved. Blend in the peach purée and lemon juice. Place over a bowl of ice and stir the mixture until it is the consistency of uncooked egg whites. Pour the cold water into a deep 1-quart mixing bowl; sprinkle the nonfat dry milk over the surface, then beat with a rotary beater or electric mixer until stiff—about 8 or 10 minutes. Fold the whipped milk into the gelatin mixture; pour into 2 small refrigerator trays. Freeze until almost firm, then turn the mixture into a chilled bowl and add the ginger; beat with a rotary beater until smooth and fluffy but not melted. Return to the trays and freeze until firm—about 2 hours. Serves 8.

For lack of wood the fire goes out;
and where there is no whisperer,
quarreling ceases.

—Proverbs 26:20

Obed Lemon Custard
Lemon Custard

1 egg yolk	pinch of salt
⅓ cup sugar	1 egg white
¼ teaspoon grated lemon rind	⅓ cup water
3 tablespoons lemon juice	⅓ cup nonfat dry milk

¼ cup graham cracker crumbs

Mix in a small bowl the egg yolk, sugar, lemon rind, lemon juice, and salt. In a one-quart bowl, put the egg white, water and nonfat dry milk and beat with a rotary beater at high speed, until the mixture stands in peaks. Gradually beat in the lemon mixture. Turn into a 1-quart ice tray, sprinkle the graham cracker crumbs over the top, and freeze without stirring, at the coldest temperature, until firm. Serves 4.

Bashan Nog
Banana Nog

1 large ripe banana	1 tablespoon sugar
⅓ cup instant nonfat dry milk	1 cup ice cold water

½ teaspoon vanilla

On a piece of waxed paper, mash the peeled banana with a fork until it makes a paste. Turn into a jar or pitcher holding 3 or 4 cups. Add the remaining ingredients, then stir or shake until well blended. Serve very cold, topped with a scoop of vanilla ice cream, if you like it. This is especially good if mixed in an electric blender.

We remember the fish we ate in Egypt for nothing, the cucumbers, the melons, the leeks, the onions, and the garlic.—Numbers 11:5

CHAPTER EIGHT

POTHERBS

According to the story of Genesis, man lived at first on vegetables alone (Genesis 1:29, 2:16); animal food is not mentioned specifically until after the flood.

So then, as we have opportunity, let us do good to all men.—Galatians 6:10

THE housewife of biblical times used the word "herb" in its true sense, i.e., any plant that does not form woody tissue, any green plant. Thus, in biblical terminology we find the word covering all of the green plants that were eaten. Potherbs were those that were cooked, and green herbs were those that were eaten raw.

Among the potherbs, the housewife of Jesus' time had the whole gourd family: cucumbers, pumpkins, squash, and the like, including the colocynth—a bitter ground fruit somewhat like an orange. Young grape leaves were often used as a vegetable in stews and pottage; pulse, a word we come across often in tracing both Old and New Testament cookery, probably meant grain or seeds used as vegetables—the implied meaning is any simple food.

She had, too, four varieties of beans, including the chick-pea; she had various sorts of chicory and endive, and the leaves of the mustard plant. She had saffron, a common plant in Palestine, a sort of crocus, which was used both for flavoring and for eating raw. She had onions, and these were highly prized as food. She had mint; this was one of the bitter herbs of the paschal feast, as was horse-radish. She had melons of many varieties, all of them a favorite food as they are today in countries where the weather is hot.

In addition, she had the spirit of adventure; she was willing to try something new. We read in 2 Kings 4:39, "One of them went out into the field to gather herbs, and found a wild vine and gathered from it his lap full of wild gourds, and came and cut them up into the pot of pottage, not knowing what they were." You try something new for dinner; see what fun it is.

Ten Commandments for Vegetable Cookery

1. Don't confine yourself to fresh vegetables in season; frozen and canned vegetables are often cheaper and better. They are quicker and easier, too.
2. Concentrate on developing a skill with your paring knife so that you peel your vegetables only skin deep. Or buy one of the patented vegetable peelers that are so easy to use.
3. Never soak fresh vegetables, no matter what your cookbook says; the largest part of the valuable vitamins and minerals go down the drain when vegetables are soaked to freshen them. Prepare them just moments before you plan to cook them.
4. Prepare just enough for one meal unless you are cooking ahead for planned leftovers. Freshly cooked vegetables taste better and are better.
5. Don't drown the poor things in the cooking—the less water the better. A couple of tablespoons of butter or margarine or oil plus the water that will cook out from the leaves will give a better-flavored dish.
6. Cook them quickly so as to seal in all the good food values. Use heavy, tightly covered saucepans, bring to a boil over high heat, and then reduce the heat to finish cooking. Don't lift the lid to test for doneness or you will lose all the steam that is doing the cooking.
7. Remember that there are other methods for cooking vegetables than plain boiling; try deep-fat frying in batter (page 130), baking, pan frying, braising.
8. Cook for the shortest possible time; overcooking is the one unforgivable sin with vegetables. They should come to the table just tender-crisp, never soggy or mushy. You'll soon learn the difference.
9. Rush them from saucepan to table—every minute of waiting after cooking allows precious vitamins to escape.
10. Save the cooking water, no matter how little it is. Use it to dilute canned soups, as the liquid in gravies and stews, and as a refreshing and healthful drink.

Artichokes

Long before the time of Christ, Mediterranean peoples cultivated a gigantic thistle, cardoon, for its leafy shoots, which
were grown in the dark to make them white and tender. It was
in Italy, at the time of Paul's journeys, that the form of artichoke that we know, with its fleshy edible flower parts, was
developed.

Artichokes are available in frozen form now, all cleaned and
neatly packaged, as easy to prepare as a can of corn. If you are
using these, disregard the paragraph below on preparation of
the artichoke; all that is necessary is to put the dish together.

Wash the artichokes thoroughly; cut about 1 inch off the tops,
then set them upside down to drain. This is a very necessary
step; if the artichokes are not thoroughly drained, liquid will
cling inside the leaves and run out when serving, diluting the
sauce. Cut off the stem about 1 inch from the base, leaving a
stub. With scissors, clip off any thorny tips on the leaves. Rub
the cut edges with lemon juice. While doing this, bring a pan
of water to a boil; drop in the artichokes and scald for 5 minutes. Drain.

To eat an artichoke, simply pluck off the leaves one by one,
dip the base of each leaf into sauce. Eat only the tender base
end, scraping off the soft pulp with the teeth, and discard the
rest. When you reach the center, use knife and fork to pick out
the fuzzy "choke." Discard this; cut the remaining heart or
bottom with your fork, dip in sauce, and eat. You'll find it
delightful.

*The Old Testament poem known as the Book of Job is
an incomparable literary masterpiece of our Bible. Read
it and thrill to it.*

Thistle Delecta
Stuffed Artichokes

6 medium French artichokes
¼ cup lemon juice
¾ pound fresh or 1½ cups
    canned mushrooms

½ cup olive oil or vegetable oil
¼ cup cracker crumbs
¾ cup tomato juice or liquid
    from canned mushrooms

3 pimentos, chopped

Chop the mushrooms and pimentos coarsely, then heat the oil in a small skillet and sauté the chopped vegetables for about 10 minutes. Add cracker crumbs and mix well. Stuff the artichoke shells with this dressing. Place in a well-oiled baking dish, pour tomato juice or mushroom liquid over and around them. Cover and bake at 350° for 60 to 75 minutes or until tender. Then uncover and bake for another 5 minutes to finish. Serve at once. Serves 6.

Aven Thistle
Steamed Artichokes

Prepare artichokes as directed on page 113, then stand them upright in a deep saucepan just large enough so they will fit snugly and not tip over. Sprinkle with ¾ teaspoon salt and 3 teaspoons salad oil for each artichoke. Now pour boiling water over them to a depth of 1 inch in the pan; add 1 or 2 minced, peeled cloves of garlic and 1 peeled, sliced onion; cover tightly and boil gently for 45 to 60 minutes, depending upon size. Test by pulling out a leaf and tasting; when the base of the leaf is very tender, the artichoke is done. Lift out with tongs, drain, then serve hot or cold.

If anyone will not work, let him not eat.—2 Thessalonians 3:10

Sauces for Artichokes

Lemon Butter

Melt ½ cup butter or margarine and add 2 tablespoons minced parsley and 2 tablespoons lemon juice.

Onion Butter

In ½ cup butter or margarine, sauté ¼ cup minced onion. Add ½ teaspoon marjoram, if you like herbs.

Parmesan Sauce

Blend ½ cup mayonnaise with 1 tablespoon grated Parmesan cheese and serve cold on cold artichokes, or heat in the top of a double boiler and serve hot on hot artichokes.

Mustard Sauce

Blend ½ cup mayonnaise with 2 teaspoons prepared mustard and 2 tablespoons lemon juice. Serve cold or hot.

Green-Pepper Sauce

Blend ½ cup mayonnaise with 1¼ cups grated Cheddar cheese and 2 tablespoons minced green pepper. Serve on cold artichokes as a salad. All of these sauces are sufficient for 4 artichokes.

The number of servings obtained from a given vegetable varies from family to family and also according to usage. As a general rule, figure for one serving, ½ to ⅓ pound of raw vegetable; ½ to ¾ cup canned vegetable; ¼ to ½ package (10 to 16 ounces) frozen vegetable.

"The child grew and became strong, filled with wisdom; and the favor of God was upon him."—Luke 2:40. These 17 words are all we have to tell us what happened from Jesus' babyhood to his twelfth year.

Asparagus

This vegetable delicacy grows wild over much of the biblical country even today, thriving along riverbanks and on the shores of lakes. The Romans as early as 200 B.C. gave detailed instructions for growing it, and it was not only eaten fresh, but was used in dried form. There is no doubt but that it appeared on the table of the housewife in biblical times.

If you are using frozen asparagus, don't defrost before cooking. Simply drop into a small amount of boiling water and cook 10 to 12 minutes after the water comes back to a boil.

If you are using the canned variety, drain and cook uncovered until the liquid is reduced by half. Then add asparagus and cook, covered, until just heated through.

For fresh asparagus, wash thoroughly to remove any sand that may be under the scales. Cut or break off tough ends. Use a deep pan with a tight cover—a tall percolator or the bottom of a double boiler with the cooking top inverted as a cover is excellent. With about 2 inches of water in the pan, add 1 tablespoon salt and bring to a boil. Tie the asparagus in a bunch and stand upright in the water—the steam will cook the tips. Cook, covered, with the water boiling rapidly, 15 or 20 minutes, or until tender.

Asparagus Bernice
Asparagus with Sauce

2 cups cooked, cut asparagus	1 teaspoon soy sauce
1 tablespoon salad oil	1 tablespoon cornstarch
½ cup finely chopped bacon	2 tablespoons cold water
1 cup chicken bouillon	1 teaspoon Accent

Heat the salad oil in a skillet; add bacon and cook, stirring, until the bacon is golden and crisp. Add the asparagus and cook until heated through, then slowly add the bouillon and soy sauce and cook for 3 minutes. While this is cooking, stir the cornstarch into the cold water until it forms a smooth paste,. then stir this into the mixture in the skillet and continue cooking, stirring constantly, until the sauce is smooth and thick and clear. Add the Accent, give it one last stir, then serve. Serves 4.

By adding any diced, cooked meat or fowl, this may be served over rice for a tasty main dish.

Asparagus Nadab
Asparagus with Cream

2 cups drained cooked or
  canned asparagus
½ cup commercial sour cream

½ cup bread crumbs
butter or margarine
salt and pepper to taste

Set the oven at 325°. Arrange the asparagus in a shallow, buttered baking dish. Cover with the sour cream; add just a sprinkling of salt and pepper, then top with the bread crumbs and dot generously with butter or margarine. Bake about 20 minutes, or until the crumbs are nicely browned. Serves 4. This is a delicious company dish, elegant and easy.

> Try topping asparagus with any of these taste teasers: a few drops of lemon juice, horse-radish blended into sour cream, or chopped hard-cooked egg.

Green Beans . . . Wax Beans

Your family will never turn up their noses at green beans if you will serve them in new and striking ways—and some of these are quicker and easier than the old tried and true methods! There has been continued controversy as to whether the green bean as we know it might have been included in the pulse of biblical writings; we could find nothing to settle the question one way or the other, and so include these few bean recipes simply because we think you will like them.

Green Beans Gozan
Quick Green Beans

2 pounds snap beans, or 2 cans   salt and pepper
  or 2 packages frozen   1 teaspoon Accent
1 tablespoon butter or mar-   ½ cup pecan halves
  garine

If you are cooking fresh beans, wash well, snip off the stems, then sliver, French style. Both canned and frozen beans may be bought already Frenched. Put fresh beans into a pot, add boiling water to not quite cover, cover tightly, bring to a boil over high heat, then remove the lid and cook until crisp tender. For frozen beans, simply turn them into a pot, add ½ inch hot water and proceed as above. For canned beans, drain, cook the liquid down to half over high heat. For all, turn a few times during the cooking; you want to prevent scorching as the liquid cooks away. When finished, there should be barely a spoonful of liquid in the pot.

While the beans are cooking, sauté the pecans in the butter or margarine over low heat until very crisp. When the beans are tender-crisp, add 2 tablespoons butter or margarine, salt and pepper to taste, and then the Accent. Add the pecans, toss lightly, and serve at once. Serves 4-6.

Eleazar Beans
Beans with Gravy

2 slices bacon, diced   1 teaspoon sugar
1 small onion, minced   salt and pepper to taste
1 tablespoon flour   2 cups cooked or canned string
1 teaspoon prepared mustard   beans with ½ cup liquid

Sauté the bacon in a saucepan until almost crisp; add the onion and continue cooking until the bacon is done and the onion a nice tender, golden brown. Add the flour and blend well; stir in the mustard, sugar, salt, and pepper. Last, add the string beans. Simmer for a few minutes to heat through, stirring until smooth. Serves 4.

Prophet's Pulse
Herbed Scramble

1 sliced garlic clove	1 pound string beans cut in
1 onion, minced	pieces
1 tablespoon salad oil	salt and pepper to taste
1 tomato, cut in small chunks	½ teaspoon dried basil

1 egg

Lightly sauté the garlic and onion in the oil. Remove the pieces of garlic, add tomato, cover, and simmer until soft. Arrange the beans on top the tomato and salt and pepper, cover, and simmer for 10 minutes. Add basil. Beat the egg slightly and pour over the beans; toss until the egg is cooked and blended throughout. You'll love it.

Beets and Swiss Chard

Chard, a primitive, leafy beet that produces no root, and common beets, the kind that we know, are of the same species. Both were well known to the Romans of Old and New Testament times, and there is evidence that the seeds were carried back to Egypt and to Palestine for cultivation.

Ahira Greens
Beet Top Greens

Beet greens may be prepared in the same ways that you prepare spinach or Swiss chard, but they must be young and small to be tasty. Try cooking 1 pound greens in boiling salted water for 5 to 8 minutes. Drain, chop, add 2 tablespoons butter or margarine, and toss with a fork until the butter is melted. Add 1 tablespoon prepared horse-radish and 1 teaspoon lemon juice and mix well. Season with salt and pepper. Serves 4. Husbands love this dish with boiled smoked tongue.

Beets Husham
Sweet-Sour Beets

3 cups cooked or canned beets
¼ cup sugar
2 teaspoons cornstarch
½ teaspoon salt
2 tablespoons lemon juice
grated rind of ¼ orange
2 tablespoons orange juice
grated rind of ½ lemon
1 tablespoon butter

If you are using fresh beets, scrub well and cut off tops, leaving about an inch of stem on the beets, then cook in boiling water until tender—45 to 60 minutes, depending upon size and age. Drain, saving ⅓ cup cooking liquid. Peel and dice. Make a sauce by stirring the sugar and cornstarch together until well blended, then stirring in the remaining ingredients and the ⅓ cup beet liquid. Stir and cook until smooth and thick (you may need a bit more liquid) and clear. This is a variation of the famous Harvard, or sweet-sour beets. Serves 4.

Beets Elimelech
Beets with Cream

I like to use canned baby beets for this dish—they look prettier and are less·work than fresh beets cooked at home.

3 tablespoons butter
3 tablespoons flour
1 cup liquid drained from beets
¼ cup tarragon vinegar
1 cup sour cream
1 tablespoon caraway seeds

Melt the butter in a saucepan, stir in the flour and cook, stirring, until smooth. Gradually stir in the liquid from the beets, then add the tarragon vinegar, and cook, stirring, until thick and smooth. Turn the beets into the sauce and heat through over low heat. To serve, pile the beets in a serving dish, top with the sour cream, and sprinkle with the caraway seeds.

"The Lord rewarded me according to my righteousness."
—2 Samuel 22:21

Cherith Chard
Cheesed Chard

2 pounds Swiss chard
boiling water
2 teaspoons salt
2 tablespoons butter or margarine

2 tablespoons flour
½ cup milk
¼ pound (1 cup) diced Cheddar cheese

Heat the oven to 325°. Cut the stalks from the washed chard into one-inch pieces; cook, covered, for 5 minutes in a half inch of boiling water and the salt. Then add the leaves, torn into pieces, and cook 5 minutes longer. Drain well, turning into a colander and using a fork to press out the liquid. While this is draining, melt the butter in a saucepan, stir in the flour, slowly add the milk and cook, stirring constantly, over medium heat until thickened. Add the cheese; add the chard and toss well. Turn into a 1½-quart casserole and bake, uncovered, for 45 minutes. Serves 4.

The middle ribs of the chard stalk are too thick and fleshy to cook in this way; cut them out and cook and serve as you would asparagus.

Broccoli

Broccoli and cauliflower stem from a common ancestor, a sort of cabbage that is native to biblical countries. Long before heading cabbage was known, the ancients of biblical lands were cooking and eating these cabbage flowers; broccoli has been known there for 2,000 years, and we have a record of cauliflower dating back to the 6th century B.C. Both of them must have been served often in biblical times.

"If any man would come after me, let him deny himself and take up his cross daily and follow me."—Luke 9:23

Broccoli Apollos
Broccoli with Soy Sauce

1 cup chicken stock or consommé	1 teaspoon soy sauce
2 teaspoons cornstarch	2 pounds broccoli
	¼ cup salad oil

Make a sauce by cooking the chicken stock with the cornstarch which has been rubbed smooth in about 2 tablespoons cold water. Cook, stirring, until thickened. Add the soy sauce. Wash the broccoli thoroughly and cut off the flowery tops. Slice the stems at a slant in pieces about ½ inch thick. Measure the oil into a heavy saucepan or skillet, add the stems, and cook for about 5 minutes, stirring. Add the tops cut in small pieces and cook 5 minutes more. Pour the thickened sauce over the broccoli, cover, and cook for 2 minutes. Remove the cover and cook 4 minutes. Try this with roast pork; it was probably in such simple ways as this that broccoli appeared on the tables of biblical times.

Broccoli Superba

Broccoli Superba is simply the vegetable cooked tender-crisp, drained, then topped with a few tablespoons melted butter and a thick sprinkling of crumbled blue cheese. Elegant as can be; every man loves it.

Jadon Casserole
Broccoli Casserole

8 deviled-egg halves	1½ cups medium white sauce
2 cups cooked broccoli buds	

Butter 4 individual casseroles. Add a few grains of nutmeg to the white sauce, then add the broccoli and mix carefully so as not to break the vegetable. Divide the creamed broccoli evenly between the 4 casseroles. Press 2 deviled-egg halves into the top of each, pushing the eggs well down so that only the golden yolk shows. Heat at 325° for about 20 minutes. Eggs are delicious with broccoli.

Caphtor Ring
Luncheon Ring

3 eggs	1 tablespoon chopped onion
½ cup milk	1 teaspoon salt
½ cup coffee cream	pinch of pepper
1½ cups cooked broccoli	dash of paprika

Beat the eggs slightly; stir in the remaining ingredients. Try adding a few grains of nutmeg. Grease a 1-quart ring mold, set it in a pan containing an inch of hot water, then fill the ring and bake at 350° for about 45 minutes, or until set. Serves 4.

Cabbage

The ancient and honorable cabbage in the form that we know it, had not come into existence in biblical days, but various loose-heading varieties were known in Egypt and along the Mediterranean Sea; it has been known here for more than 2,000 years. The housewife of biblical times probably used it most frequently as the wrapping for her dolmas, a hearty, flavorful dish that made fine use of the tiny bits of meat and grain that she had saved. She may have used grape leaves or lettuce leaves, as well as cabbage leaves, in making her *dolmades,* and if you would like to follow her recipe faithfully, you may use fresh grape leaves, which are ready on your own vines, or grape leaves obtainable now in 15½-ounce jars at specialty shops. Grape leaves add a subtle flavor to the stuffing of dolmas; they're well worth going to a little trouble to obtain.

Dolmades Lydia
Cabbage-Beef Rolls

Wash the cabbage and cut out the stem end and core. Put in a large kettle, cover with boiling salted water, and cook until the leaves are loose enough to separate with a fork—about 20 minutes more or less, depending upon size. Remove the cabbage, drain, and separate the leaves. Or, use one 15½-ounce jar grape leaves.

1 pound ground beef	2 medium onions, chopped fine
½ cup butter or margarine	½ cup uncooked rice
1 cup canned tomatoes	2 tablespoons chopped mint
1½ cups hot water	salt and pepper

Simply mix together all of the ingredients except the tomatoes and the water. Salt and pepper to taste. In the center of each leaf, place a heaping teaspoon of the mixture. Starting from the stem end (if stems are very thick, cut them out), roll, turning in the ends and rolling tightly to keep the filling from coming out. Form into oblong rolls.

Arrange in compact layers in a large saucepan, and place a plate over the rolls to prevent breaking up when the water boils. Add the water and tomatoes, bring to a boil over high heat, then reduce the heat and simmer 25 minutes. Remove from the heat and drain off the broth into a separate bowl to be used in this delicious sauce:

Tryphosa
Egg and Lemon Sauce

This is the famous Greek egg and lemon sauce. This amount of lemon juice gives a very tart sauce; if you want one less tart, use only 1 lemon. The secret in preparing it without curdling is to pour the hot broth from the *dolmades* into the eggs while they are being beaten; this heats the eggs to the same temperature and eliminates curdling—a good procedure to remember when making any sauce.

4 eggs	3 tablespoons water
juice of 2 lemons	¾ cup broth from food to be used

Beat the eggs and water until light and fluffy, then, still beating, add the hot broth gradually. When the eggs are light and foamy, pour in the lemon juice and beat again. Pour at once over the *dolmades,* allow to stand a few moments, and serve hot. Serves 5 or 6.

Another delicious idea for dolmas will be found in the chapter on Savory Meats, page 74.

Cabbage Mark
Sweet-Sour Cabbage

5 cups shredded cabbage	2 tablespoons flour
4 slices bacon, diced	½ cup water
2 tablespoons brown sugar	⅓ cup vinegar
1 small onion, diced	salt and pepper

Cook the cabbage in boiling, salted water for exactly 7 minutes; it will be tender-crisp. Drain. In a skillet, sauté the bacon, add the brown sugar, onion, and flour and stir until completely blended with the fat. Add the water and vinegar, and cook, stirring, until smooth and thick. Add seasonings to taste and turn the sauce over the drained cabbage. Toss over low heat until heated through. This serves 4-6, depending upon appetites.

This sweet-sour idea works perfectly with any of the leafy potherbs, so it is a valuable recipe to have fixed in your mind. German cooks make a huge egg pancake (4 eggs, ¼ cup milk, 2 tablespoons flour, salt, and pepper, beaten together) the full size of the skillet, fried brown in a little butter, then turn lettuce prepared with this sweet-sour sauce over it. It's delicious.

Cainan Leaves
Cabbage and Bacon

3 slices bacon	juice of 1 lemon
4 cups chopped cabbage	salt and pepper

Dice the bacon; cook in a skillet until golden brown and crisp. Spoon the bacon from the fat. Add the chopped cabbage to the bacon fat, reduce the heat, and toss the cabbage until just tender—about 10 minutes. Add the lemon juice and seasonings to taste and turn into a warm serving dish. Garnish with bacon.

Asaph Shred
Curried Cabbage

6 cups finely shredded cabbage	1 teaspoon minced garlic
2 tablespoons butter	1 teaspoon curry powder
1 teaspoon salt	

Wash the cabbage and shred as for slaw. Heat the butter in a large skillet, add the garlic, curry powder, and salt, and sauté for about 2 minutes. Add the cabbage and cook, covered, until tender—about 10 minutes—stirring occasionally. Some cooks like to add a cup of canned tomatoes just before the cabbage is done. If it seems to stick during cooking, add just a little water. Serves 4-6.

Cabbage Cornelius
Cabbage with Caraway

Here is a way of fixing cabbage that was probably one of Paul's favorites. Cook shredded cabbage in a small amount of salted water, tightly covered, until just tender. Drain and toss 3 cups of the cabbage with ½ cup sour cream and 1 teaspoon caraway seeds. Add a little salt and pepper and heat over hot water or very low heat about 10 minutes to blend the flavors.

The women who cooked for Paul would have used the cream from goat's milk, but our commercial sour cream is even better. You'll like this.

Carrots.

The humble carrot, so rich in Vitamin A, is another native of Mediterranean countries; it was cultivated in biblical lands even before Christ's time, but it was not considered an important food until much later. As a matter of fact, it is only in the past thirty years that the carrot has been treated with respect in this country; prior to 1920 or thereabouts, it was strictly a poor man's dish. How much the rich were missing!

Carrots Festus
Braised Carrots

3 cups sliced fresh carrots
½ teaspoon salt
1 inch boiling water in pan
½ cup onion rings
2 tablespoons butter or margarine

1 tablespoon flour
½ cup chicken bouillon
½ teaspoon salt
pinch of black pepper
2 tablespoons parsley

Place the carrots in a saucepan with the salt and boiling water and cook, covered, until almost tender—about 6 minutes. Drain if there is any water remaining, then set aside. In a small skillet, sauté the onion rings in butter or margarine until limp. Stir the flour into the carrots, then add to this the onion rings. Cook until the carrots begin to brown, then add bouillon, salt, and pepper. Cook slowly until carrots are tender—not more than 10 minutes. Add chopped parsley. Serves 4 or 5.

> *Did you know that verses 8, 15, 21 and 31 of Psalm 107 are alike? Look and see!*

Carrots Dorcas
Herbed Carrots

1 bunch young carrots	½ cup boiling water
2 green onions	¼ teaspoon basil
2 tablespoons butter or margarine	¼ teaspoon marjoram
	¼ teaspoon savory

4 strips bacon

Scrub the carrots, cut in half lengthwise and crosswise. Cut the onions, including tops, into 1-inch pieces. Melt the butter or margarine in a saucepan; add carrots, onions, water, and herbs, plus a little salt and pepper. Cover and cook until tender —about 20 minutes. Cut bacon into 1-inch pieces, fry until crisp, and add to carrots just before serving. Serves 4.

Hammath Carrots
Carrot Relish

1 bunch large carrots	½ teaspoon pepper
2 cloves garlic, crushed	¼ cup olive or salad oil
½ teaspoon salt	2 tablespoons wine vinegar

1 teaspoon orégano

Scrape the carrots, cut into thick slices, and boil in salted water until barely tender—8 or 10 minutes. Drain well and place in a bowl with remaining ingredients, mixing well. Let stand in this marinade for at least 12 hours, then serve as an accompaniment for meat, or as a salad. Serves 8.

Whatever is true, whatever is honorable, whatever is just, whatever is pure, whatever is lovely, whatever is gracious, if there is any excellence, if there is anything worthy of praise, think about these things.

—Philippians 4:8

Cauliflower

Cauliflower Philippi
Cauliflower Salad

This traditional salad, handed down from the Romans, is still served in Naples at Christmas dinner.

1 cauliflower—about 3 pounds
8 anchovy fillets, chopped fine
20 ripe olives pitted and chopped or 1 cup canned chopped olives
1 tablespoon capers
8 tablespoons olive oil
4 tablespoons vinegar
salt and pepper

Remove the green leaves from the cauliflower; break into flowerets. Cook in 2 inches of salted boiling water for not longer than 5 minutes so that it is tender-crisp. Drain, then place in a bowl with a few ice cubes to chill quickly. While this is chilling, mix the anchovies, olives, capers, olive oil and vinegar and blend well. Pour over the drained cauliflower and season with salt and freshly ground black pepper. Serves 6.

Mattan Flower
Cauliflower Crisp

This is just the sort of quick dish that Martha would have loved. Wash and remove lower stalks from a small or medium-sized head of crisp cauliflower. With a sharp knife, cut across the head in thin slices. Place in a skillet; sprinkle with a little salt; add about ½ cup hot water, cover, and cook 7 minutes, or until tender-crisp. Do not drain. Add 2 tablespoons butter or margarine, 2 tablespoons heavy cream. Heat over medium heat, tossing lightly with a spoon. Serve at once, sprinkled with chopped parsley or chives. Serves 4.

> *Thou dost cause the grass to grow for the cattle,*
> *and plants for man to cultivate.*
>
> —*Psalm 104:14*

Hananiah Fritters
Cauliflower Fritters

1 cup flour	1 cup milk
1/4 teaspoon salt	1 tablespoon salad oil
2 eggs, beaten	cauliflower

For 4 use one small head cauliflower broken into flowerets. Cook just 5 minutes in boiling salted water. If using frozen cauliflower, simply defrost and separate into flowerets. Make a batter by beating together the above ingredients, using a rotary beater. Dip vegetable into the batter and fry in deep fat (365°-375°) for 2 to 5 minutes. This is a fine fritter batter for any fruit or vegetable.

Celery

Celery was medicine to the ancients; it has been known in Mediterranean and biblical lands for thousands of years. The form in which the housewife of that day knew it was probably what we, today, call "smallage"; this is the wild celery that is cultivated for flavoring purposes.

Gerizim Crisp
Braised Celery

5 cups celery, cut into 1-inch pieces	1/2 teaspoon salt
	2 teaspoons cornstarch
1 small onion, sliced	1/4 cup milk
1/2 inch boiling water in saucepan	1 teaspoon salt
	1/4 teaspoon black pepper
1 cup grated Cheddar cheese	

Place celery and onion in a saucepan with the boiling water and salt. Cover and cook until the celery is just tender-crisp— 15 to 20 minutes. Drain, if necessary. Blend the cornstarch with the milk and add to the celery. Add salt and pepper. Cook, stirring, until slightly thickened. Sprinkle with the cheese and toss lightly until the cheese begins to melt. This is delicious as a luncheon or supper dish with crisp bacon. Serves 4.

Sheerah Celery
Stewed Celery

2 cups diced celery	4 tablespoons chopped onion
1 cup water	4 tablespoons chopped green
2 tablespoons butter or mar-	pepper
garine	⅔ cup canned tomatoes
½ teaspoon salt	

Boil the celery in the water for 10 minutes or until just tender-crisp. Drain. Melt the butter, add the chopped onion and green pepper, and sauté for about 5 minutes. Stir in tomatoes and salt, then add the celery. Simmer for 15 minutes longer. This serves 4; it is very inexpensive and nice for a buffet supper for it serves two vegetables at once. The recipe may be doubled or tripled without difficulty.

Whether you prefer the white celery or the green pascal, buy straight firm stalks with crisp leaves and no discoloration. Serve hearts and center stalks raw as a relish or salad, outer stalks in these celery dishes.

Celery Timothy
Baked Celery

3 cups diced celery
½ cup boiling water
milk
1 tablespoon butter or margarine

1 tablespoon flour
½ teaspoon salt
¼ cup chopped almonds
1 9-ounce can chow mein noodles

Cook the celery in a saucepan with the water for 10 minutes; drain the liquid into a measuring cup and add milk to make 1 cup. Make a thin cream sauce by melting the butter, stirring in the flour, then blending in the celery liquid and milk, and cooking, stirring, until thickened and smooth. Add the salt. Place half the cooked celery in a buttered 2-quart casserole, sprinkle with half the almonds and half the noodles, add remainder of the celery, almonds, and noodles. Pour the sauce over all. Sprinkle with paprika and bake at 375° for 20 minutes. Serves 6.

Cucumbers

Memucan Relish
Cucumber Relish

2 large cucumbers
⅓ cup fresh mint, chopped
¼ cup vinegar

1 tablespoon sugar
2 teaspoons salt
¼ teaspoon pepper

2 tablespoons water

Peel and dice the cucumbers; combine with the remaining ingredients. Cover and chill in the refrigerator; some cooks like to add a tablespoon or two of oil, just as the housewife of biblical times did. This is delicious with fish or lamb; it will keep for a week. Makes 2 cups.

Betharbel Bowl
Braised Cucumbers

2 large cucumbers	salt and pepper
2 cups celery, diced	2 tablespoons margarine
1 onion, sliced	¾ cup water

Peel the cucumbers, remove seeds, and dice. Have the celery diced in about the same size pieces. Melt the margarine in a skillet, add the onion, cucumbers, celery, and a sprinkling of salt and pepper. A teaspoon of dried dill weed adds immeasurably to the flavor of this dish. Cook gently, turning so that the vegetables become golden on all sides. Add the water, cover tightly, and simmer until tender—not more than about 10 minutes. A fine variation of this dish is to let the water cook away altogether, then sprinkle the vegetables with a tablespoon of flour, add a tablespoon butter or margarine, and toss lightly until the flour is well blended. Add gradually, stirring constantly, a cup of cream. Cook, stirring, until the mixture is smooth and thick. Serve either version on snippets of toast, with sliced ham or sausages.

> For as the earth brings forth its shoots,
>   and as a garden causes what is sown in it to
>   spring up,
> so the Lord GOD will cause righteousness and praise
>   to spring forth before all the nations.
>   —*Isaiah 61:11*

Cucumbers Titus
Stuffed Cucumbers

2 large cucumbers	1 tablespoon minced parsley
1 egg	1 tablespoon horse-radish
½ cup fine bread crumbs	1 teaspoon salt
2 tablespoons melted butter	¼ teaspoon pepper
1 tablespoon minced onion	1 cup hot water

Wash the cucumbers; don't peel, but cut in half lengthwise. Using a teaspoon, scoop out the center pulp. Place the shells in cold salted water for 30 minutes. Chop the pulp, add the egg, and the remaining ingredients except the hot water. Blend this into a stuffing. Now, drain the cucumbers thoroughly, and fill the centers with the stuffing. Place in a skillet, add the hot water and cook slowly, covered, for 30 minutes, or until tender. Serves 4.

An easy way to wash mushrooms is to douse them up and down in a bowl of heavily salted water for a minute or so.

Eggplant

The numerous Arabic and North African names for this pot-herb, and the lack of ancient Greek and Roman names for it, seem to indicate that while it was known in Old Testament lands, it didn't reach the Mediterranean countries until the early Middle Ages. However, we are fairly certain that the housewife of Old Testament times, in Egypt and the Holy Land, prized it as a food. You will, too, once you try it in these delicious ways.

> *Look at the birds of the air: they neither sow nor reap nor gather into barns, and yet your heavenly Father feeds them.—Matthew 6:26*

Eggplant Elkanah.
Eggplant Stacks

1 medium eggplant, pared	6 tablespoons salad oil
1 egg, beaten	¼ pound sliced Cheddar cheese
1 teaspoon salt	1 cup (8 ounces) tomato sauce
	¼ cup minced onion

Cut the eggplant into crosswise slices about ¼ inch thick; dip in the beaten egg to which ½ teaspoon salt has been added, then sauté slowly in the oil until brown on both sides but not completely cooked. In a shallow baking pan or dish, arrange the cooked slices in stacks of 3, like pancakes, with slices of cheese between and on top. Heat the tomato sauce with the onion and the remaining ½ teaspoon of salt, then pour around the eggplant. Bake at 375° for about 25 minutes, or until the cheese is melted and lightly browned on top. Each stack makes a serving; this will serve 4. An inexpensive and hearty main dish.

Spaghetti Agag
Eggplant with Spaghetti

2 onions, sliced	1 cup water
1 clove garlic, minced	1 medium eggplant, cubed
¼ cup salad oil	pinch of basil
1 green pepper, sliced	salt, pepper, and cayenne
1 6-ounce can tomato paste	1 8-ounce package spaghetti
1 No. 2 can tomatoes	grated Parmesan cheese

Sauté the onions and garlic in the oil until tender; add green pepper, tomato paste, tomatoes, and water, and simmer 10 minutes. Add cubed eggplant and seasonings; cook until eggplant is tender—about 30 minutes. Cook the spaghetti according to the directions on the package, drain, then arrange a layer in a 2-quart casserole. Top with the sauce, then alternate spaghetti and sauce, ending with sauce. Bake at 375° for 15 minutes. Serve with the grated cheese in a side dish. Serves 4.

Zedekiah Fritters
Waffled Fritters

1 medium eggplant, peeled and sliced thin	½ teaspoon salt
1½ cups pancake mix	½ teaspoon Vegetable Herb Blend
1 cup cool water	1 egg white

1 tablespoon salad oil

Drop the slices of eggplant into salted water until the batter is ready. Mix a batter by combining the pancake mix, water, salt, herb blend. Mix until smooth and then beat the egg white stiff and fold in gently. Last of all, fold in the salad oil. Drain the eggplant slices, dry between paper towels, and dip into flour so that they are lightly coated. These may be dipped in batter and then fried in a skillet in ¼ inch of hot fat, but an easy and very different way of frying them is to heat the waffle iron as you would for waffles, dip the eggplant slice in the batter until coated, place in the waffle iron, close, and cook as you would a waffle. This is a tricky dish to make for Sunday night supper; with a hearty salad it will make a reputation for you.

Hannah's Eggplant
Eggplant Casserole

1 medium eggplant	1½ cups tomato juice
1 large onion, peeled and diced	1 teaspoon salt
3 tablespoons butter	½ teaspoon pepper
1 6-ounce can tomato paste	½ teaspoon garlic salt

1 cup fine bread crumbs

This is one of the finest eggplant dishes I have ever eaten. Peel the eggplant, cube into 1-inch cubes, and boil in salted water until tender—about 10 minutes. Drain. Heat the butter in a large pan, add the chopped onion and sauté until golden and tender. (I sometimes add a diced green pepper; you might like to try this.) Add the can of tomato paste, the juice, and the seasonings; bring to a boil, then remove from the heat. Add the cooked eggplant and the bread crumbs; toss lightly until well mixed. Turn into a buttered 1½-quart casserole, top with ¼ cup buttered crumbs, and heat at 350° until hot and bubbling. This is a good company dish because it may be made hours ahead of time, and merely heated when you are ready to serve.

Kale, Collards, and Spinach

Kale and collards, really primitive cabbages, have been in cultivation in biblical lands for so long and have been so shifted around by migrating tribes that it is difficult to know exactly where they originated. We know, however, that the Greeks had them well before Christ's time and that long before the Christian Era the Romans grew several kinds. Spinach, on the other hand, hails from Persia and we find no mention of it in the writings of biblical times until the beginning of the New Testament Era; even then, it was still unknown to the Greeks and Romans to whom Paul was preaching.

Greens vary in tenderness, and therefore in cooking time; cook beet tops, 5 to 15 minutes; dandelion greens, 10 to 20 minutes; escarole, 10 to 12 minutes; mustard greens, 7 to 10 minutes; swiss chard, 3 to 10 minutes; turnip greens, 8 to 15 minutes.

Books are first mentioned in the Bible in Exodus 17:14 when the LORD *said to Moses, "Write this as a memorial in a book."*

Spinach Zechariah
Garden Spinach

½ pound slice raw, smoked
  ham
1½ cups bread cubes

3 tablespoons butter or margarine
1 pound spinach or 1 package frozen spinach

salt and pepper

Cut the ham slice into finger-sized strips, then fry quickly until brown. Remove from the pan. Have your bread cut into neat half-inch cubes. Add the butter or margarine to the "meat essence" left in the pan after frying the ham; when melted, add the bread cubes and sauté until crisp and golden. If you are using fresh spinach, wash, pick over, and cook 3 to 5 minutes in a covered pan with no added water. If you are using frozen spinach, simply thaw. Add the seasoned spinach to the ham and bread cubes and toss together over medium heat until the spinach is tender. Check the seasoning, but be careful of the salt; the ham will salt this dish some.

Spinach is delicious with the sweet-sour sauce on page 125. Try it that way, with baked pork chops and boiled new potatoes.

Malachi Leaves
Kale or Collards Savory

Both kale and collards can be most delicious greens, but you will enjoy them more if you will strip off and discard the heavy veins and stems from the leaves before cooking. If you are going to chop the leaves, always do this after cooking.

2 pounds young, tender kale
  or collards
¼ cup water
2 tablespoons butter or margarine

⅔ cup minced onion
1 tablespoon flour
2 teaspoons salt
¼ teaspoon pepper
1 cup milk

Wash the leaves well; then cook, covered, in a deep kettle with ¼ cup water. The water that clings to the leaves will add to the liquid. It will take about 8 to 12 minutes to cook leaves tender. Meanwhile, melt the butter in the top of a double boiler or in a saucepan over low heat. Add onion and sauté until limp and golden. Add flour and blend smooth, then add salt, pepper, and stir in the milk slowly. Cook, stirring, until smooth and thickened. Drain the cooked greens, chop coarsely, add sauce, and toss lightly. Makes 4 servings. A teaspoon of Worcestershire sauce makes a nice flavor accent. Cook an extra quantity; both kale and collards are even better when left over and reheated the next day.

Spinach Symeon
Spiced Spinach

2 packages frozen spinach	10 green olives, minced
6 tablespoons olive oil	8 ripe olives, minced
1 clove garlic, minced	1 tablespoon capers
2 tablespoons raisins	2 tablespoons chopped nuts

salt and pepper to taste

Cook the spinach in a very little water until thawed and barely tender. Set aside. In a 6-inch skillet, heat the oil (salad oil may be used as well), then add the remaining ingredients, except the salt and pepper. Cook until just heated through. Drain the spinach thoroughly; season with salt and pepper to taste, then add the oil and olive mixture and toss lightly. Turn up the heat and bring to the boiling point. Serves 6-8.

More things are wrought by prayer
Than this world dreams of.

—Tennyson

Shepherd's Pie
Vegetable Casserole

8 medium white potatoes
1 medium onion
2 tablespoons butter or margarine
2 teaspoons salt
¼ teaspoon pepper

¾ cup milk
2 pounds fresh or 2 packages frozen spinach
1 can condensed cream of celery soup
¼ teaspoon nutmeg

¼ pound sharp Cheddar cheese

Peel the potatoes and peel and slice the onion. Then boil both together until the potatoes are tender, add butter, salt, pepper, and milk, and mash until fluffy. Cook the spinach, covered, without water, until tender—frozen spinach need only be thawed. Drain thoroughly and chop fine. Heat the undiluted soup over a low flame; stir in the nutmeg, then the spinach. Save out about ¾ cup of the potato mixture for a border; spread the remainder in the bottom of a buttered casserole. Top with the spinach mixture. Cut up the cheese into inch-wide strips and arrange on top the spinach like spokes. Border the edge of the casserole with the rest of the potatoes, fluffing them up with a fork. Place under the broiler to melt and brown the cheese. Serves 6. This makes a delicious and satisfying meatless meal, as economical as it is different. Add a platter of cold cuts, sliced tomatoes, and cake for dessert, and you'll have a wonderful meal.

Another easy and delicious spinach casserole is made by cooking spinach as directed above, putting it in a buttered baking dish, adding a tablespoon of tarragon vinegar, and covering with Mornay sauce (page 179). Over the sauce, arrange mushrooms—a 6-ounce can will be plenty. Top with grated cheese, bits of butter, and brown in the oven.

2 Kings, chapter 19, Isaiah, chapter 37, are alike.

To clean any greens, cut off root ends and discard. Re-move any tough stems or yellowed leaves. Place remaining leaves in a large amount of warm water; move about gently but thoroughly, then lift out. Repeat at least twice, then drain.

Lettuce

We are fairly certain that lettuce in one of its many forms was served on biblical tables; it seems to have originated, many thousands of years before Christ, in what we now think of as biblical countries, and by the time of the New Testament it was a great favorite as far west as Rome. In the first century after Christ, Roman writers described a dozen different sorts.

Haggai Greens
Braised Lettuce

4 firm heads Boston lettuce	1 small carrot, minced
3 tablespoons butter	½ cup canned consommé
2 slices fat bacon	¼ cup water
1 small onion, minced	salt and pepper
chopped parsley	

Remove the outside leaves of the lettuce and wash the heads. Place in a pan, cover with cold water, and bring to a boil. Drain immediately and place on a tea towel to dry. Cut the heads in half. Butter an oven dish well and place the bacon on the bottom. Sprinkle onion and carrot over the bacon. Place the lettuce on top, pour the consommé and water over the lettuce, then add a bit of salt and pepper to taste. Cover with foil; bake at 350° about 45 minutes. Serve to 4, with the gravy in the dish, garnished with parsley.

"I am with you always."—*Matthew 28:20*

Achaia Bake
Lettuce au Gratin

3 small heads lettuce	2 cups buttered crumbs
1 recipe Béchamel sauce	1 teaspoon Accent

Remove the outside leaves from the lettuce heads and save them for salad. Cut the heads in half and place in a colander; pour a kettleful of boiling water over them, then drain thoroughly. While they are draining, make up one recipe of Béchamel sauce (page 179); for a variation, try a Mornay sauce with this dish, too; it's an excellent flavor combination. In the bottom of a buttered baking dish, arrange 3 of the lettuce heads; top with half the sauce. Mix the Accent with the buttered crumbs, about half a teaspoon of salt and a few grains of pepper. Sprinkle half the crumbs over the sauce. Top with remaining lettuce, sauce, and finally the rest of the crumbs. Dot with butter, and bake until brown in a moderate oven (350°).

Olives

Abib Bowl
Dried Beef Curry

¼ cup chopped onion	¼ teaspoon curry powder
1 cup sliced celery	2 cups milk
3 tablespoons butter	⅓ cup chopped ripe olives
4 tablespoons flour	1 2½-ounce jar dried beef
cooked rice	

Cook the onion and celery in butter very slowly for 10 minutes; blend in the flour and curry powder. Add the milk, stirring contantly, and cook, stirring, until smooth and thick. Add olives and dried beef and heat thoroughly. Serve on rice. Serves 4.

If God is for us, who is against us?—Romans 8:31

Micah Supper
Quick Bologna Supper

⅓ cup ripe olives
1 10½-ounce can cream of
   chicken soup

¼ cup milk
1 cup diced bologna
2 tablespoons chopped parsley
crisp toast

Cut the olives from the pits in large pieces. Turn the soup into a small saucepan and gradually blend in the milk; add bologna (chicken, ham, or any well-flavored leftover meat may be used here) and heat thoroughly. Stir in olives and chopped parsley and cook a minute longer. Serve on toast or biscuits. Serves 4.

Parsnips and Salsify

Both these root plants grew wild in great abundance in the biblical countries, just as carrots did; we have nothing to prove that they were cultivated, but we know that Greeks, Romans, and Egyptians collected both from the meadows and pastures in which they grew and used them for food.

Both parsnips and salsify (oyster plant) should be scraped, then dropped at once into water in which 2 tablespoons of flour have been rubbed smooth. This prevents discoloration. Slice about ¼ inch thick and cook, covered, in about an inch of boiling salted water 20-25 minutes for salsify, 25-40 minutes for parsnips, depending upon age and tenderness. Test with a fork; when tender, remove from the heat.

These are delicious baked. To bake them butter a shallow baking dish, arrange a layer of the tender vegetable. Sprinkle with salt and paprika and a coating of brown sugar. Cover with a thin layer of bread crumbs, dot generously with butter, and pour in cream to cover just the bottom of the dish. Bake at 400° until the top is brown.

Cakes Philemon
Parsnip Cakes

This dish may be made from salsify, turnips, or the parsnips for which it was named. It is most economical and very good.

4 medium parsnips (about 1 pound)	dash of pepper
	milk
2 tablespoons margarine	3 tablespoons flour
1 teaspoon salt	2 tablespoons drippings

Prepare the parsnips or salsify and cook until tender. Mash thoroughly or force through a food mill or ricer. Add margarine, salt and pepper, and just a bit of milk, only enough to moisten the mixture. Shape into 8 cakes about ½ inch thick, dip in flour, and brown slowly on both sides in the drippings.

Any cooked root vegetable is delicious served with white sauce. Try varying the seasonings by adding a little onion, green onion tops, parsley, pimento, or thyme.

Galilee Pot
Braised Root Vegetables

3 cups prepared vegetables	2 tablespoons chopped celery
2 tablespoons margarine	½ cup water
1 small onion, chopped	salt and pepper

Carrots, knob celery, salsify, parsnips, or turnips are delicious when cooked this way. Prepare the vegetables by peeling and cutting into inch cubes or strips. Brown lightly in the margarine in a heavy saucepan. Add onion and celery, cook 2 minutes, then add water, season with salt and pepper, cover and simmer until tender—about 20-25 minutes. Remove cover and allow liquid to evaporate. Serves 4.

Onions

The Israelites, after fleeing from Egypt, pined for onions while they were in the wilderness; these and their cousins, the chive, the garlic, and the leek, have been one of man's favorite foods since the dawn of time. Both economical and delectable, they should be in your cooking repertoire in many uses other than simply as seasoning.

Cook them, always, in enough boiling water to cover. The cooking time will vary with the type of onion; with tender green onions it will be 8 to 10 minutes, while large dried onions will take twice as long.

Onions Balaam
Luncheon Onions

4 large onions	⅛ teaspoon pepper
4 thick slices bacon	1 egg
2 tablespoons sugar	2 tablespoons vinegar
¾ teaspoon dry mustard	1 tablespoon water
¼ teaspoon salt	4 slices toasted bread

Peel the onions, cut in half crosswise, and cook gently in boiling salted water until almost tender. Cut the bacon slices in half and broil or fry until crisp. Mix 3 tablespoons of the bacon drippings in a small saucepan or skillet with sugar, mustard, salt, and pepper. Heat, then add the egg which has been beaten with vinegar and water. Cook over very low heat, stirring constantly, until slightly thickened. Brush the onion halves with bacon drippings and cook under the broiler until tender and browned. Put 2 onion halves on each piece of buttered toast, pour the sauce over, and top with bacon. Garnish with parsley. This dish, too, may be varied by spreading the toast with one of the following: deviled ham, hard-cooked egg, any fish *pâté*, chopped and seasoned liver.

Chislev Casserole
Onion Casserole

12 small whole onions	1½ cups sliced fresh mushrooms
½ cup boiling water	1 teaspoon lemon juice
1 teaspoon salt	1 cup medium white sauce
3 tablespoons butter or mar-garine	½ cup grated sharp cheese
	½ cup bread crumbs

Peel onions and place in a saucepan with boiling water and salt. Cook over medium heat 10 minutes. Drain and arrange in a 1½-quart casserole. Sauté mushrooms in 2 tablespoons of the butter or margarine and the lemon juice. Add to the cream sauce. Pour over onions. Cover and bake in a preheated oven (375°) for 15 minutes. Remove cover, sprinkle with the grated cheese mixed with the bread crumbs. Reduce heat to 350° and bake, uncovered, 20 to 25 minutes or until browned. Serves 6.

Onions Seraphim
Onions with Sausage

6 medium onions	2 tablespoons water
½ pound ground beef	½ teaspoon salt
¼ pound pork sausage	¼ teaspoon black pepper
2 tablespoons chopped onion	½ cup grated cheese

Peel the onions, cover with boiling water, add 1 teaspoon salt, and cook, uncovered, until barely tender—about 15 minutes. Cut an X almost through the onion and gently open the quarters, without breaking. Mix the remaining ingredients, except the cheese, blending thoroughly. Stuff about 2 tablespoonfuls into each onion, arrange in a shallow baking dish, cover with aluminum foil, and bake at 350° for 30 to 40 minutes. Uncover, top with cheese, and bake a few more minutes until the cheese melts. This is a delicious main dish, fine enough for a company meal. Try adding a few herbs to the stuffing. Or fill the onions with canned baked beans and top with catsup.

It is a simple matter to glaze onions. Peel 12 or 15 small ones, cook tender. Melt 5 tablespoons butter in a heavy skillet, add 2 tablespoons molasses and the onions. Cook, turning, 15 minutes.

Amaziah Supper
Scalloped Onions

4 medium onions, cut in ½-inch slices
½ cup grated sharp cheese
1½ cups cooked ham, cubed
3 slices buttered toast, cubed
1 can cream of mushroom soup
1 cup milk
½ teaspoon salt
¼ teaspoon pepper

Place the first four ingredients in a 2-quart casserole, in even layers. Combine soup, milk, salt, and pepper and pour over all. Cover and bake at 350° for 45 minutes, then remove cover and bake for 15 minutes more. Serves 6. This dish may be made with any sausage, cooked meat, or fish instead of the ham, or even with layers of leftover vegetables instead of meat. It is a delicious and valuable "basic" dish.

Nowhere in the Bible is there any explanation of the reason for prayer; prayer is dealt with as a fact—as plain as day.

The words "boy" and "boys" are mentioned three times in the Bible, but "girl" and "girls" are mentioned only twice.

Peas

Peas Rahab
Buttered Peas

2 pounds peas or 2 packages
    frozen peas
4 small onions, minced fine
½ head lettuce, shredded
1 teaspoon sugar

½ teaspoon salt
¼ teaspoon grated nutmeg
2 tablespoons chopped parsley
3 tablespoons salad oil
¾ cup boiling water

Put peas, onions, lettuce, sugar, salt, nutmeg, parsley, and oil in a heavy saucepan. Add boiling water, cover tightly and cook on high heat for 10 minutes. Turn the heat to low and cook 10 minutes more or until peas are tender. Serve with some of the broth over them. Serves 4.

Ephesian Peas
Herbed Peas

½ cup sliced green onions
2 tablespoons butter or margarine
2 cups shelled peas
½ teaspoon sugar

¼ teaspoon savory
¼ teaspoon marjoram
1 tablespoon minced parsley
½ cup water
¼ teaspoon pepper

Sauté the green onions in the butter in a saucepan for 5 minutes or until they are tender but not browned. Add the remaining ingredients, cover tightly, and cook over low heat 25 minutes or until the peas are tender. Serves 4.

Peas Aenon
Peas with Tomato

1 can peas
¼ green pepper, minced
1 small onion, minced

3 tablespoons canned tomato
    sauce
salt and pepper

Drain the liquid from the peas into a saucepan; cook over high heat until reduced to half. Add the remaining ingredients, seasoning with the salt and pepper. You might like to add a tablespoon of butter or margarine. Cook just 2 minutes, then serve hot. Serves 4.

Squash

Eranites Gourd
Baked Acorn Squash

Cut the squash in half across the ribs. Take out seeds and fiber. Dust with salt and pepper and put a generous chunk of butter in each half. Barely cover the bottom of a baking pan with water. Set the squash on a rack in the pan, cover, and bake at 400° for about 1 hour or until soft. One squash will make 2 servings.

Baked acorn squashes are delicious used as cups for many economical creamed dishes using small amounts of leftovers: creamed mushrooms, creamed dried beef, and so forth.

Casserole Jonah
Savory Squash

1 yellow crookneck squash	1 tablespoon water
6 slices bacon	1 cup crushed corn flakes
1 beaten egg	salt and pepper
2 tomatoes, sliced	

Slice the squash ¾ inch thick; pare. Fry the bacon until crisp, then remove from the pan and keep warm. Dip the squash into the egg mixed with water, then into the crushed corn flakes. (Crumbs will do as well.) Brown in hot fat, turn, season with salt and pepper, and cook until tender. Remove to a hot platter and fry the tomato slices which have been dipped in flour. Top the squash with tomato slices and crisp bacon. This is a delightful vegetable serving. Serves 6.

Zucchini Julius
Stuffed Zucchini

2 pounds medium zucchini
2 eggs, slightly beaten
⅓ cup fine bread crumbs
⅓ cup grated goat's cheese
 (Parmesan, Romano, etc.)

1 small onion, minced
¼ cup salad oil
1 tablespoon minced parsley
½ teaspoon salt
½ teaspoon thyme

Wash the zucchini; trim the ends as necessary, then parboil whole in boiling salted water for about 15 minutes. Drain and when cool enough to handle, cut lengthwise in halves. With a teaspoon, carefully scoop out the pulp, leaving a thin wall of the squash. Arrange the shells in a greased shallow baking dish. Mash the scooped-out pulp; add all the remaining ingredients and mix thoroughly. Sprinkle the zucchini shells with salt and pepper, then fill with the pulp mixture. Bake at 350° for 25 to 30 minutes.

. . . what does the LORD *require of you,
but to do justice,
 and to love kindness, and to walk humbly with
 your God?—Micah 6:8*

Every moving thing that lives shall be
food for you; and as I gave you the
green plants, I give you everything.
—Genesis 9:3

CHAPTER NINE

GREEN HERBS

May my teaching drop as the rain,
  my speech distil as the dew,
as the gentle rain upon the tender
    grass,
  and as the showers upon the herb.
        —Deuteronomy 32:2

Is there a thing of which it is said,
"See, this is new"?
                              —Ecclesiastes 1:10

MAN UNKNOWINGLY ate his first salad back in the time of Genesis, when he gathered a handful of tender young herbs and grasses and combined them with the juice of his favorite berries. The word "salad" itself is derived from the Latin *sal*, or salt, and was originally applied to uncooked leaves of herbs and vegetables eaten with a salt dressing.

Through both the Old and the New Testaments we find references to green herbs, and since we know from the writings that have come down to us that the Jews ate many vegetables raw, it seems logical to assume that they were dipped in vinegar and oil and became, thus, a "salad."

By the time of Christ the food of the masses had become much more varied than in the time of Elijah, for example; housewives of biblical times had radishes which had been known in Egypt since the pyramids were built.

During the Christian Era the cucumber was prized as a food, and it seems likely from references to dishes making up the meals of the time, that it made its appearance on the table in a bath of vinegar and oil. The Roman emperor Tiberius, who is mentioned in Luke 20:20-25 under the title of Caesar, insisted upon eating cucumbers every day of the year, and his subjects had perfected artificial methods of growing them.

Lettuce of several varieties were in use; at the beginning of the Christian Era the familiar leaf had been brought to a fairly advanced state of culture and improvement, and in the first century after Christ, Roman writers described a dozen distinctly different sorts.

Asparagus was used for both food and medicine, and wild celery and parsley were there for the hunting, too, as was endive, which was a favorite salad ingredient.

Ten Commandments for Salad Making

1. Remember first of all that salad ingredients must be fresh, fresh, fresh. Stale, dull flavor will give you a stale, dull salad.

2. Remember secondly that they must be clean, clean, clean. Wash gently but thoroughly before storing in the refrigerator. Dry gently between clean towels.

3. The old Spanish proverb, "Four persons are wanted to make a good salad: a spendthrift for oil, a miser for vinegar, a counsellor for salt, and a madman to stir all up," is still a good one; remember it.

4. Choose your vinegar with as much care as you choose your husband; quality vinegar should have a bouquet and a flavor all its own.

5. Choose your oil with the same care that you choose your vinegar; the housewife of biblical times had only one oil, and so she couldn't make a mistake. You have at least six and must know which is best suited for which dish.

6. Remember that the alpha and omega of all dressings is simplicity.

7. Some wit has said that there is no such thing as a little garlic. This is not true; with care and discrimination you can learn to measure a little garlic and a little of any other seasoning, and this is the amount you must learn to use for salad.

8. Dress salads a split second before serving them. The worst gastronomical abomination in the world is a green leaf that has been wilted into submission by too long an intimacy with the dressing.

9. Provide an ample bowl. Who can put life and charm and gaiety into the tossing of a salad if the boundaries of the bowl are constantly hemming in her efforts?

10. Wash the bowl; oil left to grow rancid in the pores of the wood will make your salad taste rancid, too.

Salad Dressings

The Oils

Our housewife of biblical times, of course, dipped her green herbs in olive oil and, while I personally prefer a lighter oil for salad dressings, there is no question but that the great majority of discriminating cooks prefer olive oil. Remember that there are at least three or four grades; the one marked "virgin" olive oil is from the first press, and is most expensive and best. A second oil is obtained by adding boiling water to the pulp residue and subjecting it again to pressure. This will become rancid more quickly than the first.

Corn oil, which has become very popular in our country, is not particularly good for salad dressings; it is light and pleasant but it has no flavor to recommend it.

Cottonseed oil and, to some extent, poppyseed oil, are now widely used for salad dressings. This oil does not become rancid and, although its flavor and fragrance differ from that of olive oil, high quality oil of this type is delicious.

Nut oils are made in wide variety. Most of them have an excellent flavor, but they must not be kept too long as they turn rancid quickly. Peanut oil has a fine flavor when pure and it is used by fine cooks everywhere, particularly in Chinese cookery.

The Vinegars

All vinegars are not alike; a vinegar skillfully made and aged is superior to the ordinary run. You should enjoy using a good vinegar, for it is as romantic and colorful a food as any we know.

In the Bible, vinegar is mentioned often; reapers, in those days, freshened their bread by soaking it in vinegar.

Lemon juice is the best substitute for vinegar.

By pouring one teaspoon of salt into a quart of any kind of good vinegar, you can prevent the formation of the mother; the vinegar will keep perfectly clear and free.

The Seasonings

Next to salt, the seasonings you will find most useful in salad preparation are pepper and mustard. You will use garlic, too, in many dressings, and you may like to get the flavor by placing a peeled clove in a quart of vinegar for 6 or 7 days. The bowl in which you make your salad may be rubbed with garlic, or a crust of bread which has been rubbed with garlic may be tossed with your greens.

Try to build up a small shelf of salad seasonings. Begin with a good grade of paprika (only the best of anything is good enough for a salad) and then add, one by one, cracked black pepper instead of ground, cayenne, mayonnaise mustard, orégano, basil, tarragon, lemon, thyme, and any others that appeal to you.

The Greens

Thanks to rapid transportation by rail and plane, we have a huge variety of salad greens fresh in our markets every day. If you think of Iceberg lettuce as the beginning and the end of the salad greens, you are definitely missing something. Try them all: celery, chicory or green endive, dandelion greens, dill, French endive, fennel, water cress, tender beet tops, carrot greens, turnip greens, and mint leaves. The housewife of biblical times picked whatever looked appetizing to her as it grew along the creek bed or the roadside. You can enjoy experimenting, too.

The Old Testament is referred to in the New Testament as the scriptures. (See Luke 24:32; Mark 12:10; Acts 1:16)

As soon as you get salad greens home, look them over, discarding all wilted portions. If you want to prevent rusting, store them, unwashed and uncut, in the refrigerator. Just before using, clean as follows:

BOSTON LETTUCE: Cut out the core end; hold, head down, under running water until water forces the leaves apart. Shake off as much water as possible, then dry gently.

ICEBERG OR SIMPSON: Separate leaves as in Boston lettuce, then pull apart or shred. Be sure to dry well.

ROMAINE, ENDIVE, ESCAROLE, LEAF LETTUCE, ETC.: Separate leaf by leaf, then wash gently and dry thoroughly between paper or clean towels.

WATER CRESS: Pick over water cress, then wash under running cold water, dry, and store like Boston lettuce. Some good cooks prefer to store water cress as they do parsley, stem end down in a covered jar in the refrigerator.

The Dressings

There are four basic dressings—French, mayonnaise, cooked dressings, and cream, either fresh or sour. Each, however, must be good to start with—smooth, well blended, perfectly seasoned and flavored.

French Dressing

For 1 quart, use 3 cups olive, peanut, or other oil, 1 cup vinegar, 2½ tablespoons salt, and ½ generous teaspoon cracked or ground pepper. Shake violently before using. It will keep well in the refrigerator.

GARLIC DRESSING: Add a peeled garlic clove to French dressing and let stand from 4 to 7 days before using.

> *Weeping may tarry for the night,*
> *but joy comes with the morning.—Psalm 30:5*

ROQUEFORT OR BLUE CHEESE DRESSING: To a generous ½ cup French dressing add 1 rounded tablespoon Roquefort or blue cheese crumbled fine with a fork. Mix thoroughly before using.

DIJON DRESSING: To a generous ½ cup French dressing add ½ teaspoon each chervil, chopped onion, parsley, chives, green pepper and pimento, all finely chopped, then 1 teaspoon prepared mustard. Place a cube or two of ice in the bowl and stir until the dressing thickens. Remove ice before serving.

VINAIGRETTE DRESSING: To ½ cup French dressing add ½ teaspoon each finely chopped green olives, capers, chives, parsley, sweet pickle, and ½ hard-cooked egg yolk.

FRUIT DRESSING: To ½ cup French dressing, add 1½ tablespoons red currant jelly and 1 tablespoon creamed cottage cheese. Finish with ¼ teaspoon grated orange rind.

LORENZO DRESSING: To ½ cup French dressing add 2 tablespoons finely chopped water cress, 1 tablespoon chili sauce, and 1 teaspoon Worcestershire sauce.

CHIFFONADE DRESSING: To 1 cup French dressing add 3 finely chopped hard-cooked eggs, 1 tablespoon grated onion, 1 tablespoon chopped parsley, 2 tablespoons chopped pickled beets, and 1 teaspoon chopped olives.

Mayonnaise

Rinse a small mixing bowl with hot water and dry thoroughly. Place 2 egg yolks in it, and beat with a rotary beater. Add ½ teaspoon salt, a pinch of white pepper, ½ teaspoon dry mustard, and 1 teaspoon lemon juice or vinegar. Mix well.

Add about 1 cup olive or other oil, drop by drop at first, beating all the while. When about ¼ cup has been added, add ½ teaspoon more of vinegar. Then, beating constantly, add the rest of the oil in a very thin stream, never letting up on the beating. When all the oil has been added and the mayonnaise is quite thick, add another ½ teaspoon vinegar.

If you add the oil too hastily without beating it in thoroughly as it is added, the dressing will separate. If this happens, try adding 1 tablespoon boiling water and beating again; this sometimes rectifies the error. Once you have eaten homemade mayonnaise, you will never again tolerate the commercial type, for this dressing gives a meaning to salads that they never had before.

MAYONNAISE VERTE (Green Dressing): Into 2 cups mayonnaise fold 1 tablespoon chopped chives, 1 tablespoon tarragon leaves (1 teaspoon dried), 2 tablespoons chopped parsley, 1 teaspoon chervil, and 1 teaspoon dill, all finely chopped. Chill before serving.

SAUCE REMOULADE: Fold into 1 cup mayonnaise 1 clove crushed garlic, 2 chopped gherkins, 1 teaspoon dry mustard, 3 tablespoons finely chopped parsley, 1 teaspoon tarragon, and 1 chopped hard-cooked egg.

RUSSIAN DRESSING: To 1 cup mayonnaise, add 2 chopped hard-cooked eggs, 3 tablespoons chili sauce, 1 tablespoon each chopped parsley and chives, 1 teaspoon grated horse-radish, a pinch of salt and freshly ground black pepper to taste. Chopped pickle relish, pimento, ripe or stuffed olives may also be added.

SAUCE TARTARE: Into 1 cup mayonnaise, blend 1 teaspoon each finely chopped parsley, shallots, tarragon leaves, capers, sweet gherkins, and green olives. Add salt and freshly ground black pepper to taste plus 1 teaspoon prepared mustard. Fine for fish.

Do you know the riddle that Samson offered his wedding guests? See Judges 14:14

RAVIGOTE DRESSING: Into 1 cup mayonnaise blend 1 tablespoon each finely chopped chives and tarragon (1 teaspoon each if dried) and 1 teaspoon each finely chopped chervil and parsley. Stir in 1 tablespoon spinach juice for color. Add a few capers if you wish.

Cooked Dressings

Since cooked dressings, as well as mayonnaise and French varieties, keep well, I'd suggest making the full recipe, even though you cook for a small family. However, any of these recipes may be halved with good results.

2 tablespoons flour	pinch cayenne pepper
2 tablespoons sugar	1 cup water
3 tablespoons salad oil	2 eggs
1¼ teaspoons salt	6 tablespoons lemon juice or
1 teaspoon prepared mustard	vinegar

In the top of the double boiler, combine all ingredients except eggs and lemon juice. Mix well. Set over boiling water in the bottom of the cooker and cook, stirring constantly, until thickened to the consistency of custard. Break the eggs into a cup; beat lightly with a fork. Gradually add the lemon juice, beating all the while, then stir in half the hot sauce. Now stir the egg mixture very slowly into the rest of the sauce in the double boiler. It is necessary to do this very slowly and thoroughly to prevent the egg from separating.

Reduce the heat so that the water in the bottom of the cooker is hot, not boiling, and cook the dressing, stirring constantly, until thick enough to mound when dropped from a spoon. Remove from the heat at once; pour into a bowl or jar, cool, and store in the refrigerator. Makes about 1½ cups. This is much less trouble than it sounds; when you've made it once, you'll make it often. Here are some variations.

SOUR CREAM DRESSING: When cold, fold in 1 cup sour cream, whipped with a rotary beater until stiff.

CURRY DRESSING: Stir ½ teaspoon curry powder and ¼ cup pickle relish into the hot dressing. Use on broccoli, rice, cauliflower, etc.

COLESLAW DRESSING: Increase the mustard in the above recipe to 2 tablespoons, and add ½ teaspoon paprika.

CHIFFON DRESSING: Make dressing with 2 egg yolks instead of whole eggs, then whip the whites stiff and fold in after the mixture cools. Delicious on asparagus or vegetable salads.

Sour Cream Dressing

For sour cream dressing, simply add 2 tablespoons lemon juice or cider vinegar, to 1 cup sour cream. Season with salt and a dash of cayenne. This may be varied by the addition of 1 tablespoon chopped chives, 1 small clove garlic finely chopped, or 2 tablespoons grated onion. It is perfect with any raw vegetable salad.

Appetizer Salads

There is a growing tendency to serve salads as the appetizer or first course of our meals. This is a good thing; it reduces our hunger, thus discouraging us from eating too much, and it gets all the wonderful greens and mineral-vitamin foods into us before we're filled up with heavier foods. Here are some suggestions:

Teman Plate
Antipasto Appetizer

plum tomato	boneless sardine
deviled egg half	marinated artichoke heart
ripe olives	sweet gherkin

Arrange one of each of the above on a small bread-and-butter plate, garnish with a sprig of parsley, and serve very cold as a first course. Makes one serving.

Macedonian Ripple
Lettuce Ripple

2 3-ounce packages cream cheese	½ teaspoon orégano
	salt and pepper to taste
¼ pound Roquefort or blue cheese	large head Iceberg lettuce
	French dressing

Soften the cream cheese and whip until fluffy—you may have to add a tablespoon or so of milk. Beat in the crumbled Roquefort cheese and the orégano. Season to taste with salt and pepper. Wash the lettuce. Cut out the core in a large cone, then let cold water run into the cut head. Turn over, cut side down, and drain thoroughly. Now reach into the cone and carefully separate the leaves, folding each back carefully so the head doesn't come apart. Spread each leaf with the cheese mixture, beginning at the center and folding the leaves together again as they are spread. Push leaves back together to re-form the head. Wrap in foil and chill several hours. To serve as an appetizer, slice crosswise and pass French dressing.

Eunice Tidbit
Curried Cheese Salad

2 8-ounce packages cream cheese	2 dashes Tabasco
1/4 cup undiluted evaporated milk	1/2 teaspoon salt
	3 teaspoons curry powder
1 tablespoon Worcestershire sauce	8 small lettuce cups
	4 tomatoes

Cream the cheese with the milk until smooth, then blend in the remaining ingredients except the lettuce and tomatoes. Taste; you may want to add more salt and curry powder, depending upon your preference. Have lettuce cups (small inner leaves of lettuce washed and crisped in the refrigerator) ready. At serving time, place a base of shredded lettuce leaves in the lettuce cup on each plate. Garnish with half a tomato, cut in wedges. Top with the curry sauce. Serve very cold. Pass a tart French dressing. Serves 8.

Artemas Spread
Guacamole

3 tablespoons minced onion	1 teaspoon salt
1 tomato, peeled and chopped	2 teaspoons chili powder
2 avocados	1 tablespoon lemon juice

Chop together the onion, tomato, and avocados until smooth. Add remaining ingredients and mix well. Scoop out little tomatoes or green peppers, one for each person to be served, and fill with the guacamole. Serve on a lettuce leaf, with rye thins. Or, simply pile the guacamole in a bowl and serve with rye thins for dipping.

Green Salads

Zarephath Greens
Wilted Greens

4 slices bacon
¼ cup mild vinegar
¼ cup minced onion

½ teaspoon mixed herbs
¼ teaspoon cracked pepper
1½ teaspoons sugar

Cut the bacon fine with the kitchen shears. Sauté in a small skillet until crisp, then remove the bacon with a slotted spoon. Break up a head of washed and dried lettuce with your fingers, then place lettuce, onion bits, and a little salt in a bowl. If you like garlic flavor, use garlic salt. Add remaining ingredients to the bacon fat in the skillet, bring to a boil, then pour over the lettuce and toss until each leaf is coated. Serve at once to 4. A garnish of hard-cooked eggs is nice with this, and some old-time cooks used to break an egg over the lettuce before adding the hot dressing.

For variation, try using young spinach greens or any other tender green that is available in the market. Dandelion greens, picked while they're very young, are delicious.

Salad Sarah
Lettuce Salad

1 clove garlic
1 hard-cooked egg yolk
½ teaspoon salt
⅛ teaspoon dry mustard
⅛ teaspoon pepper
dash of paprika

3 tablespoons tarragon vinegar
½ teaspoon Worcestershire
    sauce
½ cup olive oil
3 sprigs parsley, chopped fine
3 green onions, chopped fine

1 head lettuce

Rub the salad bowl with a cut clove of garlic, then put the egg yolk, salt, mustard, pepper, paprika, vinegar, and Worcestershire sauce in the bowl and blend thoroughly. Add oil and blend again. Add the greens and the lettuce torn into bite-sized chunks, and toss lightly. A few spoonfuls of Roquefort cheese, crumbled, make this extra special. Use this basic recipe for any crisp greens that you are able to come by. Add a few strips of cold leftover meat, and you have a delicious Chef's Salad. Add a cupful of toasted croutons, ¼ cup grated Parmesan cheese, and a raw egg beaten into the dressing mixture in the bowl, and you have a Caesar Salad.

Salad Nathan
Broccoli Salad

2 pounds broccoli   pinch of pepper
1 clove garlic   ⅓ cup lemon juice
¼ teaspoon salt   ⅔ cup olive or salad oil

Cut the broccoli into 3-inch lengths. Split ½ inch up from the stem ends. Cook in a covered saucepan in an inch of boiling water until tender—8 to 10 minutes after the water starts to boil. DO NOT OVERCOOK. Remove gently from the water; drain, and chill. Make a dressing of the remaining ingredients, pour over the chilled broccoli, and let stand an hour or more before serving. This serves 6; it is beautiful for a buffet dinner, and a nice way to use leftover boiled broccoli. Try it, too, with cauliflower or Brussels sprouts.

Soufflé Salads

This most versatile of salads was originated by the people who make Jello. I've always found it useful since it sets quickly, and may be used in many ways.

1 package Jello or similar gelatin dessert
1½ cups boiling water   1 cup mayonnaise

Add the boiling water to the gelatin; stir until dissolved. Chill until the mixture begins to set (about as thick as the whites of eggs) then fold in the mayonnaise and any additions you may wish to make. Here are some possibilities you might like to try.

Holiday Salad

Substitute ¼ cup vinegar for the same quantity of water in the basic salad. Fold in 2 cups cooked peas, 1 cup cooked diced carrots, 1 cup cut celery, and 1 tablespoon chopped green pepper. One teaspoon salt and 1 tablespoon chopped onion are nice additions for flavor.

Waldorf Soufflé Salad

Use pineapple-flavored gelatin for the basic mixture, then add 1 tablespoon lemon juice, 1 cup chopped, unpeeled apple, 1 cup chopped celery, and ½ cup chopped walnuts. Garnish with mayonnaise into which a little paprika has been folded.

Blueberry Cheese Salad

Use lemon-flavored gelatin for the basic salad, dissolving it in 1 cup hot water. Then add ¼ cup cold water and ¼ cup pineapple juice. When it begins to set, add 2 tablespoons lemon juice, ¼ cup mayonnaise, ¼ teaspoon salt, 1 cup blueberries, ½ cup cottage cheese and ½ cup drained crushed pineapple. This is a delightful main-dish salad for a luncheon to be served with dainty finger sandwiches.

Carolina Salad

Use apple-flavored gelatin for the basic salad, with 1 cup hot water and ½ cup tomato juice to dissolve it. When it begins to set, add 1 cup ripe olives cut in large pieces, ½ cup mayonnaise, 1 tablespoon grated onion, 1 teaspoon salt, ¼ teaspoon celery seed.

Fruit Salad

Use lime-flavored gelatin for the basic salad, with 1 cup hot water and ½ cup orange juice to dissolve it. When it begins to set, fold in 1 cup mayonnaise, whip with a rotary beater until thoroughly blended, then fold in 2 cups of any diced fruit, well drained.

Cheese Soufflé Salad

Use lemon-flavored gelatin dissolved in 1 cup hot water, then add ½ cup cold water, ½ cup mayonnaise, 1 tablespoon lemon juice and ½ teaspoon salt, plus 3 or 4 drops Tabasco sauce. Blend well; when it begins to thicken, fold in ¾ cup grated American cheese, 3 hard-cooked eggs sliced, ¼ cup each diced fresh green pepper and canned pimento, and 1 teaspoon grated onion.

Salad Suppers

There is an increasing trend to make a salad the main dish of the meal, particularly during the warm months. Such a dish is not only stimulating to the appetite, but a real economy move since many leftovers may be used. Here are some basic formulas.

> *in God I trust without a fear.*
> *What can man do to me?*
>
> *—Psalm 56:11*

Zenas Supper
Potato Salad

4 cups cooked potatoes
2 tablespoons salad oil
2 tablespoons good vinegar
¼ cup vinegar drained from
  pickles
½ teaspoon dried dill weed
1 tablespoon finely chopped
  onion

1 small clove garlic, crushed
2 green onions
3 radishes
3 hard-cooked eggs
2 tablespoons minced parsley
¼ teaspoon paprika
salt to taste
¼ cup mayonnaise

Combine the potatoes, either hot or cold, with oil, vinegar, pickle liquid, dill, onion, and garlic. Set aside to marinate for several hours in the refrigerator. Chop the green onions fine; slice radishes thin; quarter hard-cooked eggs. Add to the potatoes with remaining ingredients and mix lightly. Serves 6.

This is the classic French potato salad. To use as a salad supper, add any cold, cooked meat in julienne strips, a garnish of cold shrimp or lobster, or additional deviled eggs. All of these may be leftovers.

Apphian Supper
Macaroni Supper

½ cup cubed cold meat
1 8-ounce package macaroni,
  cooked
1 cup diced celery
¼ cup minced onion

¼ cup stuffed olives, sliced
4 hard-cooked eggs, chopped
¾ cup salad dressing
2 tablespoons vinegar
dash of garlic salt

salt and pepper

Combine vinegar, garlic salt, and salad dressing and blend thoroughly. Combine other ingredients, then add salad dressing mixture and toss lightly. Chill thoroughly for best flavor. Serves 8. This is delightful with half-inch cubes of any sausage, particularly hard salami or frankfurter chunks; it is also delightful turned into a casserole and heated at 350° until bubbling.

Salad Gaza
Chicken Salad Supper

2 cups white chicken meat, cooked, cubed

1 can whole-kernel corn, drained

1 can kidney beans, drained

2 hard-cooked eggs

1 cup mayonnaise

1 cup whipped cream

1 small onion, minced

1 red apple, unpeeled

1 cup chopped celery

Cut eggs, apple, and celery into uniform pieces. Drain the kidney beans, then rinse in a little hot water. Combine all the ingredients and toss lightly; serve in a lettuce-lined salad bowl to 6. This is an old family recipe, and one of the most delicious supper dishes you ever tasted. It is beautiful to use for a buffet party, too.

Gelatin Salads

Basic Molded Gelatin

2 tablespoons lemon juice or good mild vinegar

1 to 2½ cups vegetables, fruit, seafoods, etc.

1 package flavored gelatin

Prepare the gelatin (choose a flavor to make an interesting combination with the foods you are going to add) according to the directions on the package, adding the lemon juice or vinegar for sharpness. Use 1¾ cups liquid instead of the 2 cups called for in the directions. Chill, and when partially set (about the consistency of cold egg whites) add the food to make the salad. Pour into 6 or 8 individual molds and chill. Double this quantity will fill a 9-inch ring mold for 12 servings.

Seafood Mold

Use lemon-flavored gelatin for this, and for extra flavor add an extra tablespoon of vinegar, a half teaspoon of prepared mustard, and a pinch of salt. From here on, your imagination will complete the dish; you'll find one cup of crabmeat, lobster, salmon, shrimp, tuna, or any cooked fish—flaked, plus 1 cup thinly sliced celery, cucumber, green pepper, and so forth—is just about right.

Perfection Salad

This is the perfect cabbage combination. Use lemon-flavored gelatin and 1 cup very finely shredded or chopped cabbage, plus 1 cup other vegetables for flavor: celery, pimento, carrots, sweet pickles, stuffed or ripe olives, etc.

Fruit Combinations

Omit the lemon juice or vinegar, and use any of the red gelatins such as strawberry or raspberry. Use whole or cut-up fruit, well drained. The new frozen fruits for salad are exceptionally good for this; thaw before using. With toasted-cheese sandwich strips, this is the most delightful luncheon in the world.

Garden Salads

Use lemon-, aspic-, lime-, or apple-flavored gelatin and 2 cups of any garden vegetable chopped and well drained, a half cup of diced cucumber, a quarter cup of finely chopped green or white onion, and 1 cup of any vegetable sliced thin as paper: cauliflower flowerets, radishes, celery, mushrooms, artichoke hearts.

Cottage Cheese Molds

Use any flavor gelatin, omitting the lemon juice or vinegar. Add ½ teaspoon salt, 1 tablespoon minced onion, 1 tablespoon minced green pepper, 2 tablespoons chopped celery, and 1 cup smooth cottage cheese. This is another delightful luncheon salad.

Hot Salads

This is a whole new branch on the salad family tree; we have just recently discovered that the spicy smooth flavor of mayonnaise is delicious hot, as well as cold, and that some salads served in this way make delicious main dishes. You'll enjoy experimenting with these, I can promise you.

Arabian Salad
Hot Crab Salad

¼ cup butter or margarine	2 egg yolks, beaten
½ cup all-purpose flour	2 cups flaked, cooked crabmeat
1 teaspoon dry mustard	1 cup chopped celery
pinch of paprika	¼ cup chopped green pepper
1 teaspoon salt	¼ cup chopped pimento
1 cup milk	¼ cup mild vinegar

Melt the butter in a saucepan, blend in the flour and seasonings, then add the milk slowly, stirring all the while. Cook, stirring constantly, until smooth and thick. Remove from the heat, add some of the hot sauce to the lightly beaten egg yolks, blend thoroughly, then stir into the rest of the sauce. Add the remaining ingredients. Turn into a buttered 1½-quart casserole or into 8 individual baking dishes and bake at 425° for about 15 minutes or until hot and bubbly.

Try this with potato chips, corn on the cob, avocado and tomato salad with black olives, and for dessert, melon balls so cold they hurt your teeth. That's real eating!

The God who made the world and everything in it, being Lord of heaven and earth, does not live in shrines made by man, nor is he served by human hands, as though he needed anything, since he himself gives to all men life and breath and everything.—Acts 17:24-25

Salad Miriam
Baked Chicken Salad

2 cups cubed cooked chicken	½ teaspoon salt
2 cups thinly sliced celery	2 teaspoons grated onion
1 cup Pepperidge Farm packaged dressing	1 cup mayonnaise
	2 tablespoons lemon juice
½ cup toasted almonds, slivered	½ cup grated cheese

Combine all ingredients except the cheese, then pile lightly into a 1½-quart buttered casserole or into individual baking dishes. Sprinkle lightly with the grated cheese and bake at 450° about 15 minutes or until hot and bubbly. This amount will serve 6. Vary this basic recipe by using leftover ham, turkey, pork, veal, or any of the spicy sausages such as bologna, salami, or ham loaf.

Either of these hot salads may be served in avocados by cutting the avocados in half, removing the stones, and heating in the oven at 375° for 10 minutes. Remove from the oven, fill with the salad mixtures, and return to the oven to bake until the filling bubbles. This is a smaller, richer serving, especially nice for company luncheons. The above quantities will serve 12 in avocado halves.

Happy is the man who finds wisdom,
and the man who gets understanding.
—Proverbs 3:13

. . . the broth he put in a pot, and brought it to him under the oak and presented it . . .—Judges 6:19

CHAPTER TEN

SAUCES

From Esau's pottage to the 'cunning sauces of ancient Rome,' from Gideon to Escoffier, a good sauce has been the hallmark of a good cook.

If you are willing and obedient,
    you shall eat the good of the land.
    —Isaiah 1:19

OUR WORDS "sauce" and "salads" derive from the Latin *salsus*, meaning salted; thus, even in biblical times, a sauce was designed to add flavor to a dish, just as salt does.

Butter was probably the original basic sauce; it was used more than 2,000 years before the Christian Era and we find it mentioned throughout the Bible, accompanying some of the earliest of Old Testament foods.

We read of other sauces of biblical days, too; broth, the gravy from stewed meat, is mentioned in the sixth chapter of Judges, and probably the first brown sauce resulted when some ancient *saucier* ladled a quart or so of such a broth from the pot, boiled it down to a cupful, and then tasted the enhanced flavor with delight.

The housewife of biblical times had a variety of other sauce ingredients at hand, and surely must have used them but, for some reason or other, we find not one mention of a sauce as such in either the Old or the New Testament. The most likely conclusion is that the word "salt" was intended to mean "sauce" and was so included in biblical writings.

The most widespread use of a sauce in biblical times was almost identical with a custom of ours—both Hebrews and Arabs used a piece of thin bread, a "sop," bent to make a sort of spoon, at every meal. This was dipped into a sauce and eaten from the fingers; it was a food so generally accepted that two or more friends honored each other by ceremoniously dipping from the same earthen "sop" dish.

It is not hard to imagine the housewife of Jesus' time experimenting with a bit of broth from the lamb, a little oil, a bit of meal, and a handful of herbs, and delighting in the added interest this sauce brought to her meal.

Ten Commandments for Making Sauces

1. The first function of a good sauce is to enhance flavor; make it with this in mind. A sharp sauce will make up for lack of flavor in a food, and a bland sauce will make a nice background for strong-flavored food.

2. Never plan a sauce to disguise an unpleasant taste, or to cover up the flavor of overripe game and tired fish.

3. Sauce making is an art, and is simple, like all great art. All that is necessary is a little care, plus the freshest and best of ingredients.

4. There are two cardinal sins in sauce making. The first and greatest of these is making a sauce with water. Use soup, bouillon, drippings, stock, or milk.

5. The second of these two cardinal sins is carelessness in making the roux, the blending of flour and butter that thickens the sauce. Make it with care, brown it with wisdom, and it will repay you with satiny smoothness.

6. Cultivate your judgment as to the proper moment at which a sauce has reached perfection.

7. Remember that you are judging this moment at boiling temperature; it will be cooler, hence thicker, when it reaches the table, and it must flow from spoon to plate.

8. Use commercial sauces to pep up your homemade specialties.

9. Remember that your sauce must never be too "long" as the French describe it; it must garnish and accent the food, not drown it.

10. Never fall into a rut with your sauces; a pinch of herbs, a drop of vinegar, or fleck of spice will make yesterday's leftover seem like a new creation.

Sauces, like most other things in life, are continually changing in details, but the foundations upon which they are built change little, if at all. If you will master the five basic sauces, you will find it simple to turn out masterpieces that even Carême and his disciples might have envied. The first is:

Sauce Onesimus
Brown Sauce

2 tablespoons butter or margarine
½ onion, coarsely chopped

2 tablespoons flour
¾ cup stock or bouillon
¼ cup tomato paste

salt and paprika

Melt the butter in a small saucepan; add the onion and sauté over medium heat until a light brown. Scoop out the onion pieces with a slotted spoon, then stir the flour into the butter and cook, stirring, until the mixture takes on the color of a brown paper bag. Stir in the stock or bouillon and cook, stirring, until smooth and thick. Add tomato paste and cook and stir again. Season to taste. This is not the classic French recipe, which is lengthy and complicated; it is a modernized version similar to what the housewife of biblical times may have used.

For smoked meats, add a tablespoon of vinegar and a quarter cup of chopped pickles.

For roast lamb or game, add ¼ cup currant jelly to the basic sauce and cook, stirring, until melted.

Every good endowment and every perfect gift is from above, coming down from the Father of lights.—James 1:17

Sauce Obadiah
Sauce Allemande (Blonde Sauce)

This is the ubiquitous "white sauce" of today; it may be made with half chicken or veal stock and half cream, or with milk. Made properly, it is a fine dressing for egg dishes, vegetables, fish, grains, or pastas. Made as it usually is, it is fit for nothing but to paste wallpaper on the wall (and it is not recommended for that, may I hasten to add).

2 tablespoons butter	¼ teaspoon salt
2 tablespoons flour	few grains pepper
1 cup milk	½ teaspoon scraped onion

Melt the butter in a small saucepan over moderate heat; add the flour and blend thoroughly, then slowly stir in the milk. Cook, stirring, until the mixture thickens and is smooth. Then add salt, pepper, and scraped onion or onion juice. Some cooks like to add a little chopped parsley or chives; a half teaspoon of Worcestershire sauce or a little nutmeg is also good.

For a medium sauce, use 3 tablespoons each of butter and flour to 1 cup milk. For thick sauce, used for croquettes and such molded dishes, use 3 tablespoons butter, ⅓ cup flour to each cup of liquid.

Sauce Nahum
Sauce Velouté

This classic sauce is made exactly like Sauce Allemande except that all of the liquid is good rich chicken broth. I like to add a small green onion, chopped, 1 clove, and half a bay leaf. Simmer 10 minutes, then fish out the spices. This makes a delicious gravy or sauce for any meat dish. It is delightful, too, on sweetbreads or chicken, and adds a nice sublety of flavor to vegetables.

Sauce Habakkuk
Sauce Béchamel

This is the basic "cream" sauce; it should be made according to the directions for Sauce Allemande and 3 tablespoons cream stirred in after the sauce has thickened. This is a delicious sauce for almost any food. The great chef Carême added the yolks of 2 eggs to it, beating them thoroughly, stirring in a bit of the hot sauce, and then stirring this into the pan of sauce just before removing from the heat.

For use with fish, try adding a cup of mayonnaise to a cup of Béchamel sauce and blending thoroughly.

Mornay sauce, so good on eggs, vegetables, or any of the grain dishes, is simply made by stirring 3 tablespoons grated Parmesan cheese and ¼ teaspoon paprika into a cup of this basic sauce.

Swedish sauce is made simply by adding grated horse-radish to taste, plus 1 tablespoon vinegar to each cup Béchamel.

Sauce Egyptian
Garlic Sauce

Crush to a pulp 4 cloves of garlic and mix thoroughly with the raw yolk of an egg. Add a pinch of salt and work in slowly, with a fork, ¼ cup olive oil. Continue to beat, adding the oil very slowly until the sauce reaches the consistency of mayonnaise.

This sauce is always served in a separate dish to use or not, according to taste. The garlic lover will like it on baked potatoes, any cooked vegetable, and almost any fish. A Grecian version which dates from New Testament times adds a half cup finely ground almonds (I whirl them in my blender), and one cup hot, creamy mashed potatoes. For this version, make the garlic paste by blending garlic with the egg yolk, then beat this into the potatoes and add the olive oil very slowly, until completely absorbed.

Sauce for Seafood Cocktails

Various sauces are especially adapted for use with cold crab meat, shrimp, oysters, or clams for a first course. Try mixing ½ cup chili sauce, ¼ cup catsup, 1 tablespoon olive oil, 1 raw egg yolk, 1 teaspoon lemon juice, 1 teaspoon Worcestershire sauce, ½ teaspoon chili powder, and about ½ teaspoon salt. Beat for 5 minutes with a rotary beater, then chill.

Lucius Sauce
Tomato Sauce

This is the most wonderful tomato sauce you ever tasted; because it has so much meat in it, it is a complete meal when served over a starchy dish such as spaghetti or macaroni, gnocchi, lasagne, or polenta, or rice. You will use it in a thousand combinations.

¼ cup oil	½ cup water
2 medium onions, chopped	½ cup chopped celery
2 cloves garlic, minced	¼ cup chopped parsley
2 pounds ground beef	1½ tablespoons salt
3 No. 2 cans tomatoes (7 cups)	2 teaspoons sugar
2 6-ounce cans tomato paste	¼ teaspoon pepper
2 bay leaves	1 teaspoon basil

Heat the oil in a large kettle or Dutch oven; add onions and garlic and sauté 5 minutes. Add the ground beef; cook until brown, breaking the meat up with a fork as it cooks. Stir in the remaining ingredients. Bring the mixture to a simmer, then cook over low heat until it is thick and rich—45 minutes or an hour. Then remove the bay leaves and skim off the fat.

This makes about 10 cups—plenty for two hearty family dishes. It freezes perfectly, and you should have at least a quart of it on hand for emergencies. Just try it, for instance, over a split loaf of Italian bread, buttered and toasted, for an open-faced sandwich!

Sweet Sauces

Abishag Sauce
Lemon Sauce

½ cup sugar
1 tablespoon cornstarch
1 cup water
1½ tablespoons lemon juice

⅛ teaspoon salt
⅛ teaspoon nutmeg
2 tablespoons butter or margarine

Combine sugar and cornstarch in a small saucepan, stir in the water. Cook until clear and thickened, stirring constantly. Remove from the heat, add remaining ingredients, and stir until the butter is melted. Serve hot. This same sauce is delicious made with 1 teaspoon vanilla in place of the lemon juice.

Achsah Sauce
Quick Chocolate Sauce

Add 2 squares melted unsweetened chocolate to 1 cup corn syrup, either light or dark, stir until well blended, then stir in ¼ teaspoon vanilla.

Sauce Cilicia
Quick Butterscotch Sauce

⅓ cup brown sugar, packed
¾ cup corn syrup, light or dark

1 tablespoon butter
1 tablespoon water

Combine all ingredients in a small saucepan, bring to a boil and boil 1 minute. Remove from the heat; the sauce will be thin until it cools. Serve cold over ice cream or pudding.

"Take heed, watch; for you do not know when the time will come."—Mark 13:33

Butterscotch Sauce

Boil together 1 cup brown sugar, ¼ cup heavy cream, a pinch of salt, 2 tablespoons light corn syrup, and 2 tablespoons butter for about 3 minutes (to 220° on the candy thermometer).

Ginger Sauce

Another easy and delicious sweet sauce is made by creaming ⅓ cup butter well, blending in 2 cups powdered sugar and ¾ teaspoon ground ginger, and ¼ cup corn syrup. Chill before serving over bread and fruit puddings. Cloves, cinnamon, or ⅛ teaspoon each allspice, nutmeg and mace may be substituted for the ginger.

Fruit Sauce
Hot Fruit Sauce

⅔ cup apple juice	2 tablespoons sugar
⅓ cup mincemeat	1 teaspoon lemon juice

Boil the apple juice in a small saucepan until it is reduced to about ⅓ cup; add mincemeat and sugar and simmer 5 minutes. Remove from the heat and stir in lemon juice. Makes ⅔ cup—enough for 4 or 5 servings. This is a delicious sauce over cake.

They brought beds, basins, and earthen vessels, wheat, barley meal, parched grain . . . for David and the people with him to eat.—2 Samuel 17:28

CHAPTER ELEVEN

GRAINS

No one knows where, or in what year, the first grain sprouted; to biblical peoples, grain was life, and wheat is mentioned very early in the Bible in Genesis 30:14.

*Do not be deceived; God is not mocked, for whatever
a man sows, that will he also reap.—Galatians 6:7*

CEREAL grains are among man's oldest foods, and to biblical peoples, grain was life. The worst revenge an enemy could wreak was to sow weeds among the wheat and thus strangle the season's supply of food.

The early methods of threshing grains were crude; the biblical way was to set aside a large area of beaten and hardened earth, place the grain upon it, and drive oxen over it to crush out the grain (Deuteronomy 25:4) while at intervals the sheaves were lifted up and turned with a fork, and the chaff was carried away by the wind.

During Old Testament times, however, and even in Jesus' time, in the countryside which he loved, it seems likely that most of the grinding of grain was done with hand mills on the housewife's doorstep by use of a peculiar mill called a "quern." This was made by fitting two large, flat stones together; wheat was poured through a hole in the upper stone to trickle down between the upper and lower stones. A stick served as a lever to turn the upper stone against the lower one, grinding the grain.

What a wonderful renaissance in enjoyment of food would be brought about if we could learn to use the rough, whole grains of biblical times again! The good unpolished rice, still rich with the brown coating that makes it such an unequalled food, the rough whole wheat that needs no enriching for the simple reason that its rich appealing taste and health-giving food properties haven't been processed out of existence, the rye and barley and millet, eaten as God meant them to be eaten!

"Amen" is from an ancient Hebrew word whose root suggests "So be it."

Ten Commandments for Grain Cookery

1. Plan your cooking ahead so that cooking whole grains becomes part of your daily routine.

2. If rice is your choice, insist upon brown rice, which is the grain with only the outer husk removed.

3. True stone- or water-ground corn meal, processed without heat, has a taste and mind of its own. Use it in combinations, but never try to submerge its individuality.

4. Remember that the pastas are a product of the grains, too; cook them lovingly in plenty of water—at least eight times the amount of the macaroni, spaghetti, or noodles called for.

5. Sometimes the biblical ways are the best. Never rinse the cooked grains; to do so is like washing good food down the drain.

6. Never, never, never sift a whole-grain flour; simply stir lightly before measuring. (We DO sift if we're using the flour in cakes, but then we return the husks to the unused flour for use in bread.)

7. If you are trying to adapt a recipe calling for all-purpose flour for use with whole grains, a good general rule is to add ⅓ more liquid and cut the shortening 10 per cent.

8. If you must use modern all-purpose flour, try adding ⅓ cup of wheat germ to ⅔ cup all-purpose flour, for each cup of flour called for.

9. Remember that the ancients cooked all of the whole grains in oil, rather than in water as we do. Try it, and enjoy the added richness in flavor.

10. You will find that you will enjoy combinations of the various grains. Experiment with this, and as your taste matures many new dishes will develop.

Barley

Barley was cultivated by the Hebrews and used a great deal for bread, especially among the poorer classes. (See Judges 7:13.) It was so important that the barley harvest, preceding the wheat harvest, also marked a division of the year.

Pearl barley, which is the whole grain, is packaged and found in nearly all food shops today. You should have no trouble in finding it.

Barley in Soup

One hour before any pot of soup is done, add about 4 table-spoons of pearl barley which has been soaked for an hour, then drained. It will take about an hour to cook tender and will make the soup cloudy, but the cloudiness adds heartiness.

Barley à la Ruth
Barley Consommé

1 cup pearl barley	4 cups consommé or bouillon
3 tablespoons butter	½ pound mushrooms
½ cup chopped onions	salt and pepper

This is probably the way the biblical housewife cooked her barley. Place the butter and the barley in a very heavy pot or skillet and heat, stirring, over the flame until it browns a lit-tle and gives off a fragrant, nutty flavor. Add the bouillon or consommé very slowly, then the onions. Cover tightly and sim-mer until the barley has absorbed all the liquid and is tender —about an hour. Stir occasionally to prevent sticking; you may need more liquid. Add the washed and sliced mushrooms which have been sautéed in a little butter and toss lightly.

This is a fine dish to serve instead of potatoes. Mary or Martha probably hoarded bits of leftover meat until she had a cupful or two, and stirred these into the barley, thus making a main dish of it.

Jude Bowl
Barley Kasha

1 cup pearl barley	½ pound smoked pork or
3 tablespoons butter	sausage
6 cups stock or consommé	1 large onion, chopped
	½ teaspoon salt

Toast the barley in the butter as directed above over a low flame, but don't brown. Turn into a covered casserole or pot, add the heated stock or consommé, then add the meat which has been cut in half-inch cubes and sautéed with the onion in 2 tablespoons oil until brown. Add the salt and stir until well mixed. Cook at 350° until the barley is soft and the liquid has baked away—about an hour. Stir occasionally to prevent sticking. This fits nicely into a 2-quart casserole, and will serve 4.

For variations, use chicken fat instead of butter and chicken broth instead of consommé. Or omit 1 cup stock or consommé and substitute 1 cup canned tomatoes, 1 tablespoon brown sugar, and a minced clove of garlic. Then proceed as before.

Wheat

Although we see more and more of healthful whole-grain flour in our markets because there is an increasing demand for grain used as God meant it to be, you may have trouble in locating just what you want. The Byrd Mill, Route 5, Louisa, Virginia, will supply this by mail; you can write them for information. They have been millers since 1740 and make a variety of flours and meals in the old buhrstone way.

Wheat was cultivated as the chief food crop throughout Egypt, Palestine, and Mesopotamia; the wheat harvest time, April to June, was so important that it marked a division of the year. Here are some of the good main dishes with which the housewife of biblical days filled her table.

Gittith Pottage
Gnocchi

½ cup farina (Cream of
   Wheat)
1½ cups milk

2 tablespoons butter
¼ cup grated cheese
1 teaspoon salt

2 eggs, beaten light

Scald the milk over a low flame; stir in the farina slowly, then simmer, stirring occasionally, for 10 minutes. Add salt, butter, and cheese, stir until blended, and simmer another 5 minutes. Remove from the heat and add the eggs, beating thoroughly until blended. Butter a platter, then spread the gnocchi on it, about half an inch thick. When cold, cut into squares. All of this can be done ahead of time. When the rest of the meal is under way, lay the squares in a buttered baking pan or casserole, spread tomato sauce (page 180) between the layers, then bake at 400° until crisp and brown on top. Corn meal or hominy grits may be used instead of wheat. Serves 4 or 5.

A delicious meat accompaniment may be made by cooking ½ cup farina in 1½ cups water until thickened—about 15 or 20 minutes—seasoning with salt and curry powder, shaping into balls, and French frying until crisp and brown. Wonderful for stews and ragouts.

Sower's Pilaf
Wheat Pilaf

5 cups meat stock or consommé	¼ teaspoon pepper
2 cups cracked wheat, soaked overnight	1 tablespoon butter
	½ onion, sliced
½ teaspoon salt	½ cup buttered crumbs

Bring the meat stock (if stewing hens are reasonable and you have stewed a quantity for your freezer, use the broth in this dish) to a rapid boil in a 2-quart saucepan. Drain the wheat in a colander, then stir gradually into the boiling stock. Add the salt and pepper and simmer until tender—about 30 minutes. Melt the butter, cook the onion in it until tender and golden, then stir this into the pilaf. Turn into a casserole and bake at 350° uncovered so that remaining liquid evaporates. We like the buttered crumbs, to which a teaspoon of any herb has been added, sprinkled over the top. Serves 6.

The Pastas

The use of wheat flour to make a paste that could be shaped, dried, and kept for future use is so old that its origin is lost in antiquity. Nowhere do we have a hint that the people of Bible lands used this food, and still we know that the people of ancient Rome did; we know that the biblical housewife had flour and had eggs . . . we feel that we are justified in including the pastas in this book.

Don't limit yourself to noodles, macaroni, and spaghetti. The great variety of forms in the pastas arises from the fact that each different form has its own way of absorbing the sauce. You should know them all.

ROPE OR CORD PASTA: This includes spaghetti or spaghettini; the sauce should be a thick one, since this pasta absorbs from the outside only.

Tubular Pasta: This is hollow macaroni of all sizes. A thin sauce that flows through the tube and carries flavor with it is best for this.

Flat or Ribbon Pasta: This includes all the different noodles; any of them are fine for casseroles, soups, and various combinations.

Envelope Pastas: Ravioli, manicotti, and canelloni are included here.

Fancy-shape Pastas: This includes stars, diamonds, bows, shells, alphabets, and other shapes. They are used for soups, but the larger shapes may be used with almost any sauce.

For the first variety, serve with our tomato sauce (page 180) or in the following classic version:

Silvanus Supper
Pasta Supper

1 medium onion, chopped	1 cup water
1 clove garlic, minced fine	1 teaspoon salt
3 tablespoons olive or salad oil	¼ teaspoon pepper
1 can tomato sauce	pinch of cayenne
1 pound can red kidney beans	1 tablespoon orégano

2 cups pasta in any fancy shape

Cook the onion and garlic in the oil until tender but not brown; then add tomato sauce, undrained kidney beans, water, and seasonings. Cook about 30 minutes, covered, until the mixture thickens a bit. Meanwhile, cook the pasta according to package directions, drain, then stir into the tomato mixture just before serving. Serves 4. You might like to stir in a tablespoon of chili powder, or a little grated cheese.

If your enemy is hungry, give him bread to eat;
and if he is thirsty, give him water to drink.
—Proverbs 25:21

Spaghetti Nineveh
Spaghetti Tetrazzini

1 8-ounce package fine noodles
1 cup fresh mushrooms
  or 1 small can, sliced
¼ cup butter or margarine
1 medium onion, chopped
3 tablespoons flour
2 teaspoons salt

dash of pepper
dash of cayenne pepper
2½ cups milk
2 cups cooked meat: ham,
  chicken, etc.
2 tablespoons grated Parmesan
  cheese

Cook the noodles until chewy but not quite tender. Drain. Wash fresh mushrooms by dousing up and down in salted water; drain on a towel, then slice. Or drain canned mushrooms. Melt the butter in a skillet, add mushrooms and onion, and cook until tender but not brown. Stir in the flour as smoothly as possible, add the seasonings, then gradually stir in the milk. Cook, stirring constantly, until the sauce is smooth and bubbling. Add the meat cut in thin strips, and the cheese. Arrange the noodles in a thick border around the edge of a shallow baking dish which has been buttered thoroughly. Pour the meat sauce in the center. Bake at 400° about 15-20 minutes. Serves 6.

This dish can be varied by using any leftover meat; roast pork is delicious in it, as is roast veal; chicken or turkey is superb. It is a good basic dish that should be in your collection.

Shinar Pie
Macaroni Pie

Pastry for a 1-crust pie
2½ cups cooked macaroni
¼ cup butter or margarine
¼ cup flour
2 cups milk

1 teaspoon salt
dash of pepper
¼ cup heavy cream
2 cups grated cheese
1 tablespoon butter

Prepare your pastry either from your favorite recipe or from a mix, and place in the refrigerator until you are ready for it.

While this is chilling, make a sauce by melting the butter in a saucepan, stirring in the flour, and adding the milk slowly, stirring all the while, until thick and smooth. Add the seasonings, remove from the heat, and stir in the cream. I like to add a teaspoon of herb poultry seasoning here; suit your own taste. Arrange alternate layers of macaroni and cheese in the pie shell (save a little cheese for the top of the pie; Cheddar is the best cheese to use for this dish). Pour the hot sauce over the pie, top with the cheese you saved, and bake 15 minutes at 425°, then 20 minutes longer at 375°, or until brown. Serves 4-6.

If you don't want to take time to make the pie shell, bake it in a casserole for the best macaroni and cheese you ever tasted. Try it in the shell, though, for a luncheon main dish with a tart green salad and a rich dessert.

Lystra Supper
Vegetables with Pasta

1 medium onion, chopped
3 celery stalks, diced
2 medium zucchini, diced
1 small eggplant, peeled and diced

2 green peppers, seeded and diced
3 tomatoes, peeled and diced
2 tablespoons oil
1 teaspoon salt

3 tablespoons grated cheese

Cook the onion and all the vegetables in the oil, which has been heated in a skillet, until tender and reduced to half the volume. Season with salt and cook slowly for 10 minutes longer. Mix in the grated cheese, then serve over hot, freshly cooked macaroni, spaghetti, or noodles. This is different and delicious. Try it, using almost any vegetable you have on hand.

Spaghetti Merida
Savory Liver

1 pound beef liver	1 8-ounce can tomato sauce
¼ pound bacon, diced	1 No. 2 can tomatoes
1 clove garlic, minced	2 teaspoons sugar
3 tablespoons minced onion	1 teaspoon salt
1 green pepper, minced	¼ teaspoon pepper
½ cup minced celery	1 bay leaf
⅛ teaspoon cayenne pepper	1 pound spaghetti
1 6-ounce can tomato paste	grated Parmesan cheese

This is a Spanish dish, named after one of the first of the Spanish towns in which Christianity appeared. You'll find it nutritious, economical, and of delightful flavor.

Cover the liver with hot water; simmer 15 minutes, then drain. Put through the food chopper, using the coarse blade. Now, sauté the bacon until crisp, add garlic, onion, green pepper, celery, and cayenne, and simmer 10 minutes over medium heat, stirring frequently, until the vegetables are tender. Add the ground liver and all remaining ingredients except spaghetti and cheese, and simmer 15 minutes. All of this may be done ahead of time. When ready to serve, cook spaghetti tender in boiling salted water, drain, and turn onto a hot platter. Spoon the tomato-liver sauce over and toss until thoroughly blended. Top with cheese, or pass cheese separately. Serves 6 or 7, and you'll find that even people who won't eat liver will eat this.

For a delicious sauce for spaghetti, combine a 15-ounce can spaghetti sauce with 1 can condensed clam chowder. Thin to the consistency desired.

Did you know that Ezra 7:21 contains all the letters of the alphabet except J? Check it and see if it doesn't!

Elijah Loaf
Macaroni Custard

1½ cups uncooked elbow
    macaroni
3 quarts boiling water
5 teaspoons salt
3 cups milk
⅓ cup butter or margarine

2 cups soft bread crumbs
⅓ cup chopped pimento
3 cups grated Cheddar cheese
⅓ cup minced parsley
¼ cup minced onion
¼ teaspoon pepper

6 eggs, beaten

Cook the macaroni in the boiling water to which 4 teaspoons salt have been added for about 9 minutes or until the pasta is tender. Drain. Combine milk and butter and heat until butter is melted; pour over bread crumbs. Add all remaining ingredients except eggs. Now add beaten eggs and macaroni and stir until blended. Turn into a 10×5×3-inch loaf pan (Pyrex pans give a nice crust) and bake at 325° for 1 hour and 10 minutes or until a knife inserted in the center comes out clean. Cool 10 minutes, then unmold onto a platter. Serves 8.

For a delicious variation, try adding a teaspoon of basil, orégano, or marjoram to this dish. Serve it with the tomato sauce (page 180) or with the beef liver sauce (page 194) or with Gennasaret Sauce. If you have any left over, it is delicious chilled, sliced ¾ inch thick, and sautéed in butter.

Gennasaret Sauce

1 can condensed cream of
    celery soup
1 teaspoon prepared mustard

¼ cup milk
3 tablespoons sweet-pickle
    relish

1 hard-cooked egg, chopped

Empty the soup into a small saucepan, blend in the mustard and the milk. Add relish and egg and heat over low heat. This sauce is also excellent with seafood.

Nehum Casserole
Noodle Eggplant Casserole

1 small eggplant, sliced thin	1 5-ounce package broad
2 eggs, beaten	noodles, cooked
flour	⅔ cup grated Parmesan cheese
⅓ cup salad oil	salt and pepper
	2 cups milk

Dip each slice of eggplant in egg, then in flour; brown in hot oil in a skillet. Arrange alternate layers of eggplant and noodles in greased 1½-quart baking dish, sprinkling each layer with cheese and salt and pepper to taste. Pour milk over all and bake at 375° about 40 minutes. Unless you've tried one of these baked eggplant dishes, you have no idea of the wonderful flavor that develops; this is truly a New Testament combination.

Job's Pudding
Raisin Pudding

2½ cups milk, scalded	1 teaspoon grated lemon rind
¼ cup sugar	½ cup seedless raisins
½ teaspoon salt	⅛ teaspoon nutmeg
1 teaspoon vanilla	1½ cups fine noodles, uncooked

Combine milk, sugar, salt, vanilla, lemon rind, raisins, and nutmeg in the top of a double boiler. Add the uncooked noodles and place over boiling water. Cover and cook 30 minutes, stirring once when half done. Remove from the heat and spoon into 5 or 6 dessert dishes. Serve warm. Because the noodles require no eggs for thickening, this is a wonderfully economical dessert, as well as being nutritionally valuable.

> *Thou dost keep him in perfect peace,*
> *whose mind is stayed on thee.—Isaiah 26:3*

Rice

Rice cultivation is as old as civilization itself; it is a water-tolerant plant, so it is unlikely that it was known in Jerusalem, but we find it mentioned in ancient Jewish records and we know that it was (and is) grown extensively in Egypt. From here it was carried into Spain and Italy, so it is very likely that the missionary travelers of the New Testament knew and liked it.

Let's learn to cook rice properly, first of all. Few people in this day and age know that the ancient method was best. Today many cooks wash the rice, thus washing a good deal of food value down the drain. Washing is unnecessary because modern rice is machine-milled and comes to us ready to cook.

DON'T wash or rinse rice. DON'T peek while rice is cooking. And DON'T stir rice after it comes to a boil.

DO, however, keep the liquid at boiling point to prevent sogginess. DO add a bit of lemon juice to polished rice to enhance snowy whiteness. And DO keep rice hot until it is served. It stays fluffier.

Here is the ancient method of cooking. Today, we call it the 1-2-1 fluff method. Combine 1 cup of rice, 2 cups water, and 1 teaspoon salt in a 3-quart saucepan that has a tight-fitting lid. Bring to a boil, stirring once or twice as the water comes to a boil. Lower the heat to simmer. Cover pan and cook about 14 minutes without removing lid or stirring. If the rice is not quite tender enough to suit your taste, replace lid and cook 2 to 6 minutes longer. Remove from the heat.

For drier rice, fluff lightly with a fork and let stand in the covered pan 5 to 10 minutes to steam dry. For extra tender rice, start with ⅓ cup more water and increase the cooking time 4 or 5 minutes.

Rice cooked in this manner will keep well in the refrigerator for a week; cook enough for several dishes, so that it will be ready when you want it, or for an emergency meal.

Pilaf Timothy
Chicken Pilaf

½ cup butter or margarine	1 cup uncooked rice
2 cups cooked chicken, ham, or other meat cut in strips	2½ cups chicken stock or 2½ cups water and 3 bouillon cubes
¼ cup diced onion	
2 teaspoons salt	½ cup chopped tomatoes, drained
⅛ teaspoon pepper	
½ teaspoon orégano or thyme	½ cup chopped walnuts

Melt the butter or margarine in a large saucepan. Add meat and onion and cook until the onion is tender. Add salt, pepper, and orégano, then add the rice and cook, stirring occasionally, for 5 minutes. Slowly add the chicken stock or water and bouillon cubes, then add tomatoes and walnuts, bring to a boil, cover and simmer for about 20 minutes, or until the rice is tender. Do not stir while cooking. Serve very hot with crisp hot bread, a green salad, and a fruit dessert. Serves 8.

Rice Ring, Ebal
Rice Ring

½ cup grated cheese	5 cups hot, cooked rice
2 tablespoons butter or margarine	

Add the cheese and butter to the rice; toss lightly with a fork until cheese and butter are melted. Pack lightly into a buttered 8- or 8½-inch ring mold. Cover with aluminum foil; set in a pan of hot water and keep warm until ready to use. This may be made a couple of hours ahead of serving time; when ready to serve, loosen the edges with a spatula, invert onto a platter, and fill the center with Chicken Priscilla (page 86), Haddock Stew (page 42), or any good basic meat stew such as Rich Beef Stew (page 67), Peppered Pig (page 79), or Kettle Meal (page 88). Serves about 6.

Jorim Platter
Lamb Platter

½ cup salad oil	2 tablespoons salt
2 pounds lean lamb, cubed	1 tablespoon ground allspice
2 large onions, peeled and sliced	4 cups uncooked rice
1 large head cauliflower, sliced	1 green pepper, sliced
	few grains pepper
	¼ cup sesame seeds

If you are looking for a truly delicious dish that will serve a party beautifully and economically, this one should have your attention. It is truly of biblical origin, is still a favorite dish in modern-day Jordan, and this quantity will make 10 or 12 servings at reasonable cost.

Heat ¼ cup of the oil in a 4-quart kettle, then add the lamb and brown lightly. Add the remaining ¼ cup oil, the sliced onions and cauliflower, and sauté until the onions are tender and transparent. Add 2 quarts (8 cups) boiling water, the salt, and the allspice. Heat until the water boils, then add the rice slowly so that all of the rice is covered by the water. Boil 5 minutes, then cover, reduce the heat and simmer about 20 minutes, or until the rice is tender and all the water is absorbed.

Now comes the trick. Place a large round chop plate or platter over the top of the kettle, hold the kettle and plate on each side, and flip over. The lamb will come out on top of a mound of rice. Garnish with strips of green pepper, sprinkle with sesame seeds and a little pepper, and help yourself to a dish that Paul himself probably enjoyed in his time. All it needs is a green salad to make a meal.

> the ants are a people not strong,
> yet they provide their food in the summer.
> —*Proverbs 30:25*

Salem Soup
Supper Soup

1 cup diced celery	salt to taste
2 small onions, chopped	6 eggs
1 green pepper, diced	½ cup sharp grated cheese
2½ cups canned tomatoes	2 cups hot, cooked rice
3 cups water	

Combine the first five ingredients and simmer 15 minutes; add salt to taste. Remove from the heat and break the eggs into the hot soup; sprinkle with the cheese. Cover and keep warm for about 5 minutes. Serve very hot in individual soup dishes over mounds of the cooked rice. With crackers and pickles, this is a whole-meal supper that children love. Serves 6.

For extra flavor, try adding a bouillon cube to the water in which you cook rice, or use broth in place of water.

Tirzah Pudding
Plum Pudding

⅔ cup uncooked rice	2 teaspoons vanilla
1 teaspoon salt	3 eggs, separated
1½ cups milk, scalded	½ cup milk
1 cup juice from plums	1 can purple plums, halved and drained
½ cup water	
½ cup sugar	6 tablespoons sugar
1 teaspoon pumpkin pie spice	½ teaspoon vanilla

Put the rice, salt, 1½ cups milk, plum juice, and water in a greased 2-quart baking dish. Place in a pan of hot water, cover and bake at 350° for 45 minutes. Remove from the oven and stir. Cover and bake 15 more minutes or until the rice has absorbed the liquid. Remove from the oven and stir in the ½ cup sugar, pumpkin pie spice, and vanilla. Beat egg yolks well, beat in the ½ cup milk, then stir this mixture into the pudding. Mix thoroughly. Stir in the the halved plums. Return to the oven and bake at 400° for 15 minutes. When baked, top with a meringue made by beating the egg whites with the 6 tablespoons sugar and the ½ teaspoon vanilla, and return to the oven for 12 to 15 minutes, or until nicely browned. Serve warm or cold. This makes 8 or 10 servings.

Crème Enoch
Coffee Creme

1⅓ cups water
1 teaspoon salt
⅔ cup uncooked rice
1 cup milk
½ cup sugar

1 cup very strong coffee
1 cup whipping cream
½ teaspoon vanilla
toasted pecans, unsweetened
   chocolate, or cherries

16 marshmallows, cut up

Combine water, salt, and rice, and cook as directed on page 197. Stir in the milk, cover, and cook over very low heat 10 to 15 minutes or until the rice absorbs the milk. Stir occasionally. Now stir in the sugar, marshmallows, and coffee, and cook, covered, over medium heat 15 minutes, stirring frequently. The mixture will be creamy. Cover and cool. When cool, whip the cream until stiff and fold this, together with the vanilla, into the rice mixture. Serve topped with toasted nuts, shavings of unsweetened chocolate, or chopped maraschino cherries. This very impressive dessert serves 8.

> *And what does the* Lord *require of you,*
> *but to do justice and to love kindness,*
> *and to walk humbly with your God?*
> *—Micah 6:8.*

Gibbethon Custard
Fruit Custard

2 eggs	1 teaspoon vanilla extract
2 cups milk	2 cups cooked rice
1 tablespoon melted butter	1/4 cup raisins
3 tablespoons sugar	1/4 cup chopped dates
1/4 teaspoon salt	1/4 cup chopped nuts

1/8 teaspoon nutmeg

Beat the eggs lightly; stir in milk and remaining ingredients. Pour into buttered cups or 1½-quart casserole, set in a pan of hot water, and bake at 350° about 1 hour or until a knife inserted in the center of the custard comes out clean. Serve hot with Lemon Sauce (page 181), or very cold with hot Butter Sauce (page 275).

Azgad Squares
Rice Squares

3 cups cooked rice	1/2 teaspoon Accent
1 cup chopped parsley	3 beaten eggs
3/4 cup shredded sharp cheese	1½ cups milk
1/3 cup finely chopped onion	1½ teaspoons Worcestershire
1 teaspoon salt	sauce

Mix the rice, parsley, cheese, onion, and seasonings. Combine eggs, milk, and Worcestershire sauce, add to the rice mixture and mix thoroughly. Pour into a greased 10×6×2-inch baking dish and bake at 325° for 40 minutes or until just set. Cut into squares and serve with any creamed mixture of chicken, meat, or vegetables. Makes 6-8 servings. This is an invaluable basic dish for lunches or Sunday night suppers, since it is economical to make and may be served with a creamed sauce which uses up as little as 1 cup leftover meat, etc.

Lentils

Esau's Pottage
Pottage of Lentils

This is said to be the very same dish for which Esau sold his birthright; it is a sort of stew, a cheap dish much used by the lower classes, thus stressing the fact that he made a very bad bargain indeed.

½ cup oil	1 green pepper
6 onions, diced	2 cups tomatoes
1 pound lamb or beef, in small cubes	1 cup water
2 carrots	1 pound lentils
2 stalks celery	1 teaspoon salt
	¼ teaspoon black pepper

Heat the oil; add the onions and sauté until tender but not brown. Turn in the cubed meat (it should be lean as possible) and let simmer gently while you wash and dice the vegetables. Add the vegetables and lentils to the meat, with the cup of water, and simmer gently until lentils are tender. It will take about 1½ hours; if you have a pressure cooker, cook at 15 pounds' pressure for 30 minutes. Add salt and pepper when the lentils are cooked. If simmered in an ordinary pan for the longer length of time, you may have to shake the pot occasionally or add a little water, to prevent sticking. Serves 6.

This gets very thick after it is chilled; a favorite Lebanese dish is the chilled pottage shaped in patties or croquettes, rolled in cracker crumbs, and fried.

> *Better is a little with righteousness*
> *than great revenues with injustice.*
> *.—Proverbs 16:8*

Abigail's Dish
Spicy Lentils

1 cup dried lentils	3 tablespoons oil
3 cups water	1 cup cooked rice
1 bay leaf	1/4 teaspoon mace
3 sprigs parsley	salt and pepper
1 onion chopped	1 1/2 cups tomato sauce (page 180)

Wash the lentils and soak in water overnight; do not drain. Add bay leaf and parsley and cook until tender—about an hour. Meanwhile, brown the onion in the heated oil, then add the remaining ingredients with the exception of the sauce. Heat through, and serve with sauce in a side dish. For a meatless dish, this may be served with other sauces. Serves 4.

For Spicy Lentils and Sausages, a fine economy dish that is as delicious as it is easy, make the above except for the tomato sauce. Turn into a shallow buttered baking dish (10×6×2). Top with 2 peeled and sliced tomatoes and 8 pork sausages and bake at 350° for 25-30 minutes. Serves 4 or 5.

Corn

The Indian maize that we know was unknown in biblical days, but how foolish it would be to omit this great gift of God here when it serves us so well!

Corn meal, either white or yellow, may also be obtained from the Byrd Mill in the rich stone-ground state. Until you've tasted it in spoon bread and muffins, you just don't know real corn flavor. We are not including breads made from corn meal in this chapter; they will be found in the chapter on Bread, page 228.

"Agree with God, and be at peace."—Job 22:21

Mush-Scrapple-Polenta

1 cup corn meal	1 teaspoon salt
4 cups water	1 tablespoon butter

Here is the basic recipe for corn-meal dishes; mix the corn meal with 1 cup cold water. Stir until smooth, then add the remaining liquid boiling hot. Cook 30 minutes in the top of a double boiler, stirring occasionally. Add salt and butter, and serve as desired. Served as described here, this is corn-meal porridge—a wonderfully nourishing dish when served with milk and sugar, or syrup, for breakfast.

SCRAPPLE: Buy a nice soup bone with about a pound of meat on it; cover with boiling water in a kettle, bring to a boil, and simmer until the meat falls from the bone. This is a lengthy job; if you have a pressure cooker, cook under 15 pounds' pressure for about 40 minutes, and the job will be done. Cool, remove meat from stock and cut into fine pieces. Measure the stock; add water to make 4 cups. Mix 1 cup cold stock with the corn meal as directed above, then stir into remaining 3 cups boiling stock. Add diced meat and ½ cup grated carrots and cook as above. Pour the mixture into a loaf pan (9×5×3) which has been rinsed with cold water, pressing down to form an even, solid loaf. Refrigerate overnight, then turn out of the pan, slice about ½ inch thick, and fry in hot bacon or pork fat until golden brown on both sides. Serve for breakfast with syrup or with a green salad for supper.

> *Beloved, let us love one another; for love is of God, and he who loves is born of God and knows God. He who does not love does not know God; for God is love. In this the love of God was made manifest among us, that God sent his only Son into the world, so that we might live through him.—1 John 4:7-9*

POLENTA: Cook corn-meal mush as directed above. When thick, add 1 teaspoon paprika and 1 cup grated Parmesan cheese. Stir until well blended. Turn into a shallow, buttered baking dish and level off the top with a spoon. Make a mixture of 1½ cups cooked leftover meat, poultry, or ham cut in thin strips, one 6-ounce can sliced mushrooms, drained, ¼ cup grated Parmesan cheese, and one 8-ounce can tomato sauce. Spread this over the top of the polenta. Sprinkle with freshly ground black pepper and bake at 350° for 45 minutes. Serves 6.

"Give us each day our daily bread."
—Luke 11:3

CHAPTER TWELVE

BREADS

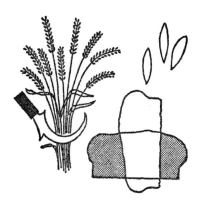

As old as written history, as diversified as mankind itself, bread is still the world's staff of life. In 6,000 years men have never lost their taste for it.

Aspire to live quietly, to mind your own affairs, and to work with your hands.—1 Thessalonians 4:11

Bread was on the table at the Lord's supper, symbolic of all the food set before men at an ordinary meal of the ancient world. In the Lord's Prayer, Jesus directed his disciples to ask for their daily bread even before they asked to be forgiven their debts, protected from temptation, and delivered from evil. Bread was life.

It is the one food that in Martha's time, or even in Sarah's, was probably better than that we have today, for the bread we call the staff of life is a pallid, limp shadow of the crusty and flavorful loaf that was baked in Palestine.

No one knows where or when the first loaf of bread was baked, but by the time of the Pharaohs two kinds of bread, leavened and unleavened, were in use. Scientists surmise that the first leavened bread was made when a primitive baker let his dough stand too long before baking and fermentation accidentally took place. In the course of time it was learned, probably also by accident, that if a portion of well-raised dough was added to a fresh batch of grain and water, fermentation was likely to take place. Thus, the leavened bread we know was born.

The biblical housewife had, of course, no solid shortening; she used oil and so you, too, may use oil. She used flour ground from whole grains, too, just as you may use flour ground from whole grains if you are willing to go to a bit of trouble to find it. Thus, bread is the one food which you may reproduce today exactly as it was in biblical times.

How long has it been since you sniffed the good earthy scent of yeast dissolving in warm milk? How long since you turned a bowl of risen dough out on the board, light and porous, and kneaded it into a shapely, living thing with which to feed your loved ones?

Promise yourself that you will bake bread at least once a month from now on, and from grains with all their God-given goodness included. Your children will bless you.

Ten Commandments for Making Bread with Yeast

1. Forget your belief that you have only two kinds of flour, all-purpose and cake. There are a dozen other kinds, and every one will delight you.
2. Discover that there is nothing difficult about making bread. A yeast dough is one of the most obliging and indestructible materials you will ever work with.
3. Remember that if the liquid in your bread is milk, it must be scalded to halt bacterial action; otherwise your bread may sour.
4. Remember that the yeast which is raising your bread is a living, breathing thing, which must be fed and kept warm.
5. Thus, your basic mixture must always contain a little sugar for feeding the yeast and must never be hotter than lukewarm.
6. We are experimenting all the time with bread that will be quicker; but as long as yeast is the leavener, the best bread will be that which has time to rise slowly.
7. When you make a so-called "no-knead" bread, you are depriving yourself of one of the greatest joys of a woman's life. Learn to knead a bread dough thoroughly and competently; it is fine exercise, and good for any neuroses you may be harboring.
8. The oven must be exactly hot enough to stop the growth of the yeast, to form a crust as the leavening breathes its last gasp, and to finish up a luscious glistening golden brown, while the inside of the loaf is cooked to a velvety crumb.
9. A loaf of bread that has baked to perfection will have shrunk from the sides of the pan; it will turn out easily; when the loaf is tapped on the bottom, it will have a recognizably hollow sound.
10. Remember to bake enough so that your family can take one loaf hot from the oven, slice it in extravagant chunks, spread it with sweet yellow butter, and eat it then and there. This is a moment that makes you feel close to God.

Nob Bread
Challah

Challah, or Challa, is the Sabbath bread of the Israelites.

It is a fine bread even today; you will enjoy the subtly different flavor imparted by the saffron.

8 cups flour	2 cakes yeast
1 tablespoon salt	2 cups hot potato water
1 tablespoon sugar	2 eggs
¼ cup vegetable shortening	¼ teaspoon saffron

Sift the flour and salt together. Into a large bowl, measure the
sugar and shortening; add the saffron and the hot potato water
and stir until the shortening is melted. If you do not have potato
water, plain hot water will do nicely, but potato water makes
such a superior bread that you should get acquainted with it.
When this has cooled to lukewarm, scoop out about a half cup
of the liquid and crumble the yeast into it; stir until the yeast
is dissolved, then stir it all into the liquid in the bowl. Mix well,
then stir in the slightly beaten eggs and half the flour. This
will make what is called a "sponge." Cover and let rise in a
warm place for 30 minutes, then add the remaining flour to
make a stiff dough. Turn out onto a lightly floured board and
knead for about 10 minutes until smooth and elastic, then return
to the bowl, cover, and let rise until doubled in bulk—about one
hour.

Turn out of the bowl and knead again for a few moments.
Now divide the dough in two; take a piece of dough the size of
a large bun from each piece. Divide the remaining large pieces of
dough into thirds and roll each piece with your hands to a long

The plans of the diligent lead surely to abundance.
—Proverbs 21:5

rope about 1½ inches thick. Fasten the three ropes together at the end by pinching together, then braid, fastening the ends again at the end of the braid. Place this in a greased and floured bread pan.

Now divide each of the bun-sized pieces into three parts; roll each part into a rope ½ inch thick, braid this and place on top of the large braid. Brush with beaten egg yolks, sprinkle with poppy seeds, and allow to rise in a warm place for 1 hour. Bake at 400° for 25 minutes, then reduce heat to 375° and bake 15 minutes; reduce heat to 350° and bake 20 minutes or until done. Makes 2 loaves.

In some countries, the small braid on top of the loaf is shaped like a ladder, symbolic of the ladder which appeared to Jacob in his dream.

Angel's Bread
Grandmother's White Bread

This is my favorite bread recipe. Even though made with today's devitalized flour, it is rich and satisfying; it is a fine recipe to begin with, and your first experience at breadmaking will, I know, be crowned with success.

2 cups liquid (milk, water, or potato water)	5 tablespoons shortening or oil
4 tablespoons sugar	2 cups water
4 teaspoons salt	2 cakes yeast or 2 packages active dry yeast
12 cups sifted all-purpose flour	

Heat the milk until you can see a puckery film over the top, but don't let it boil. If using water or potato water, merely heat. Stir in sugar, salt, and shortening. Cool to lukewarm. A solid shortening will be melted by the time the liquid cools to the proper temperature. The liquid will be lukewarm when a drop on the inside of your wrist feels neither cold nor hot. The temperature is extremely important since it must be warm enough to promote growth of the yeast but not so hot as to kill the organism.

Heat the water just to lukewarm. Sprinkle dry yeast over the water or crumble compressed yeast into it, then stir until dissolved. Now, add the yeast mixture to the milk mixture, then stir in half the flour. Beat until smooth. Then add remaining flour and work in well with your hands.

The dough will be a little sticky at this point; turn it onto a lightly floured board and knead and punch and stretch to mix all the ingredients thoroughly. As you knead, sprinkle just enough flour under the dough to keep it from sticking, but be careful not to use too much. Too much flour will make the bread coarse and heavy. Knead until the dough looks satiny smooth and springy. Oil your biggest bowl; turn in the dough, brush the top with oil, and let stand in a warm place away from drafts until doubled in bulk—about one hour. When you poke two fingers into the dough and pull them away fast, indentations should remain. Punch the dough down into the center of the bowl, pull the edges away from the bowl, then turn the dough onto the floured board and cut into 3 parts. It will be warm and responsive—almost living. Knead each part a bit, then shape into a nice loaf with the edges pulled to the bottom, and place in a greased bread pan. Cover with a clean towel and let stand in a warm place until doubled in bulk again—about 45 minutes.

Bake at 400° for 15 minutes, then reduce the heat to 375° and bake 25 minutes longer. Turn out on a rack to cool. This makes 3 large or 4 not-so-large loaves. If you like a soft, rich crust, brush the finished loaf with oil or melted butter. If you like a hard crust, bake with a pan of hot water in the bottom of the oven. For a glazed crust, brush the tops of the loaves just before baking with a beaten egg yolk into which 1 tablespoon water has been stirred.

Ephraim Cake
Rich Egg Bread

2⅔ cups milk	2 eggs, beaten
1 stick butter or margarine	8 cups all-purpose flour
2 cakes yeast dissolved in	1½ teaspoons salt
½ cup lukewarm water	1½ tablespoons sugar

Scald the milk as directed previously, but do not boil. Turn into a large bowl. Add the stick of butter or margarine (½ cup of other shortening will do, but the flavor will not be so rich) and let cool to lukewarm. Dissolve the yeast in the lukewarm water.

When the milk and butter are lukewarm, add the eggs and the yeast mixture and beat thoroughly. I like to use a slotted spoon for this; anything with a good handle that will let you go at it with all your might is all right. While you are beating, add the flour which has been sifted with the salt and sugar; it should take you about 10 minutes to get it all beaten in. Thorough beating is necessary, for this takes the place of one of the kneading operations.

Cover the bowl with a clean towel and set in a warm place to rise to double its bulk—it will take about an hour or a bit more, depending upon the warmth of the rising place. While it rises, oil 2 loaf pans. The dough will be very soft—don't worry about that; the beating took care of the kneading, and the softness of the dough is what makes the delicacy of this bread. Scoop out half the dough into your floured hands, and juggle it somehow into an oblong, and drop it into one of the pans. It won't look as you expect it to, but don't worry. Repeat with the last half of the dough.

Cover with a towel again, and when the dough has once more doubled in bulk—about 45 minutes or an hour—bake at 375° for about 50 minutes. When the bread has shrunk from the sides of the pan, it is done. Turn onto a rack and cool. This is a very rich bread; eaten warm, it is almost like cake. But for teatime with fresh strawberry preserves and softened cream cheese, or for a midnight snack with a very special brand of cheese, or for a simple dinner for which you want one distinguishing dish, it is just superb. I have served it to some of my most distinguished guests, with only a thick rich soup, a green salad, and a dessert, and had them say that they had never eaten such a meal.

For variety, you might like to add 1 cup washed, well-drained seedless raisins to this dough.

To make **Panettone**, the white fruitcake of Italy which is a very special Christmas bread, add ½ cup candied citron peel, cut in small pieces (you can buy this already diced), ½ cup seedless raisins, and ½ cup chopped nuts.

Jesus compared himself to the manna which came down from heaven to feed the wandering Hebrews. Those who ate the manna eventually died. Those who have faith in him as the bread of life will never die. See John 6:48-51.

Jeremiah's Bread
Whole-Wheat Bread

1 cake compressed yeast or
  1 envelope dry yeast
	2 tablespoons butter, lard, or
	  oil

¼ cup lukewarm water	2 teaspoons salt
¼ cup brown sugar	3½ cups whole-wheat flour
1½ cups water	½ teaspoon mace

The procedure here is the same as with other breads; soak the yeast in the lukewarm water until dissolved and while it is soaking, heat the remaining water, add shortening, salt, and sugar, and cool to lukewarm. If you have had your whole-wheat flour in the refrigerator (the best place to keep it, by the way), be sure that it has come to room temperature before using. Stir lightly with a spoon before measuring, then stir the mace into the flour.

Simply combine the yeast mixture with the shortening mixture, then stir in the flour with a wooden spoon; you may have to add just a little lukewarm water to get the last of the flour blended in, but try to do it without; this is a defeatist attitude, and should be avoided. The dough should be stiff but soft. Turn into a bowl, brush the dough with oil as directed in other recipes, cover with a clean towel, and set in a warm place to rise. After an hour, check it; if it hasn't risen well, the dough is too stiff, and a little lukewarm water should be worked into it. Complete rising will take 1½ to 2 hours.

Grease the bread pan thoroughly. Work the dough down in the bowl with your hands, then turn it into the pan, and let it rise again for 45 minutes. When well risen, it is ready to be baked. There is an important difference in baking whole grain breads; instead of putting them into a moderate oven, we start them in a slow oven (350°) and after 20 minutes reduce the heat further to 325° and bake about an hour. I have known some cooks who start whole grain breads in a cold oven, as we used to do angel cake, then light the oven, set at 350°, and have a perfectly baked loaf in one hour. Perhaps you would like to try both methods.

Lechem
Wheat Egg Bread

2 cups milk	1 tablespoon sugar
½ cup margarine	¼ cup lukewarm water
1 teaspoon salt	3 cups whole-wheat flour
½ cup sugar	4 eggs, separated
1 cake compressed yeast	½ teaspoon baking soda

Scald the milk as directed above, add margarine, salt, and sugar and let cool to lukewarm. Dissolve the yeast in the warm water, add the tablespoon of sugar, and combine with the lukewarm milk mixture. Stir in the flour. Add egg yolks which have been beaten until light and fluffy and beat well. Beat the egg whites until stiff enough to hold a peak, sprinkle in the baking soda, and beat again. Fold this into the dough, beat thoroughly, then cover with a clean towel and set to rise. Punch down with the spoon and beat again, then turn into a greased and floured loaf pan and 6 muffin tins which have been greased and floured. Let rise for about 45 minutes, then bake at 350° about 40 minutes for the loaf and 20-25 minutes for the muffins.

This is a delightful bread for tea or late breakfast; it is quite sweet and rises very high because of the amount of liquid. Your family will love it toasted, buttered, and served with fresh fruit in place of coffeecake.

Most of these breads from soft doughs (Lechem, Rich Egg Bread) can be beaten in the electric mixer.

The very first baker mentioned in the Scripture is Sarah. See Genesis 18:6

Hasshub Bread
Oatmeal Nut Bread

2½ cups liquid—milk, water, or potato water
¼ cup brown sugar, packed down
1 tablespoon salt
1 cake yeast
2 cups regular rolled oats (not quick oats)
5½ cups all-purpose flour
1 cup broken pecans
2 tablespoons oil

Heat the liquid to just lukewarm, add the sugar, salt, and oil, then crumble the yeast into the mixture and stir until dissolved. Stir in the rolled oats. Now measure the flour, then begin stirring it into the first mixture with a spoon; after adding about half, you will have to begin working the remainder in with your hands—rub them with a little oil first, and the dough won't stick. While adding the flour, add the nuts, too. Be sure to use only enough flour to make it possible to handle the dough.

Turn onto a lightly floured board, cover with the bowl, and let the dough "rest" for 10 minutes. Then knead until smooth—about ten more minutes. Place in a greased bowl, set in a warm place, and allow to rise until double in bulk—about an hour. Punch down, divide into halves, shape each half into a loaf, and place in 2 lightly greased bread pans. Cover with a clean towel and let rise again until doubled in bulk—about 1 hour. Bake at 400° for 30 to 40 minutes. The Scotch oatmeal from the Byrd Mill is delicious in this bread.

Zeresh Bread
Protein Bread

This bread, developed by nutritionists at Cornell University, gains protein by the use of soya flour. Note that it contains very little fat or sugar, and so is valuable in certain diets where these foods are forbidden.

1 package granulated yeast	1½ teaspoons salt
1 cup lukewarm water	2 teaspoons sugar
2 teaspoons vegetable oil	3 tablespoons soya flour
2½ cups all-purpose flour	3½ tablespoons powdered milk

Dissolve the yeast in the lukewarm water; add the oil. Measure the dry ingredients into a bowl, add the yeast mixture and vigorously stir until the dough is smooth—you may need your hands for this. Turn into a well-oiled bowl, cover with a tea towel, and allow to rise in a warm place for 1½ hours. Right in the bowl, punch the risen dough down, then fold over the edges in a kneading action. Cover and allow to rise again for 15 minutes. Then turn out and knead again until smooth and elastic. Shape into a loaf, place in an oiled bread pan, cover with a cloth and allow to rise until it fills the pan—it will take about an hour. Bake at 375° for about 35 minutes or until the loaf tests done. This bread freezes beautifully and keeps well. Save work by tripling the recipe and making 3 loaves at one time.

Libyan Cakes
Buckwheat Cakes

2 cups buckwheat flour	1 package dry yeast
½ cup corn meal	2¼ cups buttermilk
1 tablespoon molasses	1 teaspoon baking soda
	1 teaspoon salt

Dissolve the yeast in the lukewarm buttermilk, add the salt and molasses, then stir in the flour and corn meal, and let stand in a covered bowl overnight. In the morning stir the mixture down, add the soda, then bake as usual on a well-greased griddle or skillet. This is an old Virginia recipe, beloved by all men, and well worth the little trouble.

The longest verse in the Bible is Esther 8:9. Read it and see!

Bread of Tyre
Brown Bread

1 cup unbleached flour	1½ cups whole-wheat flour
½ cup sugar	1 egg
2 teaspoons baking soda	1 cup buttermilk
½ teaspoon salt	1 cup molasses

Sift the unbleached flour, then measure. Resift with the sugar, soda, and salt. Stir the whole-wheat flour lightly before measuring, then add to other dry ingredients. Beat the egg, add the milk and molasses, and beat again. Stir into the dry ingredients, then turn into an oiled loaf pan. Bake slowly—at 325°—about 1½ hours. This must be cooled completely before slicing.

When yeast is used in bread, use potato water instead of milk for the liquid; the bread will stay fresh much longer.

Belteshazzar Sweet Bread
Raised Coffeecake

No matter how fine our mixes and prepared foods become, no home cook should deny herself the pleasure of working with a yeast-raised dough once a month or so. The fragrance of a yeast dough rising is delightful (a young boy said to me the other day that he could smell it through the closed door), and psychiatrists tell us that the kneading rids us of all our complexes. Besides, it's fun. Just try it. This one is the finest basic sweet dough I have ever known.

2 cakes yeast	½ teaspoonful salt
½ cup lukewarm milk	1 teaspoon grated lemon rind
1½ teaspoons sugar	2 eggs, beaten
½ cup butter or margarine	½ cup milk
⅓ cup sugar	5 cups all-purpose flour

It will speed the rising greatly if you have your mixing bowl warm; prepare it by filling with hot water for a few minutes, then emptying and drying. Measure ½ cup of the flour into the bowl. Make sure the ½ cup milk is truly lukewarm (110°), then crumble the yeast into it and stir until dissolved. Add this mixture, plus the sugar, to the ½ cup flour. Stir until well blended, then cover, and set in a warm place for 20 minutes. This is called a "sponge."

While this is rising, cream the butter until fluffy and blend in the ⅓ cup sugar; add salt, lemon rind, eggs, and the last ½ cup milk. Stir this into the risen yeast mixture. Then begin stirring in the flour; after about 3 cups you will have to discard the spoon and work the flour in with your hands. You may not need the full 5 cups; flours differ in moisture content, so it is impossible to give exact amounts. Just add flour until the dough is soft but can be kneaded without sticking to your oiled hands too much. Knead it thoroughly—at least 20 times. Return it to the bowl, cover, and set in a warm place to rise until double in bulk—about 1½ hours. Now it is ready to shape as you prefer.

Try some of the following suggestions—these are the ones my family likes best.

DOUGHNUTS: Roll or pat out ½ inch thick, cut with a 3-inch doughnut cutter. Cover with a towel and let rise for 15-20 minutes, then fry in deep fat heated to 375° for about 3 minutes, or until golden brown on both sides. Drain on a paper towel and sprinkle with powdered sugar.

CINNAMON STACKS: Pat dough out to a 15 × 12-inch rectangle; brush with melted butter and sprinkle with a mixture of ¼ cup sugar, ½ teaspoon cinnamon, and ¼ cup finely chopped nuts. Cut into 8 strips 1½ inches wide and 15 inches long. Stack the strips on each other, and cut into 12 equal pieces. Place each little stack cut side down, in a greased muffin cup. Let rise about 20-30 minutes, then bake at 375° about 15-20 minutes.

Fruit Coffeecake: Pat the dough into two 8 × 8-inch pans which have been thoroughly greased. Let rise until doubled, then cover with sliced apples, peaches, plums, or other fruit. Sprinkle with cinnamon and enough sugar to sweeten, dot generously with butter, and bake at 400° until the cake is done and the fruit cooked.

Bildad Bread
Fruited Oat Bread

2 cups boiling water	6 cups sifted all-purpose flour
1 cup regular rolled oats	1 tablespoon salt
2 cakes yeast (or 2 packages)	2 tablespoons vegetable oil
1/3 cup sugar	3/4 cup chopped peanuts
1/2 cup lukewarm water	3/4 cup seedless raisins

Pour the boiling water over the rolled oats, then stir and set aside to cool. Crumble the yeast into the lukewarm water, add 4 tablespoons of the sugar, and stir until the yeast is dissolved. Stir in 1/2 cup of the flour, then set aside for 10 minutes. At the end of this time, add yeast mixture to the rolled oats, then stir in the remaining ingredients. Shape into a ball and place in a greased salad bowl, set in a warm place, and let rise until doubled in bulk—about an hour. Then turn out, knead down, shape into two loaves, and place each in an oiled bread pan. Brush the top with oil, cover with a towel and let rise again until doubled in bulk—a bit more than an hour. Bake at 375° for 50 to 55 minutes. Makes 2 loaves.

*"Why do you spend your money for that which is not bread,
and your labor for that which does not satisfy?"*
—*Isaiah 55:2*

Ten Commandments for Making Quick Breads

1. Mix lightly and quickly. The leavening in quick breads is released the moment the liquid is added, and the batter must be in the oven before it escapes.
2. Keep your baking powder fresh for best results. If in doubt, test it by mixing 1 teaspoonful with ⅓ cupful of hot water. If it bubbles gleefully, it is still good.
3. Study baking powder labels and learn the three types; each is best for a particular purpose, and a good cook should be familiar with all of them.
4. Both calcium and tartrate baking powders may be used in smaller amounts than recipes call for; the only difference in finished results will be a slightly smaller bulk.
5. Too many jests have been repeated about the bride's biscuits. If she can read and is willing to learn, she can bake a better biscuit than her grandmother could.
6. Because breads leavened with baking soda or baking powder rise only once, any gluten which is developed has no opportunity to stretch and become tender; therefore, kneading or beating, which develops gluten, should be avoided.
7. Oven temperature is even more important with quick breads than with yeast breads. If your oven isn't equipped with a regulator, buy an oven thermometer; the results will more than repay you.
8. A small roll with a large proportion of crust will taste altogether different from a roll or biscuit having little crust because the pieces are baked close together.
9. The beauty of hot breads is in serving them really hot. Have a little basket for them. Snuggle them in a napkin, with the corners drawn up so that the delicious crust will remain crisp.
10. As in every other field of cookery, use originality to stamp your breads as your very own; it takes only a moment to add a little chopped ginger to a biscuit mix, but the bloom on your reputation will last for years.

Biscuits

Biscuits Birei
Light Biscuits

The name "birei," in the ancient Hebrew, meant "my creation"; I have given it to these biscuits because the extra ingredient here makes them, truly, "my creation." I think you will find them the finest biscuits you ever made.

2 cups sifted flour	½ teaspoon cream of tartar
4 teaspoons baking powder	½ cup shortening
2 teaspoons sugar	⅔ cup milk
½ teaspoon salt	

Sift the measured dry ingredients together in a bowl; add the shortening and cut in with a pastry blender until the mixture resembles coarse crumbs. Now add the milk all at once; mix briskly with a fork until the dough pulls away from the side of the bowl and comes together. Turn onto a lightly floured board and knead gently just 8 or 10 times. Pat or roll ¾ inch thick and cut out. (Biscuits rolled thinner will be crispy; rolled thicker, they'll bake high and light.) Place on an ungreased tin and bake at 450° for 10 to 12 minutes. Makes 16.

If you are in a hurry and want to make drop biscuits, simply increase the milk to 1 cup and drop the soft mixture from a spoon onto the sheet.

Now, just consider all the things that you can do with this good basic biscuit dough (and remember that if you are in a hurry, any of these things may be done with a biscuit mix made up according to directions on the package).

NUT TWISTS: Combine ½ cup chopped walnuts, ¼ cup sugar and ½ teaspoon nutmeg in a plate. Roll biscuit dough into an 8 × 12-inch rectangle. Cut in half crosswise; cut each half crosswise into 8 strips; brush strips with milk. Roll strips, one at a time, in the sugar-nut mixture, gently pressing into the dough to make it stick. Twist each strip to form a figure 8 or an S, then bake as above.

GOLDEN CRESCENTS: Roll biscuit dough into a 14-inch circle; sprinkle with ½ cup grated sharp cheese. Cut into 12 pie-shaped wedges. Starting at the wide end of each wedge, roll up each piece, ending with the point underneath. Place about 2 inches apart on an ungreased cooky sheet; bend ends of each roll to form a crescent. Brush tops with melted butter or margarine, sprinkle with caraway seeds, and bake as above.

FRUIT PUFFS: Prepare one recipe Biscuits Birei. Lightly butter 12 muffin tins. In a small bowl, combine ½ cup sugar, 2 teaspoons grated orange rind, ½ teaspoon ground ginger. Divide the dough into quarters, then cut each quarter into 9 equal chunks; form each into a ball by rolling between the palms, then with a fork dip each ball into ¼ cup orange juice, roll in the sugar mixture, and place 3 in each muffin tin. Bake at 400° for about 20 minutes. These are delicious for tea.

SCOTCH SCONE: Increase sugar in the basic recipe to 2 tablespoons. When measuring the milk, open an egg into the measuring cup, then add milk or cream to make the ⅔ cup. Roll ½ inch thick, cut into triangles. Brush the tops with cream and sprinkle with sugar. Bake as above. These are delicious with jelly.

The bakers who gave their name to a street in Jerusalem not only baked the dough prepared in private houses, but baked and sold bread to the public, just as bakers do today. See Jeremiah 37:21

Dibri Bread
Buttermilk Biscuits

2½ cups unbleached flour
   such as Aristos
5 tablespoons shortening

1 cup buttermilk
½ teaspoon soda
½ teaspoon salt

Sift flour, salt, and soda and cut in the shortening until the mixture resembles coarse crumbs. Add buttermilk and stir until the mixture leaves the sides of the bowl. Turn out on a floured board and knead 10 times. Cut, brush with melted butter, and bake at 450° for about 15 minutes. This is a very old and very delicious biscuit.

Luke's Bread
Bran Buttermilk Biscuits

1½ cups sifted flour
1 teaspoon baking powder
¾ teaspoon salt

½ teaspoon soda
⅓ cup shortening
buttermilk mixture

For the buttermilk mixture, add ½ cup breakfast bran (100%) to ¾ cup buttermilk and let stand while measuring other ingredients. Sift the dry ingredients together, then cut in the shortening until the mixture resembles coarse crumbs, then add buttermilk-bran mixture and mix until the dough follows the spoon around the bowl. Turn out onto a lightly floured board and knead lightly about 15 times. Roll ½ inch thick, cut, and bake as above on a lightly greased sheet.

Try this hot biscuit split in two, the bottom spread with honey and the top with butter. Put together and let stand for a moment. Delicious!

Whoever knows what is right and fails to do it, for him it is sin.—James 4:17

Horeb Cakes
Muffins

You will enjoy making muffins with oil, as our biblical house-wife made her little cakes. Both measuring and mixing are easier and quicker with this new-old method.

1 egg	2 cups sifted all-purpose flour
1 cup milk	¼ cup sugar
¼ cup salad oil	3 teaspoons baking powder
	1 teaspoon salt

Set the oven at 400°. Oil 12 muffin tins. Beat the egg lightly, stir in the milk and oil, then the dry ingredients sifted together. Stir ONLY until the flour is barely moistened; the batter should be lumpy. Turn into 12 tins and bake 20 to 25 minutes.

Try some of these delicious variations:

MUFFIN JEWELS: Fill muffin cups half full of batter, drop a small teaspoonful of jelly in the center, add more batter to fill ⅔ full.

APPLE MUFFINS: Use ½ cup milk and ½ cup sugar instead of the quantities given above, and add ½ teaspoon cinnamon and 1 cup unpared grated raw apple.

CHERRY CAKES: Measure 1 cup drained, unsweetened, canned cherries to the batter and bake as directed above.

DATE MUFFINS: Add ¾ cup sliced dates to the dry ingredients, then proceed as directed above.

WHOLE-WHEAT MUFFINS: Use only 1 cup all-purpose flour and 2 teaspoons baking powder, then add 1 cup whole-wheat flour to the sifted dry ingredients in the mixing bowl.

Cracknels
Scones

The cracknels mentioned in earlier chapters are described
as small dry cakes which crumbled easily. The scones below,
while actually a Scotch bread, fit the description very well. I
sometimes add bits of dry crumbled bacon to them, or two tablespoons sugar, if they're to be eaten with coffee. You will find
them easy to make and delicious; note that they contain no fat.

4 cups flour	1½ teaspoons salt
1 teaspoon soda	1 cup buttermilk
1 teaspoon cream of tartar	

Mix all of the ingredients thoroughly. Pat out on a floured
board to ½ inch thickness; cut with a 2-inch cutter. Place on a
hot, greased griddle; cook until well risen and light brown underneath, then turn and cook on the other side until brown.
When the edges are dry, the scones are done.

Corn Breads

Our biblical housewife would have welcomed good water-
ground corn meal with open arms, for it would have enabled
her to add a great deal of interest to her meals. These are all
primitive recipes, similar to quick breads she may have made
from other meals.

Bethsaida Bread
Spoon Bread

1 cup white water-ground corn meal	2 teaspoons sugar
	1 teaspoon salt
3 cups hot milk	3 egg yolks
1 teaspoon melted butter	3 egg whites, beaten stiff

Scald the cornmeal by stirring it gradually into the hot milk.
When all is added, place over heat for 4 or 5 minutes, stirring
constantly. Cool until just warm; then stir in butter, sugar, salt,

and beaten egg yolks. Mix thoroughly, then fold in the stiffly beaten egg whites. Turn into a well-greased glass baking dish and bake at 350° for 45 minutes. Serve hot, in the same dish, serving with a spoon and topping each serving with a generous chunk of butter.

Euodia Cake
Johnny Cake

The Indians taught our colonists how to parch corn and mix it with boiling water for baking in thin cakes; these were used by hunters on their long journeys, and were called, thus, "Journey Cakes." It's easy to see how "Journey Cake" became "Johnny Cake" and easy to imagine, too, that biblical housewives probably baked just such a cake from meal made from their own grains.

1 cup corn meal	1 cup boiling water
1 teaspoon salt	¼ cup milk
1 tablespoon butter	2 tablespoons drippings

Put the drippings into a medium-sized very heavy iron skillet over low heat, while you scald (parch) the meal. To do this, add salt and butter to the meal, then pour the boiling water over, stirring thoroughly, until the corn meal has absorbed all the water it will take. Spread very thin on a greased skillet, wetting the spatula or knife from time to time in the milk, as you spread. Mark off in squares. Bake at 475° for about 10 minutes.

Some good cooks use the ¼ cup milk to thin the johnny-cake batter, then drop by spoonfuls on a hot, well-greased griddle, and bake slowly on both sides.

> *Wisdom is a fountain of life to him who has it,*
> *but folly is the chastisement of fools.*
> *—Proverbs 16:22*

Edom Cake
Corn-Nut Muffins

1 cup all-purpose flour	½ cup yellow corn meal
½ teaspoon salt	1 cup milk
3 teaspoons baking powder	1 beaten egg
1 tablespoon sugar	¼ cup crunchy peanut butter

1 tablespoon salad oil

Sift together the flour, salt, baking powder, and sugar. Stir in the corn meal. Combine the remaining ingredients, stirring until the peanut butter is well broken up, then add to the dry ingredients and mix only until the flour is moistened. Fill greased muffin pans two thirds full. Bake at 400° about 20 minutes. This makes 12.

Pancakes

The pancake was one bread which the housewife of Jesus' time loved, since it was quick, filling, and economical. She may have baked hers on a hot stone; some housewives, no doubt, used a hole dug in the ground for their oven. In this, the sides were smoothly plastered and the fire was placed in the bottom; when it was sufficiently heated, the bread or cake was stuck on the smooth sides and baked swiftly.

Mareshah Cakes
Corn-Meal Cakes

1 egg, beaten	1 cup enriched flour
1¼ cups buttermilk	1 teaspoon salt
¼ cup salad oil	2 teaspoons baking powder
1 tablespoon light molasses	½ teaspoon baking soda

½ cup yellow corn meal

Sour milk may be used here if you don't have buttermilk on hand. You can sour milk by adding 1 tablespoon vinegar to each cup sweet milk. Combine egg, milk, shortening, and molasses. Add sifted dry ingredients and corn meal; stir until just barely moistened. Bake on a hot, ungreased griddle, pouring batter from a 1/4-cup measure. Makes 12. Serve with maple sugar, or as a bread to accompany a chicken dish such as fricassee.

A cup of ham, chopped fine, or a cup of whole-kernel corn may be added to this batter to make a main dish for a noonday luncheon.

Patmos Cakes
Crumb Pancakes

1 1/2 cups bread crumbs	1/2 cup all-purpose flour
1 1/2 cups milk, scalded	1/2 teaspoon salt
2 eggs, well beaten	4 teaspoons baking powder
3 tablespoons salad oil	3/4 cup blueberries

Soak the crumbs in the scalded milk until very soft; then add the well-beaten eggs and the shortening. Sift the dry ingredients together, then stir into the first mixture. These may be made without the blueberries if you prefer, but if you have them on hand, be sure to try them. Bake on a hot griddle.

Achaia Cakes
Whole-Wheat Cakes

2 cups whole-wheat flour	2 cups milk
4 teaspoons baking powder	1 egg, well beaten
1 teaspoon salt	2 tablespoons salad oil
1 teaspoon sugar	

Mix the dry ingredients thoroughly, stirring the flour with a spoon before measuring. Beat the egg, add the milk, then add oil and stir into the dry ingredients. Drop from a large spoon on a hot, well-greased griddle. Makes about 12.

Try creaming together 2 tablespoons butter, 2 tablespoons brown sugar, and ½ teaspoon cinnamon and spreading this on pancakes.

Epaphras Cakes
Onion Pancakes

1½ cups finely chopped onion	1 cup milk
2 tablespoons drippings	2 eggs
2 cups biscuit mix	4 tablespoons salad oil

Sauté the onion in the drippings until tender and golden. Make a pancake batter by combining the remaining ingredients, then add the cooked onion to the batter. Bake as directed above, on a hot, well-greased griddle. These are delicious served with leftover roast cut fine and heated in the gravy; simply serve the roast meat sauce over the cakes, and stack in threes.

The Bible was originally written in three languages: Hebrew, Aramaic, and Greek. Today it is translated, in part or as a whole, into 1,109 languages and dialects.

And they gave him a piece of a cake of figs and two clusters of raisins.—1 Samuel 30:12

CHAPTER THIRTEEN

MANNA

Ever since the wandering shepherd tribes of Old Testament times first cooked balls of sweetened dough in oil, cake in some form has been the test of the home cook's skill.

Go to the ant, O sluggard;
consider her ways, and be wise.
—Proverbs 6:6

LET [her] . . . make a couple of cakes in my sight," we find Amnon saying to the king in 2 Samuel 13:6, and we know that the cake he meant was probably a sweetened dough, twice kneaded because by this time the cooks of the Old Testament period had found, by a process of trial and error, that two workings of their dough produced a finer loaf, so that it could be served as a sweet. They had added some aromatic seeds and perhaps a few dried grapes and figs to their dough. They must have used honey and ginger and all the good spices. Cake, as a food entirely distinct from bread, was coming into being, although it had a long way to go before it became the light and delicate creation, moist and velvety of crumb, that is the pride of every housewife today.

We have instances which indicate that they made cake as a distinctly different dish from bread. When Abraham told Sarah to make cakes upon the hearth (Genesis 18:6), for instance, he stipulated, "Make ready three measures of fine meal." Doesn't this suggest that even as far back as Genesis there was a difference in flours, or in meals, which was what the people of Abraham's time used, just as there is a difference between cake and bread flours today?

No matter how faithfully they kneaded, this was not dough to make cakes as we know them, but the women of the Bible did their best; they ground the manna and baked it into cakes which tasted as if they had been baked in "fresh oil." (Numbers 11:8.)

Whether you bake one of your fine cakes as a gesture of affection, or a pan of cookies as a gift of remembrance, or a fruitcake as a neighbor's Christmas gift, you are continuing in the pattern set by Sarah and continued throughout the Bible. It will bring you happiness.

Ten Commandments for Baking Cakes

1. A fine cake is a work of art and only the finest materials should go into it—the freshest eggs, the richest milk, the finest flour.

2. Light your oven before you begin mixing, and have your pans greased and ready. Your cake won't wait while you repair an oversight.

3. Assemble all necessary ingredients before the spoon goes into the bowl; it won't help to remember you've omitted the baking powder after the cake is in the oven.

4. Measure accurately; a cake is a delicate chemical formula which must be mixed in exact proportions.

5. Remember that flour and sugar should be sifted, the flour before measuring. To save work, sift onto a paper towel.

6. Be sure to have all ingredients, unless otherwise directed, at room temperature.

7. Learn what the word "cream" means. Your butter-sugar mixture must be actually creamy; it should drop from the spoon when you test it. This is the most important step in cake-making.

8. Learn what "fold" means. Do this gently, simply lifting and turning, so that all the air you troubled to beat in will remain to lighten your cake.

9. Cool butter cakes on a rack for 5 minutes before turning out of the pan; they will come out better. Cool sponge cakes upside down until the pan is cold; prop the pan between four cups so that the cake will hang. Any cake delicate enough to make you proud is too delicate to be handled warm.

10. Try all of the wonderful new mixes; cake is one of the things that comes out of a box in such perfection that the housewife of Jesus' day would have called it a miracle.

Here is a collection of delicious breads, very sweet and rich, which might well be served instead of cake. This is the sort of "cake" which Martha might have baked.

Bishop's Bread
Date Bread

2 cups brown sugar	1 teaspoon cinnamon
½ cup oil	½ teaspoon salt
1 egg	½ teaspoon baking soda
2½ cups sifted flour	¾ cup sour milk
2 teaspoons baking powder	1 cup chopped dates

Blend the sugar and oil together, then add the egg and beat until smooth. Sift the flour with the dry ingredients. Add to the creamed mixture alternately with the milk. Fold in the dates. Pour into a greased and floured 9 × 9-inch pan. Bake at 375° for 35 to 40 minutes. When the top springs back when pressed with a finger, remove from the oven and sprinkle with ½ cup sugar mixed with 1 tablespoon cinnamon. Serve hot. Cut 12 servings.

Eglon Butter
Lemon Butter

For tea, you might like to serve this delicious English lemon butter as a spread for the Bishop's Bread.

3 eggs	2 lemons, grated rind and juice
1 cup sugar	1 tablespoon butter

Beat eggs and sugar together until thick and light colored. Add remaining ingredients and cook in a double boiler over hot water, stirring constantly, until the mixture is of the consistency of mayonnaise. It will take about 10 minutes. Cool. This makes about 2 cups; it will keep a long time in the refrigerator.

Rabshakeh's Rolls
Honey Nut Rolls

1 package yeast
¼ cup lukewarm water
1 cup milk, scalded
2 tablespoons oil
¼ cup corn syrup

grated rind 1 lemon
3⅓ cups sifted flour
½ cup honey
1 cup ground almonds or
    walnuts

1½ teaspoons salt

Soften the yeast in the lukewarm water. Mix the milk, oil, syrup, and salt in a bowl; cool to lukewarm and add lemon rind and yeast mixture. Beat in the flour gradually. Let rise until double in bulk, then punch down the dough and pat out on a floured board into a long sheet about ¼ inch thick. Spread with honey and cover with nuts. Roll like jelly roll. Cut in inch slices; arrange on a baking sheet or in greased muffin tins. Let rise until almost double (30 minutes) then bake at 350° for about 20 minutes. Delicious!

Hanani Bread
Apricot Bread

3 cups sifted flour
3 teaspoons baking powder
1½ teaspoons salt
1 cup milk

1 egg, beaten
1 cup dark corn syrup
¼ cup oil
1 cup finely cut, dried apricots

½ cup chopped nuts

Sift dry ingredients into a bowl; mix the liquid ingredients and add to the first bowl all at once. Stir until the flour is moistened. Very quickly, stir in the apricots and nuts. Turn into a greased and floured 9 × 5 × 3-inch loaf pan and bake at 325° about 1¼ hours. Turn up the oven heat during the last few minutes if the loaf doesn't seem to be browning. Remove from the pan at once; cool on a rack and store overnight before slicing. The dried apricots should be a little moist; if they seem very dry, soak them in water for 15 minutes before cutting.

Vashti Bread
Quick Date Bread

1 cup boiling water	1 egg
1 cup chopped, pitted dates	1 cup chopped Brazil nuts
1 teaspoon baking soda	2 cups sifted cake flour
3 tablespoons oil	½ teaspoon salt
1 cup sugar	1 teaspoon vanilla

Pour the water over the dates; add the soda and let stand until cool. Add the sugar to the oil and beat until well blended; then beat in the egg with a spoon. Sprinkle 1 tablespoon of flour over the nuts to coat them; sift the rest of the flour with the salt, then add alternately to the egg mixture with the dates, beating to blend after each addition. Stir in nuts and vanilla. Pour into a greased and floured 9 × 5 × 3 loaf pan. I sometimes line the bottom of loaf pans with waxed paper, to facilitate removing. Bake at 350° for 1 hour or until done. Ice with any good caramel frosting.

There are two general classifications for cakes: butter cakes, which are made with shortening or oil, and sponge cakes, which contain no shortening. I am not going to include a recipe for angel cake in this collection, for packaged angel food mixes are so good that there is simply no point in making your own. Here are some other sponge cakes, however, that you will find delicious.

Miriam's Cake
Sundae Cake

1 cup eggs (about 5)	1¼ cups sifted all-purpose flour
1 cup sugar	1 package vanilla pudding mix
½ teaspoon salt	1½ cups milk
1 teaspoon vanilla	2 eggs
	¼ cup butter, creamed

Beat the eggs until very light and fluffy; then beat in sugar, salt, and vanilla and continue beating until light and lemon colored. Fold in the sifted flour very gently, 2 tablespoonfuls at a time, and blend thoroughly with the eggs. Have ready two 8-inch round layer pans, well greased and lined with waxed paper on the bottom. Divide the batter equally into these. Bake at 350° for 25-30 minutes, or until the cake springs back when touched with a finger. Cool in the pans.

While the cake is cooling, make up the pudding mix according to the directions on the package, using the 1½ cups milk. When it has cooked thick and smooth, beat the 2 eggs, add a few tablespoons of pudding to the eggs, stir until mixed, then stir the egg mixture into the pudding. Remove from the heat and stir in the softened butter, beating until blended. Cool.

Remove the cooled cake from the pans and split each to form 4 thin layers. Spread the cooled butter cream between the layers and, after the layers are stacked, on the sides of the cake. Frost the top with this icing:

Cream 2 tablespoons butter or margarine. Blend in 1 cup sifted confectioner's sugar. Add 1 small egg; beat well. Blend in 1 square (1 ounce) melted chocolate and ½ teaspoon vanilla. Beat until smooth and thick enough to spread.

For spiced angel cake, add ½ teaspoon each nutmeg, allspice, and cloves and 1 teaspoon cinnamon to the packaged angel food mix. Frost with caramel frosting.

Delilah Cake
Parish Cake

3 eggs, well beaten
1 cup sugar
1½ cups sifted all-purpose flour
¼ teaspoon salt

4 ounces semisweet chocolate
2 cups coarsely chopped walnuts
1 cup coarsely cut-up dates
1 cup halved candied cherries

Grease and flour a 9 × 5 × 3-inch loaf pan, and line the bottom with waxed paper. Combine the eggs and sugar and beat until light and lemon colored. Sift the dry ingredients together. Chop the chocolate into pieces the size of Lima beans. Add the chocolate, with the dates, nuts, and cherries, to the dry ingredients, then fold into the egg mixture. Pour into the pan and bake at 325° for about 1½ hours. This is not exactly like sponge cake; it's more like fruit cake, but it is delicious.

"Seek the LORD *while he may be found,*
call upon him while he is near;
let the wicked forsake his way,
and the unrighteous man his thoughts;
let him return to the LORD, *that he may have*
mercy on him."—Isaiah 55:6-7

Chiffon cakes, the first really new development in cake baking in many years, are delightful, and particularly appropriate for use in modern adaptations of biblical menus, since the Bible mentions several times a custom of "mingling flour with oil." (Numbers 15:4.)   They stay moist and fresh for days.

Silk Cake
Basic Chiffon Cake

1 cup sifted all-purpose flour	3 unbeaten egg yolks
¾ cup sugar	6 tablespoons cold water
1½ teaspoons baking powder	1 teaspoon vanilla
½ teaspoon salt	¼ teaspoon cream of tartar
¼ cup Wesson Oil	½ cup egg whites (4)

Heat the oven to 325°. Sift the first four ingredients together into a mixing bowl.   Make a well and add the oil, egg yolks, water, and vanilla. Beat until smooth with a spoon (with the electric beater, use medium speed for 1 minute).   Add cream of tartar to egg whites in a large mixing bowl. Beat with rotary beater until the whites form very stiff peaks. With an electric beater, use high speed for 3 to 5 minutes; it is important not to underbeat.   Pour the egg yolk mixture gradually over the beaten egg whites, gently folding with a rubber scraper until just blended.   DO NOT STIR.

Pour immediately into an 8 × 8 × 2-inch square pan, a 10 × 5 × 3-inch loaf pan, or a 9 × 3½-inch tube pan. Bake in square pan 30 to 35 minutes, and the loaf or tube pan for 50-55 minutes. Turn the pan upside down, free of the table, until cold. When the cake is completely cold, loosen around the sides with a spatula, turn the pan over, and hit the edge sharply on the table to loosen. The cake will drop out. Here are some variations:

SPICY CHIFFON: Omit vanilla, and sift with the dry ingredients, ½ teaspoon cinnamon, ¼ teaspoon nutmeg, ¼ teaspoon allspice and ¼ teaspoon cloves. Serve topped with 1 package butterscotch pudding made according to directions on the package, cooled, then whipped until smooth and 1 cup whipped cream folded in.

CHERRY NUT CHIFFON: Reduce vanilla to ½ teaspoon and substitute 2 tablespoons maraschino cherry juice for 2 tablespoons of the cold water. Just before pouring into the pan, gently fold in ¼ cup finely chopped, well-drained maraschino cherries and ¼ cup very finely chopped nuts.

ORANGE SUNDAE CHIFFON: Omit vanilla and add the grated rind of 1 orange (about 1½ tablespoons) to the water. Use orange juice for all or part of the liquid. Serve with vanilla ice cream and pineapple sauce.

MAPLE NUT CHIFFON: Use half brown sugar and half white sugar in the recipe; add 2 teaspoons maple flavoring, omitting the vanilla. Just before pouring the batter into the pan, gently fold in ½ cup very finely chopped nuts. Frost with mocha icing and top with finely chopped nuts.

ALMOND CHIFFON: Add 2 teaspoons almond flavoring when adding the vanilla. Serve with crushed and sweetened peaches and ice cream, or with peach ice cream.

Fruitcakes

This is my grandmother's original recipe, brought from England; many a gift cake has been made from the formula.

Star Cake
English Fruit Cake

1 cup Wesson Oil	1 cup fruit juice
1½ cups brown sugar, packed in	1 cup sifted flour
4 eggs, separated	1 cup citron, sliced thin
2 cups sifted all-purpose flour	1 cup chopped candied
1 teaspoon baking powder	pineapple
2 teaspoons salt	1½ cups whole candied cherries
2 teaspoons cinnamon	1 cup seeded raisins
2 teaspoons allspice	1 cup chopped figs
1 teaspoon cloves	3 cups chopped nuts

Heat the oven to 275° or very slow. Prepare the pans (this will fill two 9 × 5 × 3-inch loaf pans) by greasing and lining with brown paper, then greasing the paper. Place a pan containing about 2 inches of hot water on the bottom of the oven.

Now, combine the oil, sugar, and egg yolks and beat until well blended. Sift the 2 cups flour with the baking powder, salt, and spices. Stir into the oil mixture alternately with the fruit juice (this may be pineapple or orange juice). Mix the other cup of flour with the fruits and nuts so that each piece is coated with flour, then pour the batter over the fruit, mixing thoroughly. Whip the egg whites stiff and fold them into this batter, folding gently but thoroughly until they disappear.

Turn into the two loaf pans and bake 2½ to 3 hours, being careful to lower the heat if the cakes show signs of browning. When the baking time is up, remove from the oven and let stand 15 minutes before removing from the pans. Cool thoroughly on racks without removing the paper. This batter may be baked in 24 paper baking cups set in medium-sized muffin tins and baked at the same temperature for one hour. A box of these, beautifully glazed, makes a wonderful gift.

If you wish to glaze your fruitcake, combine 2 tablespoons brown sugar, 1 tablespoon corn syrup, and 2 tablespoons water in a saucepan; bring to a boil and boil 2 minutes. Cool. Brush over the tops of cooled cakes. Decorate with candied fruit or marzipan. This glaze should not be added until the cakes have aged and are ready to pack.

At our house, we bake the cakes around the first of November, then wrap them in aluminum foil and store in a cool place. Each week they should be sprinkled with 3 tablespoons of grape juice, then wrapped in a cloth moistened with fruit juice, and rewrapped in foil.

Properly aged, this cake can be sliced very thin so that it makes a very fine wedding, or groom's, cake.

Honey Cake, Esther
Sweetmeat Cake

2 sticks butter or margarine	3 cups sifted flour
1 cup strained honey	2 teaspoons baking powder
4 well-beaten eggs	½ teaspoon salt
1 tablespoon lemon juice	1 cup chopped citron
1 teaspoon grated lemon rind	¾ cup chopped nuts

Let the butter or margarine stand at room temperature until soft; then cream with the honey until light and fluffy. Add the eggs and beat thoroughly, then the lemon juice and rind. Beat until well blended. Sift the dry ingredients together, then blend gently into the butter mixture, being careful not to overmix; too much stirring will give this cake a coarse texture. Last, fold in the citron and chopped nuts. Turn into a loaf pan which has been greased and floured, and bake at 350° for about one hour or until it tests done.

Corinthian Cake
Honey Cake

3½ cups sifted, all-purpose flour	1 cup sugar
2½ teaspoons baking powder	3 eggs, separated
1 teaspoon baking soda	¼ cup peanut oil
½ teaspoon salt	1 pound honey
1 teaspoon cinnamon	1⅓ cups warm, black coffee
½ teaspoon ground cloves	¼ teaspoon cream of tartar
¼ teaspoon ginger	1 cup slivered, blanched almonds

Mix and sift the dry ingredients into a mixing bowl. Make a well in the center and add the egg yolks, oil, honey, and coffee. Beat until smooth and well blended. Add the cream of tartar to the egg whites, then beat until they stand in very stiff peaks when the beater is removed. Gently fold the yolk mixture into the whites, being careful not to beat or stir. Fold in the slivered almonds. Pour the batter into an ungreased 9-inch tube pan and bake at 350° for 55 to 60 minutes, or until the cake springs back when touched with the finger. Invert the pan by hanging it over the neck of a soda bottle, until the cake is completely cooled. Then loosen the cake with a spatula and remove from the pan. Makes 8 or 10 servings. You will notice that this is a sort of chiffon cake; it is delicious served with canned sliced peaches, drained, and topped with whipped cream or custard sauce.

Demas Cake
Applesauce Cake

2 sticks butter or margarine	1 teaspoon baking soda
1 cup brown sugar, packed	2 tablespoons cocoa
2 eggs, separated	½ teaspoon cinnamon
1 cup tart applesauce	½ teaspoon nutmeg
1¾ cups whole-wheat flour	¾ cup seedless raisins

Cream the butter and sugar until smooth and fluffy; add the beaten egg yolks and the applesauce. Sift the coarse husks out of the flour 2 or 3 times, then sift the flour with soda and the spices and mix the raisins through it. Add the dry ingredients to the first mixture, and last of all fold in the stiffly beaten egg whites. Turn into two 8-inch cake pans, greased and floured, and bake 25 minutes at 325°. Fill and frost with mocha frosting.

This is an example of the added flavor and texture you may put into your cakes by using whole-grain flours in them; it is a delicious cake, and well worth the little extra trouble of the multiple sifting of the flour. Save the husks which are sifted out, and return them to the bag of flour for use in making bread.

Gaza Nut Cake
Nut Cream Cake

1 cup sugar	2 tablespoons grated lemon rind
1 cup butter or margarine	2 cups cake flour
3 eggs, separated	1 teaspoon baking powder
2 tablespoons grated orange rind	1 teaspoon baking soda
	1 cup ground walnuts

¾ cup sour cream

Cream the butter with the sugar, then add the egg yolks and grated rinds and beat until light and fluffy. Sift the flour, baking powder, and soda together, and stir 2 tablespoons of this mixture into the nuts. Fold nuts, dry ingredients and sour cream into the egg-yolk mixture. Lastly, beat the egg whites until stiff, and fold in lightly. Butter and flour a spring-form cake pan, turn in the mixture and bake at 350° for one hour or until the cake tests done. Then remove from the oven, let stand 5 minutes, and remove the spring sides of the pan. Dust with powdered sugar.

This cake, with a name that seems to be derived from the Latin word for very fine flour, *simila,* was originally made of wheat flour, unleavened, and flavored with honey and anise. In Old Testament times, long before baked cake came into being, it was boiled in a pot. In England it has long been traditional for children to present to their mothers on Mothering Sunday, the fourth Sunday in Lent, a simnel.

Mary's Cake
Simnel Cake

½ cup milk
1 cake yeast
2 egg yolks
¾ cup sugar
1 whole egg

¼ cup butter
1¾ cups sifted flour
¼ teaspoon anise seed
½ cup candied lemon and
    orange peel

½ cup currants

Scald the milk, cool to lukewarm, then crumble the yeast into the milk and stir until dissolved. Beat the egg yolks until light and thick, then gradually beat in the sugar and the whole egg. Melt the butter, cool it a bit, then add to the egg mixture. Stir the milk and yeast mixture into the egg mixture, then beat in the sifted flour; there should be enough to make a thick batter; you may need 2 full cups. Cover, set in a warm place, and let rise until double in bulk—about an hour. While this is rising, grease and flour a large ring mold. Then stir down the risen batter. Beat in the anise, currants, and chopped peels. Turn the batter into the pan, filling half full; cover and let rise again until doubled. Bake at 350° until a cake tester comes out clean. Turn from the pan and cool on a rack. When cool, frost with a thin white confectioner's sugar icing flavored with a little almond extract.

Man does not live by bread alone.—Deuteronomy 8:3

Pentecost Cake
Black Devil's Food

⅔ cup soft shortening	½ teaspoon baking soda
1½ cups sugar	1 teaspoon vanilla
3 eggs	2 cups flour
⅔ cup cocoa	1 teaspoon salt
½ cup hot water	2 teaspoons baking powder

1 cup thick sour milk

If you do not have thick sour milk on hand, sour sweet milk by adding 1 tablespoon vinegar to a cupful. Let stand about 15 minutes. Light the oven and set at 350°. Grease and flour two 8-inch cake pans. Combine shortening, sugar, and eggs in the mixing bowl and blend thoroughly. Add the hot water to the cocoa slowly, beating until smooth, then add this to the first mixture. Beat until blended, then beat in the sour milk, soda, and vanilla. Last, stir in the dry ingredients which have been sifted together. (In this instance, the flour is measured before sifting.) Turn into the two pans and bake about 30 minutes, or until the layers test done. Cool, then fill, and frost with this good icing:

1¾ cups sugar	3 egg whites, beaten stiff
pinch of salt	12 marshmallows, quartered

½ cup water

Cook sugar, salt, and water to a temperature of 238° or until the syrup forms a soft ball in cold water. Pour slowly over the stiffly beaten egg whites, beating as you pour. While the icing is still hot, fold in the quartered marshmallows. Beat until of a consistency to spread.

> *One of the most comforting chapters in the Bible is the 23rd Psalm; the next time you're disturbed about something, read it and see.*

Scripture Cake

You may want to use this cake for church affairs where you want a biblical connection with the refreshments. It is a favorite New England recipe.

4½ cups 1 Kings 4:22 (flour)
1 cup Judges 5:25, last clause (butter)
2 cups Jeremiah 6:20 (sugar)
2 cups 1 Samuel 30:12 (raisins)
2 cups Nahum 3:12 (figs)
2 cups Numbers 17:8 (almonds)

2 tablespoons 1 Samuel 14:25 (honey)
1 pinch Leviticus 2:13 (salt)
6 Jeremiah 17:11 (eggs)
½ cup Judges 4:19 (milk)
Seasonings, 2 Chronicles, 9:9 (spices)

Follow the directions of Solomon for bringing up a child, Proverbs 23:14; that is, "beat him with a rod."

Just as a matter of accuracy, I might add that since this is a simple butter cake, but with little leavening except the air and eggs, bake it as a loaf at 325° for about 50 minutes. When it tests done, turn out on a rack until cool. Slices best after a few hours.

Adina Cake
Dark Spice Cake

4 squares semisweet chocolate
½ cup strong coffee
½ cup butter or margarine
1 cup sugar
2 eggs, beaten

1¾ cups sifted flour
2 teaspoons baking powder
1 teaspoon cinnamon
¼ teaspoon cloves
½ cup milk

1 teaspoon vanilla

Over a low flame melt the chocolate with the heated coffee, stirring until the mixture is smooth. Cream the butter thoroughly, add the sugar, and beat until light and fluffy. Beat in the eggs, then stir in the melted chocolate. Sift the flour, measure, then sift the dry ingredients together. Add to the creamed mixture alternately with the milk, stirring in the vanilla last of all. Divide the batter between 2 greased and floured layer cake pans and bake at 350° for about 30 minutes or until a tester inserted in the center comes out clean. Turn the layers onto racks to cool, then put together with whipped cream sweetened to taste with powdered sugar and a little cinnamon.

Adadah Torte
Spice Torte

Make the Adina Cake. Put layers together with a rich fruit filling (page 182) and top with this frosting:

Melt 3½ ounces chocolate chips over hot water, cool to lukewarm. Beat 2 egg whites with a pinch of salt until stiff but not dry; then fold in ⅓ cup honey, beating constantly, and finally beat in the chocolate mixture. Add ½ teaspoon vanilla and beat to a spreading consistency.

Cookies

Hadid Cookies
Carrot Cookies

⅓ cup shortening	½ teaspoon salt
⅓ cup sugar	¼ teaspoon baking soda
½ cup unsulphured molasses	1 teaspoon baking powder
1 egg	1 cup grated carrots
¼ cup nonfat skim milk	¼ cup raisins
1 cup sifted flour	1¼ cups rolled oats

¼ teaspoon each nutmeg and cinnamon

Cream together the shortening, sugar, unsulphured molasses, and the egg. Sift together the nonfat skim milk, flour, spices, salt, soda, and baking powder; stir into the creamed mixture. Add grated carrot, raisins, and rolled oats; mix well. Drop by level tablespoons on a lightly greased cookie sheet. Bake at 400° about 10 minutes. Makes about 6 dozen.

Manger Cookies
Sugar Shapes

2 cups sifted cake flour	½ cup margarine
1½ teaspoons baking powder	1 cup sugar
½ teaspoon baking soda	1 egg, unbeaten
¼ teaspoon salt	3 squares unsweetened choco-
½ teaspoon cinnamon	late, melted

2 tablespoons milk

Sift the flour, then measure. Add remaining dry ingredients and sift 3 times. Cream margarine, add sugar gradually, then cream together until light and fluffy. Add egg and chocolate; beat well. Add the flour mixture a small amount at a time, mixing well after each addition. Add milk. Chill thoroughly. Roll ⅛ inch thick on a lightly floured board. Cut out in shapes of animals, wise men, angels, etc. Brush with a glaze of 1 egg yolk beaten into about ½ cup milk. Bake on an ungreased baking sheet at 350° about 9 minutes. Remove from the oven, cool, and outline around the edges with a frosting of powdered sugar and egg white squeezed through a cone of paper.

Bethlehem Shortbread
Shortbread

2 cups sifted all-purpose flour	¼ teaspoon salt
¼ teaspoon baking powder	1 cup margarine

½ cup confectioner's sugar

Sift together the flour, baking powder, and salt. Cut the shortening into the confectioner's sugar as you do when cutting shortening into flour for pastry; then add the flour mixture and blend thoroughly; about halfway through the mixing, you will have to use your hands. Chill until easy to handle, then roll out on lightly floured board to ¼ inch thickness. Cut into squares or diamonds. Place on ungreased cookie sheet about an inch apart, and bake at 350° until a delicate brown—about 20-25 minutes. Brushing these cookies with a little milk and sprinkling with multicolored decorettes make them very bright and festive-looking. If you want to save cutting time, merely pat the unchilled dough into a 9 × 9 × 2-inch pan, sprinkle with ¼ cup sugar blended with 1 teaspoon cinnamon, bake as above, then cut into squares while warm.

Jericho Cookies
Almond Spice Cookies

1½ cups strained honey	10 cups cake flour
¾ cup shortening	1 teaspoon salt
2 cups sugar	1 teaspoon cinnamon
¼ cup fruit juice	2 teaspoons nutmeg
grated rind of 1 orange	1 teaspoon cloves
grated rind of 1 lemon	4 teaspoons baking powder

2 cups unblanched almonds, chopped

Melt the honey and shortening together over hot water. Add the sugar and fruit juice and stir until dissolved. Stir in grated rinds, chopped almonds, then the dry ingredients which have been sifted together. Chill in the refrigerator; this dough may be kept several days to ripen or may be used at once. Roll about ⅛ inch thick and cut in strips or fancy shapes. Bake at 350° about 20 minutes. While still warm, frost with an icing made by beating together 2 cups confectioner's sugar, 1 tablespoon melted butter, 3 or 4 tablespoons cream, and 1 teaspoon vanilla. This makes about 15 dozen; the recipe is easily halved.

The custom of tithing goes back to antiquity; God leaves it to each of us to decide just how much we will give of ourselves.—See Proverbs 3:9

Temptation Cookies
Brazil Cookies

½ cup butter or margarine
¼ cup sugar
½ teaspoon vanilla
1 egg yolk
1 cup sifted all-purpose flour

¼ teaspoon salt
1 egg white, unbeaten
¾ cup finely chopped Brazil
    nuts
currant jelly

Cream the butter; add sugar gradually and cream thoroughly until light and fluffy. Blend in the vanilla. Add egg yolk and beat well. Sift in flour and salt, mixing until thoroughly blended. Shape into balls ¾ inch in diameter. Dip into the unbeaten egg white and roll lightly in the chopped nuts. Place on an ungreased cookie sheet and make a small depression in each ball with the tip of a teaspoon. Bake at 375° about 15 minutes, or until a delicate brown. Remove from baking sheet immediately. Place a half teaspoon of bright red jelly in each little depression. Makes about 3 dozen.

Moab Crispies
Coffee Cookies

2 cups sifted all-purpose flour
½ teaspoon salt
¼ teaspoon soda
¼ teaspoon baking powder
2 tablespoons instant coffee

¾ cup shortening
½ cup light brown sugar
½ cup granulated sugar
1 egg
1½ teaspoons vanilla extract

1 tablespoon milk

Sift the first five ingredients together and set aside. Cream the shortening with the two sugars until light and fluffy, then beat in the egg and the vanilla extract. Add milk, then gradually blend in the sifted flour mixture. Shape into 1-inch balls. Place balls 2 inches apart on ungreased cookie sheets; flatten to ⅛-inch thickness with the bottom of a water glass. Bake at 400° about 8 minutes, or until the edges are brown. DO NOT BAKE TOO BROWN. Store in a tightly closed jar or box. Makes about 4 dozen. If you use a glass with a pretty cut pattern in the bottom to flatten these cookies, you will have a pattern in the cookie.

To measure a quarter cup butter or margarine, simply cut one stick (½ cup) in half.

Pies

We find mention of "flour mingled with oil" (Numbers 15: 4) early in the Old Testament, so it seems reasonable to assume that by the time of the New Testament, the biblical housewife would have perfected some way of serving sweets in a crust of pastry. The city woman would have had commercial bakers make sheets of pastry for her, as the Greeks did, but the woman of the countryside probably made her own. For you, it is simpler; perfected shortenings and regulated stoves leave little to chance for the modern pastry maker; a pie delicate enough to put Mother's to shame is possible for the most inexperienced bride if she makes her pastry with oil, as Martha did.

Ten Commandments for Making Pies

1. In pies, as in any other field of cookery, no amount of mixing or blending or know-how can overcome inaccurate measurements.

2. Tenderness of pastry depends a great deal upon the kind of flour and the amount of shortening and handling, but flakiness is determined by the method of combining.

3. Four laws you must remember are: use little water, fold in as much air as possible, handle lightly, and always start in a hot oven (450°).

4. Buy yourself a pastry blender; it will pay for itself in better and better pies.

5. To prevent a soggy undercrust, always brush with beaten egg before turning in fruit or custard fillings.

6. Choose pie pans fitted for their purpose; deep ones are better than shallow. Heat-resistant glass seems to give the nicest brown crust. If you have new tins, you won't get a brown crust until the shininess has worn off.

7. When you are ready to mix, have everything cold, cold, cold. Milk or water should be iced; bowls should be cold. It all adds up to better pastry.

8. In pie making, more than in anything else, excesses make trouble. Too much flour makes the pastry tough; too much shortening makes it dry and crumbly; too much liquid makes it heavy and soggy; too much handling will ruin it.

9. Remember that any seed such as poppy, sesame, dill, etc., may be added to the sifted flour for new flavor. So may a half cup of any nuts, ground or finely chopped.

10. It is no more trouble to make two or three pies than it is to make one. Make an extra to store unbaked in your freezer against the day when you're in a hurry.

Stir-n-Roll Pastry

2 cups sifted all-purpose flour   ½ cup Wesson oil
1½ teaspoons salt   ¼ cup cold whole milk

Heat the oven to 425°. Mix the flour and salt. Measure the
oil and milk into one measuring cup, but don't stir; add all at
once to the flour. Stir until mixed. Press into a smooth ball. Cut
in halves and flatten slightly. For the bottom crust, place one
piece of dough between two 12-inch squares of waxed paper
and roll gently to the edges of the paper. Peel off the top paper
and turn the crust into the pan, paper side up. Peel off paper,
ease, and fit the pastry into the pan. Trim even with the rim.
Add the filling. For the top crust, roll as above and place over
filling. Fold the edges under the bottom crust and seal.

Puff Paste

2 cups sifted all-purpose flour   6 tablespoons lard
½ teaspoon salt   ½ teaspoon vinegar
2 teaspoons butter   6 tablespoons ice water

Sift the flour and salt together, into a bowl. Cut the cold
butter and lard into ½-inch slices. Turn half of this into the
flour and cut in with a pastry blender. Add the water and
vinegar and blend lightly to make a stiff dough. Roll out in an
oblong, dot it down the center with bits of butter and lard, then
fold the left third over the center. Dot this with bits of butter
and lard as before, then fold the right third over the center.
Turn so you have folded edges at top and bottom, then roll
again. Repeat until the dough has been rolled 3 times, turning
each time. Let rest in a cool place for about 30 minutes, then
treat as you would any pastry. This rich and flasky pastry
makes a fine topping for deep-dish cobblers, meat pies, or
creamed main dishes.

Cream Cheese Pastry

1 cup all-purpose flour	1½ packages soft cream cheese
¼ teaspoon salt	or 4½ ounces dry cottage
1 stick margarine	cheese

flour to roll

Sift the flour before measuring, then add the salt and sift again. Cut the margarine and cheese in with a pastry blender or two forks. Roll between pieces of waxed paper as directed on page 257. You will find this particularly delicious with cheese pies or fruit pies. I often make it into little tarts by cutting into squares, putting a teaspoon of preserves on each square, folding crosswise, pinching the edges together, and then baking at 450°. With a filling of deviled ham, this makes a nice tea accompaniment which may be made ahead and baked as needed.

A delicious rich crust for chiffon pie fillings or ice cream is made of biblical fruits, nuts, and grains:

Date Bran Crumb Crust

1 cup pitted dates	1½ cups ready-to-eat bran
¼ cup water	2 tablespoons sugar
⅓ cup butter or margarine	½ cup chopped nuts

Run the dates through the food chopper using the medium blade; then cook for a few minutes with the water until a soft paste is formed. Add the butter and stir until well blended. On a paper towel or piece of waxed paper, roll the bran to fine crumbs. Add to date paste, together with sugar and nutmeats, and blend thoroughly. Press evenly and firmly into sides and bottom of a 9-inch pie pan. Fill with any preferred filling.

Crumb Crusts

Crumb crusts are a great boon to the pie maker who is in a hurry, as well as being particularly delicious with certain fillings. A general rule applies to all; let butter or margarine soften, mix with the measured crumbs and sugar, and blend thoroughly with a fork. Press into the bottom and sides with the back of a spoon. Bake at 375° for about 8 minutes.

Variety	Butter	Crumbs	Sugar
graham crackers (16)	1/4 cup	1 1/3 cups	1/4 cup
vanilla wafers (24)	1/4 cup	1 1/3 cups	none
chocolate wafers (18)	3 tablespoons	1 1/3 cups	none
gingersnaps (20)	6 tablespoons	1 1/3 cups	none
corn or wheat flakes	1/4 cup	1 1/3 cups	2 tablespoons

You will have have no trouble at all in rolling the crumbs if you place crackers or cereal in a clean paper bag, then close at the end and roll gently with the rolling pin. I sometimes add 1/4 cup nonfat dry milk to the crumbs before creaming in the butter; this nearly doubles the nutritive value.

NUT CRUMB CRUST: Reduce the crumbs to one cup and add 1/2 cup chopped walnuts, pecans, almonds, or Brazil nuts.

MARBLE CRUMB CRUST: Reduce the crumbs to 1 cup and add 2 squares unsweetened chocolate, grated.

COCOANUT CRUST: Melt 2 squares unsweetened chocolate and 2 tablespoons butter, then add 2 tablespoons milk and 2/3 cup sifted confectioner's sugar. Stir until smooth. Add 1 1/2 cups flaked cocoanut. Mix well. Press into a greased 9-inch pan. Serve piled high with ice cream, cream pie filling, parfait pie filling, or any chiffon filling.

Oatmeal Pie Crust

2 cups quick rolled oats
⅓ cup melted butter or margarine

¼ teaspoon salt
2 teaspoons grated lemon rind
3 tablespoons light corn syrup

Combine the quick oats and melted butter and blend thoroughly. Add salt, lemon rind, and corn syrup. With the back of a spoon, press the mixture lightly into a greased pie plate, then bake at 375° for 15 to 20 minutes or until browned. Cool before filling.

Athenian Pie
Layered Pie

This is my own version of Black Bottom Pie; I think you will find it one of the most delightful pies you ever made.

1 tablespoon unflavored gelatin
¼ cup cold water
2 cups rich milk
½ cup sugar
1¼ tablespoons cornstarch
4 eggs, separated

1½ squares bitter chocolate, melted
1 teaspoon vanilla
¼ teaspoon cream of tartar
½ cup sugar
1 tablespoon rum flavoring
whipped cream

Have ready a baked 9-inch pastry shell or a rich crumb crust of either chocolate cookies or gingersnaps. Soak the gelatin in the cold water; scald the milk. Mix the sugar and cornstarch together, then add the egg yolks and beat well. Stir this mixture into the scalded milk and cook over low heat or hot water until the custard coats the spoon. Stir constantly. Take out one cup custard and add to it the melted chocolate. Beat with a rotary beater until cool, then add the teaspoon of vanilla. Pour into the pie shell and chill.

For the top layer, while the remaining custard is still hot, blend in the dissolved gelatin. Stir until completely blended.

Beat the egg whites until stiff, then beat in the cream of tartar and half cup of sugar and rum flavoring. Fold this meringue carefully into the soft custard. As soon as the chocolate layer is set, cover with the fluffy custard and chill. Serve with a garnish of whipped cream.

Linus Pastry
Pumpkin Puddin' Pie

1 package instant butterscotch pudding	¾ teaspoon cinnamon
	½ teaspoon ginger
1 cup milk	½ teaspoon salt ·
	1¾ cups canned pumpkin

Empty the package of instant pudding mix into the cup of milk, and beat with a rotary beater for 1 minute. Blend in remaining ingredients thoroughly, then pour into Date Bran Crumb Crust (page 258). Refrigerate until served. Top with unsweetened whipped cream, sprinkle with chopped walnuts.

Orion Custard
Cheese Pie

2 eggs, separated	½ cup sugar
2 cups cream cheese or smooth cottage cheese	1 teaspoon vanilla
	pinch of salt
2 tablespoons flour	½ cup powdered sugar

Beat the egg yolks lightly, then blend into the cheese; add flour, granulated sugar, vanilla, and salt and beat well. Beat the egg whites until stiff, then fold in the powdered sugar, then fold the meringue into the cheese mixture, blending thoroughly. Pour into either a pastry or crumb crust; if a pastry crust, bake 10 minutes at 450° and about 35 minutes at 325°. If using a crumb crust, bake about 45 minutes at 325°. Makes one 8-inch pie.

Antioch Cream
Raisin Cream Pie

¾ cup brown sugar	2 tablespoons vinegar
2 beaten egg yolks	⅛ teaspoon salt
1 tablespoon melted butter	¼ teaspoon cinnamon
1½ cups seeded raisins	¼ teaspoon nutmeg
⅓ cup cream	2 egg whites, beaten stiff

Prepare either a pastry or a crumb-crust shell in an 8-inch pie pan. Combine sugar, egg yolks, and melted butter. Add raisins, cream, vinegar, salt, and spices. Fold in stiffly beaten egg whites. I like to add a teaspoon vanilla here; you taste it yourself and see if you want to use it. Turn into the pan; if using a pastry crust, bake 10 minutes at 425°, then 20 minutes more at 350°. If using a crumb crust, bake 30 minutes at 350°. Cool before serving.

Signet Pie
Rhubarb Custard Pie

1½ cups rhubarb cut into small pieces, unpeeled	2 eggs
1½ cups sugar	½ teaspoon salt
3 tablespoons flour	1 tablespoon butter
	1 recipe pastry

It will take about 2 bunches of rhubarb to make 1½ to 2 cups small pieces. Put these into a strainer and pour boiling water over them. Drain. Line a 9-inch pie pan with the pastry; pour in the blanched rhubarb. Mix together the sugar, flour, eggs, and salt and pour this over the rhubarb. Dot with the butter cut in small pieces. Cover with a lattice top of the pastry, or a plain top well pierced. Bake at 450° for 20 minutes, then at 350° for 15 minutes. Cool before serving, but don't chill in the refrigerator.

He will take your daughters to be perfumers and cooks and bakers.—
1 Samuel 8:13

CHAPTER FOURTEEN

SWEETS

Butter and honey, the principal ingredients of biblical sweets, were a symbol of plenty in the land. In every walk of life, a sweet dish to end the meal was the usual thing.

Behold, how good and pleasant it is
*   when brothers dwell in unity!—Psalm 133:1*

HOW FORTUNATE our housewife of biblical times was, in the matter of a sweet to top off the meals she spread on her table! She had honey to use; although there is no direct mention of beekeeping in the Bible, honey was found in every household. Josephus mentions honey as a product of the Plain of Jericho, both the honey "from bees," and an artificial honey made of a syrup of figs and dates which, under the name "dibs," is still common in the East.

She may even have had sugar; we know that sugar cane was imported to the Middle East about three hundred years before New Testament times, and we read in Jeremiah 6:20:

> "To what purpose does frankincense come to me from Sheba,
> or sweet cane from a distant land?"

Candies were plentiful and in Bible times, as now, were displayed in the bazaars; sweetmeats of dates, honey, nuts, and gum arabic were exported to Tyre (Ezekiel 27:17), and Hebrew women captives were employed in the making of Babylonian dainties. (1 Samuel 8:13.)

We know that nuts were plentiful; the pistachio was among the gifts sent by Jacob to Pharaoh, and in Genesis 30:37 we read of the almond. Small wonder that ancient cooks prized them in their condiments, just as vendors in Damascus valued them in the sweetmeats they sold!

Of fruits, she had a bewildering variety; grapes, figs, dates, mulberries, pomegranates, apricots, and melons all were plentiful and cheap. She often boiled the grapes, after the juice was extracted, into a thick sweet relish which she used as an accompaniment for meat, and figs were so important to her that the time of the fig harvest, in September, was a time of community social activity; she and her neighbors gathered together and picnicked out of doors while the youngsters climbed among the trees.

Ten Commandments for Making Jams and Jellies

1. Jams and jellies are almost without nutritive value, except for the sugar in them. They are the "Babylonian Dainties" of the food field, intended for delight alone.
2. Best results are obtained when slightly underripe fruit is used, since pectin content is highest in such fruit. If you are making jam to utilize ripe fruit on hand, add commercial pectin.
3. Beet and cane sugar produce the same results in preserves and jellies; don't let claims for one or the other confuse you.
4. Open your mind to new advances in jelly making, such as the use of commercial pectin. Your mother's methods (and Martha's and Mary's) may have been good, but they were decidedly uncertain.
5. Be patient, remembering Job, when you decide to make preserves; a small amount made in a large kettle will assure good results.
6. Your biggest kettle will not be too large for a batch of jelly; it needs room to roll and boil like the Red Sea when it parted before Moses and the Israelites.
7. To test jelly, place a small amount in a spoon, cool slightly, and let it drop back into the pan from the side of the spoon. As the syrup thickens, 2 large drops will form along the edge of the spoon. When these two drops come together and fall as one, the "sheeting stage" (220° to 222°) has been reached, and the jelly is ready to pour. Begin testing about 5 minutes after the sugar has been added.
8. To test jams, simply cook until the jam will stay in place when dropped from a teaspoon onto a plate to cool.
9. A jelly that contains too little or too much sugar never thickens. Measure accurately if you want to enjoy the fruits of your labor.
10. You can enjoy God's gift of summer sunshine all winter long, with a well-filled jelly closet. Make a few glasses whenever you have time, and know that this was meant to be.

Jams and Jellies

Once you master the new, quick method for making jams and jellies, you'll find yourself making them frequently. Making a few jars at a time, as biblical housewives did when fruit began to go bad, is no chore at all, and soon stockpiles into a sizeable inventory.

Homemade fruit preserves make wonderful items for sale at bazaars and fairs. Save all your prettiest jars and have someone who is artistic make personal labels. They will be a real money-maker for your church group.

Preserves Ahijah
Fig Preserve

4 pounds prepared figs	¼ cup lemon juice
3½ pounds sugar	2 lemons, sliced

The figs should be firm-ripe. Wash and peel, then add sugar and lemon juice to 8 cups boiling water. Stir until sugar dissolves. Add figs and boil until clear. Add lemons when figs are about two thirds done. If the syrup becomes too thick before the figs are clear, add boiling water, ½ cup at a time. Let stand 12 to 24 hours in a cool place, then pack into hot sterilized jars. Process 30 minutes at simmering in a water-bath canner. This is a beautiful preserve for selling at bazaars, etc.

Although the product will not be as high in quality, figs may be preserved without peeling. If unpeeled, cover with water and boil 15 to 20 minutes, then drain before adding to syrup. A few whole allspice, a piece of cinnamon or ginger may be cooked with the figs.

For every one who asks receives, and he who seeks finds, and to him who knocks it will be opened.—Luke 11:10

Jephthah Preserve
Minute Strawberry Preserves

3¾ cups prepared fruit (about	¼ cup lemon juice
2 quarts ripe berries)	7 cups (3 pounds) sugar
½ bottle liquid fruit pectin	

Crush completely, one layer at a time, about 2 quarts fully ripe strawberries. Measure 3¾ cups into a very large saucepan. Squeeze the juice from 2 lemons; measure ¼ cup juice into the saucepan with the fruit. Add sugar to the fruit in the saucepan and mix well. Place over high heat and bring to a full rolling boil and boil hard 1 minute, stirring constantly. Remove from the heat and at once stir in the liquid fruit pectin. Skim off with a metal spoon. Then stir and skim by turns for 5 minutes to cool slightly, to prevent floating fruit. Ladle quickly into glasses. Cover at once with ⅛ inch hot paraffin.

Gaius Preserve
Mulberry Jam

8 cups mulberries	6 cups sugar
¼ cup vinegar	

Wash, drain, stem, crush, and measure the berries. Add sugar and vinegar. Boil until thick. Pour, boiling hot, into a hot glass; seal at once. Elderberries may also be preserved by this method.

Endor Preserve
Carrot Conserve

4 pounds carrots put through	6 cups sugar
the food grinder, using a	¾ pound almonds, blanched
medium blade	and chopped fine
4 lemons put through the grinder with a little water	

Combine the carrots and lemons in a large kettle and cook gently until soft. Add the sugar and cook until the mixture is thick and mounds on the spoon. Turn in the almonds, then remove from the heat and spoon into hot glasses. Seal as for jelly. Makes 11 glasses.

Zabdi Sweet
Grape Jam

8 cups grape pulp   6 cups sugar

Wash, stem, drain, and crush the grapes. Add just enough water to prevent sticking; boil until grapes are soft. Press through sieve or food mill. Measure the pulp, discarding the skins. Add the sugar and boil to, or almost to, the jellying point. Pour, boiling hot, into hot sterilized glasses. Seal at once.

Babel Sweet
Cherry Relish

5 pounds not-too-ripe cherries   2 quarts wine vinegar
6 cloves   1 teaspoon tarragon
1 2-inch stick cinnamon   ½ pound honey

Boil honey and vinegar 15 minutes. Cool. Wash the cherries, pack into quart jars, divide the mixed spices equally among the jars, then pour the honey-vinegar mixture into the jars to cover the fruit. Let steep for a week or more. This is wonderful with cold meats.

Thessalonian Marmalade
Persimmon Marmalade

Cut up 2 quarts ripe persimmons and discard the seeds and cores. Mash the fruit and cook it with 1 cup sugar, 1 cup orange juice, and the grated rind of 1 orange until the mixture is thick. Seal in hot sterilized jars.

Haroseth
Apple Relish

This ceremonial complement to the Passover Feast, eaten on a piece of matzoth, symbolizes the mortar used by the Israelite slaves in the erection of the pyramids in ancient Egypt.—Exodus 1:14

1 cup chopped apple	1 teaspoon honey
¼ cup almonds	½ teaspoon grated lemon rind
¼ cup walnuts	¼ teaspoon cinnamon

about 2 tablespoons orange juice

Core the apple, but leave the skin on. Run apple and nuts through the food chopper, using the medium blade. Add the remaining ingredients and enough juice to make a paste—about 2 tablespoons. This keeps well, and makes a nice relish when packed in pretty jars. Seal with paraffin before capping.

Anab Conserve
Grape Conserve

8 cups grapes	¼ teaspoon salt
6 cups sugar	1 cup shelled walnuts

Wash, drain, stem, and measure the grapes. Press the pulp from the skins and put the pulp through a sieve or food mill to separate pulp from seeds. Put the skins through the food chopper using a medium blade, then boil 20 minutes in just enough water to prevent sticking. Boil the pulp, without water, until soft. Press through a sieve or food mill. Mix pulp, skins, sugar, and salt. Boil rapidly until it has almost reached the jellying point. Add nuts 5 minutes before removing from the heat. Pour, boiling hot, into hot sterilized glasses. Seal at once. Nice for bazaars or for gifts.

The name "Christian" was first used in Antioch.
—*See Acts 11:26*

Saints' Honey
Pear Honey

8 cups chopped pears
1 lemon, sliced thin

5 cups sugar
1 teaspoon ginger

Wash, core, pare, finely chop, and measure the pears. Add the lemon, sugar, ginger, and ½ cup water. Boil until thick as marmalade. Pour, boiling hot, into hot sterilized glasses. Seal at once. Quince honey is made in exactly the same way, using 5 cups chopped quince to 4 cups sugar, and cooking the quince with 4 cups water instead of the ½ cup directed above. Be sure to discard the core and all the gritty part of the quince.

Desserts

Issachar Mold
Fruit Pudding

1 cup sugar
3 cups water
4 tablespoons butter
1 cup Cream of Wheat, un-cooked
pinch of salt
¼ cup seedless raisins

12 blanched almonds, chopped
12 blanched pistachios, chopped
4 tablespoons candied orange and lemon peel
1 teaspoon almond extract
½ teaspoon cinnamon

Boil sugar and water together until it forms a thin syrup—about 10 or 15 minutes. Set aside. In a heavy skillet melt the butter, then add the Cream of Wheat and cook over medium heat until the grains brown lightly. Stir in the sugar syrup and the salt and cook, stirring constantly, until the liquid is absorbed. Continue to cook and stir until the mixture thickens and butter begins to show on top. When it no longer sticks to the spoon, add the chopped fruit and nuts, cover and steam for about 5 minutes. Stir in the cinnamon and almond extract, then turn into a buttered 5-cup mold. Cool, unmold, and serve with canned or fresh fruit. This makes a large mold, enough to serve 8 or 10 people. It is easily divided in half.

Stephen's Cake
Dobos Torte

This is an ancient and honored creation, too much trouble for everyday eating, but so rich and delicious that you'll say it is well worth the time you put into it. For some reason or other, it has come to be identified with Stephen I, the king who Christianized the four corners of Hungary. Here is my modernized version; it is, I think, a great improvement over the original Hungarian recipe, which took hours to complete.

Make up a plain chiffon cake; if possible, make the cake the day before you plan to serve the dessert. Using a long slender slicing knife, cut the cake into as many thin layers as possible. In the Middle East, layers number from seven to fifteen; you should get about nine half-inch layers.

Make up 1 package vanilla pudding according to the directions on the package, using 2 cups milk. Cut into pieces ¼ pound bittersweet chocolate; put these in a small bowl with 2 tablespoons hot water, and set in a pan of boiling water until dissolved. Keep the chocolate warm.

Now, cream until light ⅞ cup butter (1¾ sticks). When the butter is light and fluffy, add butter and melted chocolate alternately to the pudding mixture, beating after each addition. This will thicken as it cools; when thick enough to spread, put the layers together with the chocolate filling.

Some cooks ice top and sides also, but the traditional icing is a caramel glaze. Simply melt 3 tablespoons sugar in a small skillet over low heat. Stir carefully until light brown. Then spread over the top of the cake, working quickly. Store the cake in the refrigerator at least 12 hours before slicing. It will serve 10 or 12 people, and will keep at least a week in a good refrigerator.

It is unlikely that any "made" desserts such as these were known in New Testament times; in early Rome, however, meals were elaborate beyond anything that we can imagine, and the sweets were often intricate creations.

Honey Pudding
Honey Rice Custard

2 cups whole milk	¾ cup converted rice
1 cup water	¼ cup honey
2 egg yolks, beaten	nutmeg and cinnamon

Measure milk and water into a saucepan and bring to the boiling point. Stir in the rice and simmer gently until tender, stirring occasionally to prevent sticking. (This may be cooked in a double boiler without stirring, but it takes much longer.) When the rice is tender, stir in the honey; add some of the hot rice to the egg yolks and stir thoroughly, then stir the yolks into the rice. Turn into the serving dish, sprinkle with cinnamon and nutmeg and serve very cold. This is delicious with stewed dried fruit.

Pudding Anna
Fruit Charlotte

3 cups cooked fruit	¼ teaspoon cinnamon
½ cup light cream	¼ cup chopped nuts (optional)
6 slices toast	whipped cream for garnish

This is a dessert much used in Palestine, and is so delicious, easy, and economical that it will be one of your favorites. The fruit may be stewed fresh fruit, drained canned fruit, or stewed dried fruit. I prefer the dried, for flavor. Cut each slice of toast into 3 strips. In a 1½-quart saucepan arrange a layer of toast strips, then one of fruit, cinnamon, and nuts alternately until used. Pour in enough cream to moisten the bread and cover the bottom of the pan. Cover and cook over low heat for about ten minutes. Serve warm, with cream or whipped cream, like a pudding. This will serve 6.

Sweet Syntyche
Date-Nut Candy

This is a dessert such as Martha might have prepared; you will find it easy to serve as a dessert, nice to wrap in waxed paper and include in boxes of cookies as gifts, and a nutritious snack that the children will welcome.

| 2 cups pitted dates | 2 cups walnuts |

Both dates and walnuts must be chopped very fine; I put them through the food chopper, using the fine blade. They are even nicer if whirled in the electric blender, but it is hard to keep the dates from gathering on the blades. Mix them together, rubbing with the back of a spoon until smooth. Then spread about ½ inch thick on a buttered plate. Let it dry a bit, then cut into small square or diamond shapes. Sprinkle with powdered sugar, or if used for dessert, serve topped with whipped cream.

Tabitha Pudding
Date-Nut Pudding

1¼ cups sifted all-purpose flour	1 package dates cut in small
¼ teaspoon baking powder	pieces
¼ teaspoon salt	1 cup boiling water
1 cup chopped pecans or wal-	¼ cup butter or margarine
nuts	1 cup sugar
1 teaspoon baking soda	1 egg

Heat the oven to 300°. Sift the flour with baking powder and salt, then stir in the nuts. Mix the soda into the dates, then pour boiling water over them. Now cream the butter until fluffy, add the sugar, and cream again, then beat in the egg. Add the flour mixture and mix thoroughly, then stir in the soaked dates. Pour into a buttered 9-inch square pan and bake 1 hour. Cool on a rack, then turn out and cut into squares. Serve with any pudding sauce.

Sauce Magdalene
Butter Sauce

½ cup sugar	1 cup boiling water
1 tablespoon cornstarch	2 tablespoons butter
¼ teaspoon salt	1 teaspoon vanilla

Mix sugar, cornstarch, and salt well. Stir in the hot water and cook, stirring, until clear and thick. Add butter and vanilla and cool. This is delicious with any cake or pudding.

Nympha Pie
Cocoanut Torte

Make up the contents of a package of gingerbread cake mix according to directions on the package, and bake in two 9-inch greased pans. Turn out on racks to cool. For the filling:

1 package vanilla pudding	½ teaspoon almond extract
2 cups milk	½ cup Angel Flake cocoanut
2 egg yolks	powdered sugar

Turn the pudding mix into a small saucepan, place over low heat, and stir the milk in slowly so as not to cause lumps. Cook, stirring, until boiling and thickened. Remove from the heat. Beat the egg yolks, add a little of the hot pudding and mix well, then add to the pudding in the pan and cook again for a minute or so. Remove from the heat and stir in almond extract and cocoanut. Cool.

Put the two cake layers together with the filling in the center, and dust the top with powdered sugar. If you will put a lace paper doily on top the cake and dust the sugar through this, you'll get a pretty design.

Fruit Pildash
Baked Bananas

We know, of course, that our biblical housewife did not have bananas, but she roasted a great many fruits wrapped in grape leaves, and this recipe, using honey for flavor and whole wheat crackers for dressing, is much like what she may have prepared.

6 large firm bananas
¼ cup honey
3 tablespoons brown sugar
¾ cup crushed graham crackers
3 tablespoons melted butter or margarine

Peel the bananas and brush with the honey. Place each one on a piece of aluminum foil about 6 inches wide and 2 inches longer than the banana. Sprinkle with the crumbs, sugar, and melted butter which have been mixed together. Wrap each banana loosely in foil, folding under the ends to seal. Roast on the barbecue grill over hot coals for 8 to 10 minutes, or until steam escapes from the foil. Or bake at 425 degrees in the oven for the same length of time. To serve, open the wrapping and eat from it as from a dish. The children will love it.

Berries James
Blueberry Crisp

2 cups quick rolled oats, uncooked
1 cup all-purpose flour
1 cup brown sugar, packed
¾ cup butter or margarine, melted
1 No. 2 can blueberries or blueberry pie filling
1 tablespoon flour
½ cup sugar
2 tablespoons lemon juice
pinch of salt

Mix rolled oats, flour, and brown sugar together; add the melted butter and mix thoroughly. Line the bottom of an 8-inch square pan with this mixture, reserving ½ cup for topping. If you use blueberry pie filling, turn this into the crust without further preparation. If you are using canned blueberries, drain them, add water to the syrup to make ¾ cup, then combine flour, sugar, lemon juice, and salt, stir in the juice, and simmer, stirring, for about 5 minutes. Add blueberries, and then turn this into the oatmeal crust. Top with reserved crumbs and bake at 350° for 45 minutes. Serve topped with whipped cream, light cream, or ice cream.

Zadok Pudding
Apple Pudding

2 No. 303 cans applesauce (or 2 1-quart jars)	24 zwieback, crushed
½ cup sugar	¼ cup butter or margarine, melted

Add the sugar to the applesauce. Add also, a bit of lemon juice, and about a half teaspoon each of cinnamon and nutmeg, so that it is very zesty. Crush the zwieback with the rolling pin, so that you have 2 cups crumbs. Butter thoroughly a 9-inch layer cake pan of Pyrex (these are deeper than most metal pans) or a 9-inch round pan at least 1½ inches deep. Mix crumbs and melted butter thoroughly, adding the crumbs to the skillet in which the butter was melted and stirring over heat until the crumbs are golden brown. Now make a layer of crumbs in the bottom of the pan; add a half-inch layer of applesauce, then a thick layer of crumbs, another of applesauce, and finish off with crumbs. Sprinkle with a little cinnamon. Bake at 375° for about 45 minutes. Serve warm, with cream. This makes 2 puddings. If it is cooled first, it turns out of the dish nicely, and may be served as a cake with Sauce Magdalene (page 275).

For every house is built by some one, but the builder of all things is God.—Hebrews 3:4

In Palestine and Egypt iced desserts, of course, were unknown; the Roman emperors, however, were great consumers of ices, and sent their slaves up into the mountains for snow to cool their drinks on hot summer days. The iced "granate" was their favorite; it was a tall beaker of shaved ice or snow, with fruit juice poured over it, and it took its name from the pomegranate, which was the first fruit so served. Thus, we can trace even today's ice cream soda back to biblical times.

Zion Ice
Coffee Ice

2 measuring cups hot double-
strength coffee

½ cup granulated sugar
2 teaspoons vanilla

Dissolve the sugar in the hot coffee—you may use more or less sugar, to taste. Cool. Add vanilla. Pour the mixture into the refrigerator tray and let freeze, with the control set at the coldest point, until almost hard. Take out the tray, scrape the ice into a bowl, and beat hard until smooth but not melted. Return to the refrigerator and freeze to sherbet consistency. Turn into sherbet glasses and top with whipped cream, if desired. This will serve 4.

Sherbet Idumea
Buttermilk Sherbet

1 envelope unflavored gelatin
½ cup cold water
¾ cup sugar

1 6-ounce can frozen fruit
concentrate (grapefruit,
grape, orange, etc.)

2¼ cups buttermilk

Sprinkle the gelatin on cold water to soften. Place over boiling water and stir until dissolved. Add sugar and stir until mixed. Empty the fruit concentrate into a bowl; refill the can 3 times with buttermilk. Add to the concentrate and mix well. Stir in the gelatin mixture and turn into a freezing tray. Freeze with the control set at the coldest point. When partially frozen (about 1 hour), remove to a bowl and beat until smooth. Return to tray and continue freezing until firm. Makes about 1¼ quarts.

Assyrian Ribbons
Fruit Ribbons

First Layer:
30 marshmallows (10-ounce package)
½ cup milk
1 cup whipping cream

Second Layer:
1 No. 3 can sliced peaches
1 tablespoon unflavored gelatin
¼ cup cold water
1 tablespoon lemon juice

Butter an 8 × 8 × 2-inch pan. Quarter the marshmallows with scissors dipped in water; add the pieces to the milk and cook and stir over low heat until melted and well blended. Cool, then fold in the cream whipped stiff. Pour into the pan and chill until firm. For the second layer, drain the syrup from the peaches and add enough water to measure 1⅓ cups. Soften the gelatin in the cold water. Heat the syrup, then dissolve the gelatin mixture in the syrup. Stir in lemon juice. Chill until syrupy. Arrange the peaches in pretty rows over the marshmallow layer, then carefully top with the gelatined syrup. Chill until firm. This makes 12 nice servings; it is a nice dish to plan on when serving a large group, since it can be made the day before, and has a rich homemade look.

"You are the light of the world. . . . Let your light so shine before men, that they may see your good works and give glory to your Father who is in heaven."—Matthew 4:14, 16

Amana Sweet
Wheat Sweet

6 shredded wheat biscuits	2 teaspoons cinnamon
½ cup butter or margarine, melted	2½ cups sugar
	1 cup warm water
1 teaspoon vanilla	

Arrange the wheat biscuits in a Pyrex baking dish. Sprinkle generously with the cinnamon, then pour the melted butter or margarine evenly over all six. Place in a hot oven (425°) to brown—about 20 to 25 minutes. While the biscuits are browning, prepare a syrup by cooking the sugar and warm water together until thick—about 10 minutes. Cool to lukewarm. Add vanilla. Remove the biscuits from the oven and pour the syrup over. Serve hot or cold with fruit, heavy cream, or sour cream.

An ancient Greek dessert that Paul must have encountered in his journeys, was this same sugar syrup cooled to lukewarm and poured over plain sweet cake. Serve with whipped cream.

Candy

In biblical times, all candy was made with honey; there is in existence an Egyptian scroll giving a recipe for a candy-type confection of honey, dates, figs, and nuts, which was the most favored of that time, and is very similar to those of our own day. For candy which must be cooked, I would strongly urge a modern concession—the purchase of a candy thermometer. You will use it also for jams, jellies, and frostings, and it will more than pay for itself in a very little time.

Tychicus Sweet
Farina Candy

This is a sweet that Martha herself might have made; it is not only delicious, but is easily made and a real food so that you may allow the children to eat as much as they wish.

2½ cups sugar
2 cups water
½ cup honey
½ cup butter or margarine
3 cups farina

¼ pound almonds, chopped fine
½ teaspoon each ground cloves and cinnamon
powdered sugar

Make a syrup by boiling sugar, water, and honey for 15 minutes. While this is cooking, heat the butter in a skillet until very hot, then stir the farina into it gradually and cook, stirring, until the farina browns. It will take about 10 minutes. Then stir the syrup into the farina mixture, and add the nuts and spices. Stir constantly over a low heat until the candy thickens. Then remove from the heat and cover the pan for 5 minutes. Pour out into an oiled 9 × 9-inch pan. Cool from 4 to 5 hours, then cut in squares or diamonds. Sprinkle with powdered sugar or cinnamon.

Temple Fruit
Fruit Squares

1 cup raisins or 7 ounces pitted dates
1 cup pitted, uncooked prunes or ½ pound dried figs

½ cup chopped nuts
¼ cup molasses
¼ cup nonfat dry milk
¼ cup graham cracker crumbs

Put the fruit through the food chopper, using the medium blade. Chop the nuts by hand, so that they won't be too fine. Blend with the fruit. Mix in the molasses, then combine the nonfat dry milk with the graham cracker crumbs, and mix this into the fruit with the fingers. Shape the mixture into 1-inch balls, topping each, bonbon style, with glazed cherries or nuts, chocolate sprinkles, or colored sugar. For fruit bars, shape the mixture into a cake 8 × 2 × 2 inches; roll in colored sugar. Wrap in waxed paper and chill overnight. Then cut in slices ½ inch thick.

Nectared Egoz
Sugared Walnuts

1 cup sugar
2 tablespoons honey
⅓ cup water
1 teaspoon salt

1 teaspoon grated lemon rind
1 teaspoon lemon juice
1 tablespoon butter or margarine

2½ cups walnut halves

Combine sugar, honey, water, and salt, and stir over low heat until the sugar is dissolved. Boil to 238°, or until a few drops form a soft ball when dropped in cold water. Remove from heat and blend in lemon rind, juice, and butter. Add walnuts and stir gently until the mixture becomes creamy. Turn out onto waxed paper or a buttered cookie sheet and when cool, separate the nuts. Makes about 1¼ pounds.

Here are a few more very new ideas in candy making that are so "homey" that the biblical housewife would have loved them. They are the sort of sweet, too, that you don't mind giving the children when they need some quick energy.

Dibon Delight
Apple Candy

This is a candy that looks like old-fashioned Turkish Delight, but the flavor is new and different.

2 cups sweetened applesauce (No. 2 can)
1 tablespoon lemon juice

2 packages cherry gelatin dessert
1 cup chopped walnuts

powdered sugar

Heat the applesauce to boiling. Add lemon juice and simmer gently 10 to 15 minutes, or until the sauce is very thick. Add the cherry gelatin powder and stir until dissolved. Remove from the heat and stir in chopped walnuts. Pour into an 8 × 8-inch pan which has been rinsed in cold water. Allow to cool to room temperature, then place in the refrigerator until set. Cut in 1-inch squares and remove from the pan. Dust with the powdered sugar. Makes about 64 pieces. This one, too, is good for the youngsters.

Sidon Spice
Spiced Nuts

½ cup sugar
½ teaspoon salt
1 teaspoon cinnamon

¼ teaspoon each nutmeg and cloves
2 tablespoons water

Combine all ingredients and boil gently to 235°, or until a few drops in cold water form a soft ball. Add ¼ pound of any unsalted nuts and remove from the heat at once, stirring until the nuts are completely coated and the mixture turns to sugar. Pour onto a buttered pan or cookie sheet and quickly spread thin. When cool, break the nuts apart. Makes about ⅓ pound.

Silvered Nuts
Sugared Nuts

Beat 1 egg white slightly with 2 tablespoons cold water. Mix ½ cup sugar, 2 tablespoons cornstarch, a pinch of salt, 1½ teaspoons cinnamon, ½ teaspoon allspice, and ¼ teaspoon ginger. Dip walnuts or pecans in egg, then roll in spice mixture to coat. Place on greased cookie sheet and bake at 250° for 1½ hours.

Behold, to obey is better than sacrifice,
and to hearken than the fat of rams.
—1 Samuel 15:22

Betonim Crisp
Minted Nuts

1 cup sugar
½ cup water
1 tablespoon light corn syrup
pinch of salt

6 marshmallows
½ teaspoon essence of peppermint or 3 drops oil of peppermint

3 cups walnuts, broken in half

Mix the sugar, water, corn syrup, and salt in a small saucepan and cook slowly for about 8 minutes. Just before it forms a soft ball when a little is dropped in cold water (230° on the candy thermometer) remove from the heat. Add the marshmallows and stir until melted. Add peppermint and nuts and stir with circular motion until every nut is coated and the mixture hardens. Cool on unglazed paper. These will keep about a week in a tightly covered jar.

Zabud
Potato Candy

1 cup cold mashed potatoes (leftover are fine)
1 4-ounce can shredded cocoanut

1 teaspoon almond extract
3 1-pound cartons confectioner's sugar

Cut the cocoanut fine, using two paring knives scissors fashion. Blend together potatoes, cocoanut, and almond extract, then gradually work in the sugar a little at a time. Shape into small balls by rolling a piece between the palms. May be rolled in additional cocoanut or cinnamon for added flavor interest.

Faith is the assurance of things hoped for, the conviction of things not seen.—Hebrews 11:1

... all ate the same supernatural food and all drank the same supernatural drink.—1 Corinthians 10:3-4

CHAPTER FIFTEEN

DRINKS

Milk, water, fruit juices were common in biblical times. The time of the gathering of the grapes was a recognized season of the year, and one of the most joyous for the people.

So, whether you eat or drink, or whatever you do, do all to the glory of God.—1 Corinthians 10:31

W E TURN the spigot in our shining sinks, you and I, and the water bubbles out clear and sparkling, pure as God meant it to be, ready for whatever use we may make of it. We turn to our pantry shelf or freezer, and choose the juice of a dozen fruits with which to mix this gift of God. How like we are to the women who did the very same thing, although in a very different way, when they were preparing their tables for a guest.

To the ancients, water was one of the greatest of gifts, and to the people of Palestine it meant even more than it did to others, for it was scarcer there than elsewhere. To me, the fact that Jesus paused at the well (John 4:6) is in itself significant, for it shows that this was the center of life in the town, and his resting there demonstrates the important part that the well played in the lives of the people.

A great many other beverages were available: camel's milk, mixed in a proportion of one part milk to three parts water, was a great favorite. Goat's milk and ewe's milk were generally liked and used.

We know that a beverage of some sort was an integral part of biblical meals. Although host and guests ate from a common bowl, drink was handed to each in individual bowls or cups, and when particular honor was to be paid a guest, his cup was filled until it ran over, hence the feeling of joy in the phrase, "my cup overflows." (Psalm 23:5.)

Our cups, too, should run over when we consider the gifts of health and enjoyment that come to us so generously today. Frozen juices are, of course, wonderful not only for their health-giving vitamins but for the glory of their flavor. Consider, too, the almost limitless variety of new taste experiences on the grocer's shelves in sparkling glass: apple, cherry, cranberry, pineapple, grape, prune, tomato, combinations of all the citrus juices . . . how many blessings are ours! Let us not neglect a single one of them; they were put there for our use.

Punches

Bithynia Punch
Hot Tea Punch

This is delightful to serve to a group after a meeting on a winter night. Have a batch simmering in the kitchen while you serve at the table from a container over a candle warmer.

1 pint water
1 2-inch cinnamon stick
½ teaspoon whole cloves

1 tablespoon instant tea
1 cup apple juice
1 cup cranberry juice

3 tablespoons honey

Simmer water, cinnamon stick, and cloves for 5 minutes. Add instant tea and stir until dissolved, then add apple and cranberry juices. Heat just to the boiling point, then stir in the honey. Pour through a strainer into the serving container. Makes 1 quart.

Pomegranate Punch
Kool-Aid Punch

1 package cherry Kool-Aid
⅔ cup sugar

1 6-ounce can frozen orange-juice concentrate

2 quarts water with ice cubes

Simply combine all ingredients and stir until the soft drink powder (Kool-Aid) is dissolved. Makes about 2 quarts, or 16 servings.

Ice Mold

For a pretty frozen fruit mold to serve in a punch bowl, have ready 1 sliced orange, 1 sliced lemon, and 6 red and 6 green maraschino cherries. Fill a 1-quart bowl ⅓ full of cold water.

Place several fruit slices and 4 of the cherries in the water. Freeze fairly firm. Add more water and fruit and freeze again. Then fill the bowl to the top with water, add remaining fruit, and freeze until firm—at least 8 hours. To unmold, simply place the bowl in a pan of hot water until the ice loosens from the bowl, then unmold into the punch bowl. Then add the punch. If your punch bowl is large, double quantities and freeze in a 2-quart bowl. A stainless steel bowl is best if you have one, because the ice loosens from it more quickly.

I have often frozen small flowers into the ice mold in exactly this same way; violets, rosebuds, calendula, and such make a beautiful decoration for the bowl.

Roman Nog
Hot Fruit Eggnog

½ cup light brown sugar	1½ teaspoons pure vanilla ex-
¼ cup hot water	tract
1 tablespoon butter	pinch of salt
3 cups milk	whipped cream
	grated nutmeg

Melt the sugar in a 2-quart saucepan over low heat, stirring constantly. Gradually stir in the hot water and bring the mixture to the boiling point. Add the butter and cook 2 minutes. Add the milk slowly, stirring, and heat over low heat, stirring constantly. Blend in the vanilla and salt, and serve hot in punch cups or mugs, garnished with whipped cream, a dash of nutmeg, and spiced apricots, crabapples, or peaches. The combination of fruit with the milk punch is delightful. This makes about 4 servings; it is not a drink that should be planned for large crowds.

Eggs are not often mentioned in the Bible, but we do find the word in Isaiah 10:14

Matthew Punch
Spiced Punch

We call this drink by Matthew's name because it is such a nice punch for serving at Christmas time; very festive, bright and gay.

¾ cup unblanched almonds, halved	1 teaspoon whole cloves
1½ cups white seedless raisins	3 2-inch pieces cinnamon
peel of 3 oranges	6 cups water
	3 No. 2 cans pineapple juice

6 pints cranberry juice

Tie the spices in a cheesecloth bag. Strip all the white membrane from the inside of the orange rind, then cut with the kitchen shears into slivers. Simmer almonds, raisins, spice bag, and orange peel in the water for about 15 minutes; discard the peel and the spice bag. Chill thoroughly. When ready to serve, turn into the punch bowl and add the chilled juices. Serve with a few raisins and an almond in each cup. Makes about 50 half-cup servings.

Nobleman's Velvet
Grape Punch

2 6-ounce cans frozen grape juice concentrate	6 cups cold water
2 6-ounce cans frozen orange juice concentrate	5 cups lemon-lime carbonated soda
	fruit ice mold

Simply combine all ingredients in a punch bowl and pour over the ice mold; a pretty touch, if you are serving at a season when grapes are available, is to use purple, red, and black grapes in your ice mold, with mint leaves. Serves 25.

Claiming to be wise, they become fools.—Romans 1:22

Pharaoh's Cup
Grape-Honey Drink

The children love this for lunch; have the drink piping hot and serve it at bedtime, too. Simply mix 2 tablespoons honey with ¼ cup boiling water, stir until blended and dissolved, then add enough hot grape juice to fill the glass. For variety, 2 tablespoons lemon juice may be added.

Honey Sweet
Honeyed Cocoa

1 quart milk	¼ teaspoon allspice
¼ cup cocoa	¼ teaspoon nutmeg
¼ teaspoon salt	3 tablespoons honey
½ teaspoon cinnamon	¼ teaspoon vanilla

Scald the milk in a double boiler. Mix cocoa, salt, cinnamon, allspice, and nutmeg; add 2 tablespoons of the milk and blend into a smooth paste. Pour into the scalded milk, add the honey and vanilla and reheat, stirring. Then beat with a rotary beater until smooth. Serve very hot to 4.

Milk 'n Honey

4 ounces shredded cocoanut	3 tablespoons honey
2 tablespoons butter	1 teaspoon cinnamon
1 quart milk	sugar to taste

Melt the butter in a 2-quart saucepan; add the cocoanut and cook over low heat, stirring constantly until the cocoanut is golden brown. Add milk, honey, and cinnamon; scald over very low heat. Taste it; you may prefer to add a bit of sugar. Heat 2 or 3 minutes, then strain or not, as you wish, and serve hot. Serves 6.

Iddo Ice
Spiced Iced Coffee

6 tablespoons instant coffee   1 5-inch stick cinnamon
2 cups boiling water   ½ cup sugar
15 whole cloves   few grains salt
3 cups cold water

Mix the instant coffee, boiling water, cloves, cinnamon, sugar, and salt. Bring to a boil, cover tightly and let stand for 30 minutes. Remove the spices if you prefer, then add cold water to the coffee and pour over ice cubes in tall glasses. Garnish with whipped cream and cinnamon. This is a lovely drink to serve for a ladies' luncheon. Serves 6.

Why not make coffee the day before and freeze in your ice cube tray if you're planning a drink such as this one? Coffee ice cubes will chill the drink without diluting it. The same idea may be applied to tea.

Marah Punch
Berry Punch

Add ¾ cup sugar to a pint of fresh raspberries, or ½ cup sugar to a package of frozen berries. Let stand 1 to 2 hours. Strain off the juice; you should have about 1¼ cups, or enough to make 5 or 6 drinks. Add 3 to 4 tablespoons juice to each glass of crushed ice, then fill with golden or pale dry ginger ale. Float a few berries on top. Try grape juice for a similar effect.

Shepherd's Shake
Fruit Milk Shake

Put 3 tablespoons of any sieved, canned baby food fruit in a glass. Add ½ teaspoon sugar, a dash of cinnamon, and fill with chilled milk. Shake or stir vigorously. Garnish with fruit.

Sheshai Punch
Sherbet Punch

This is the sherbet punch which so many people serve today; I like to call it *Sheshai* because the word means "whitish" which describes the appearance of the finished drink.

1 46-ounce can orange-grape-
    fruit juice blend

1 12-ounce can apricot nectar
1 quart ginger ale
1 quart sherbet

Have juices and ginger ale thoroughly chilled; empty into the punch bowl, then add the sherbet and ginger ale. Spoon the liquid over the sherbet until partly melted and whitish. This will serve about 25 half-cup servings. For orange or grapefruit juice, use pineapple or lemon sherbet; with raspberry sherbet, use cranberry or cherry juice.

". . . , '*Let days speak,*
    and many years teach wisdom.' "—*Job 32:7*

Milk Naomi
Anise Milk

1 teaspoon ground anise seed   2 cups rich milk
1 teaspoon butter

Blend the anise seed with the milk; heat gradually in a small saucepan over low heat until very hot, but not boiling. Pour the hot milk into a heavy glass with a spoon in it, and float half teaspoon of butter on top. Cold milk may be flavored in the same way; simply blend well in the electric mixer or blender, and omit the butter.

Eve's Punch
Apple Punch

2 quarts cider or apple juice   6 cups orange juice
2 3-inch sticks cinnamon   2 cups lemon juice
12 whole cloves   1 No. 2 can crushed pineapple
1 No. 2 can pineapple juice   1½ quarts ginger ale

Simmer 2 cups of the cider with the spices in a saucepan for about 15 minutes. Cool and remove spices. Chill juices until ice cold. Combine all ingredients and pour over an ice mold. Serves 25.

Only take care lest this liberty of yours somehow become a stumbling-block to the weak.—1 Corinthians 8:9

Lifting up his eyes, then, and seeing that a multitude was coming to him, Jesus said to Philip, "How are we to buy bread, so that these people may eat?"—John 6:5

CHAPTER SIXTEEN

FEEDING THE MULTITUDES

Jesus knew his people's love of gathering together, and he recognized the value of merrymaking in their simple lives. He often accepted invitations to large dinners.

One of the most sumptuous feasts of all time is described in Esther 1:1 as being given by King Ahasuerus.

COOKING FOR a crowd, whether as a project dedicated to God, to entertain for study groups, or simply to bring our friends together, is a definite part of our lives. This is no new thing; meals for large groups were important in the various social levels of life in biblical times, and harvests were reaped and kings crowned to the merrymaking that accompanied the feasts prepared by the women of the Bible.

When Laban gave his sister to Isaac, "he and the men who were with him ate and drank, and spent the night there" (Genesis 24:54). And when he gave his daughter Leah to Jacob for wife, he "gathered together all the men of the place, and made a feast" (Genesis 29:22).

Seven days was not an uncommon duration for a festival, and those that Jesus attended, he enjoyed; he joined his family in the marriage feast at Cana (John 2:2), and he dined with a group when he accepted the invitation of Simon the Pharisee (Luke 7:36).

There was little cutlery, except for serving or carving pieces, and there was usually only one dish, into which each dipped his hand (Matthew 26:23). These common meals were the confirmation and seal of brotherhood, and when the early Christians met for them, as they did regularly, they made every member of the community welcome.

There will be many, many demands upon you for help in planning and serving "common meals" today; heed them cheerfully, and give of yourself to them, for this is a privilege granted to us to demonstrate our dedication to God. The suggestions on the following pages are some which I have found helpful in planning such meals; adapt them to your purposes and measure them by the tools you have at hand, as the biblical housewife did. You will find your efforts blessed by success.

Ten Commandments for Feeding a Crowd

1. Decide at the beginning whether you are planning this affair to make money for a worthy cause or purely for social purposes. The approach for one, obviously, is different from the approach for the other.

2. Organize a committee to help you. Make one person responsible for the menu, one for preparation of each course, one for table setting and decorations, one for purchasing, one for serving, and one for cleaning up. Let each choose her own helpers; she'll work better.

3. Consider the type of guest you're preparing for; men's groups prefer plain (but good) food in ample servings while women enjoy small servings and greater variety.

4. Decide on the price, per plate, that the group will pay.

5. Plan the menu with the price in mind, making it as good (and as different) as you can for the price.

6. Estimate the number to be served, allowing for about five per cent more than you expect. After all, you may have some who are willing to pay for second servings.

7. Get acquainted with the kitchen you are to use. Check utensils, count dishes, silver, and glasses, organize refrigerator space for items which must be kept cold. Check your serving space particularly; ample space is necessary for smooth service.

8. Estimate your cost on the menu you've planned (see "How to Estimate Costs" on opposite page) if you are entertaining to make a profit.

9. Prepare food carefully; this is no time for experiments. Prepare fractional, identical recipes at home, so that you may determine seasoning, texture, etc., by actual testing.

10. Greet your guests warmly. Make them welcome. Serve them with care.

How to Estimate Costs

In planning a money-making project which includes a meal, it is of vital importance to know exactly what you are doing; neglect of the smallest detail sometimes means the difference between a sizable return for the effort involved, and abject failure. First of all, in the earliest stages of your planning, decide upon the price per plate that your group will pay; if you build a reputation for good meals at reasonable prices, the future success of your efforts is assured.

Next, you must estimate the number of people who will attend; draw upon previous experience in deciding upon this figure, then add five per cent (that is, if you estimate a hundred diners, allow for five more) to take care of unexpected guests.

With these figures in hand, turn to your menu; I consider this the most important step of all. Whether you are planning for a small, one-table committee group or for a huge every-member supper, it is important that you try to serve something tempting and different. The dishes can be ordinary, reasonably priced foods, but they should be served in new and attractive combinations, such as we suggest in the following menus. After all, peas don't always have to team up with carrots, nor is corned beef restricted to an accompaniment of cabbage; give them something different, and your guests will come back again.

Once your menu is decided upon, check your recipes and make a list of the amounts of food necessary. It won't be necessary to include staples such as salt, pepper, etc., because these are probably already in the church kitchen. Do include, however, some unusual seasoning such as a herb or a special vinegar, in such quantity that you can leave something in the pantry for the next group.

"With God all things are possible."—Matthew 19:26

Get the prices on everything needed so that you can figure the cost of each dish. Perhaps some of the food will be donated; if so, figure what it would have cost you if it had to be purchased, and add in this figure; it will increase your profit. Remember to figure on large-size containers and to buy in quantity wherever possible; sometimes such planning makes a big difference in cost.

Next list your incidental expenses. List everything—paper and cleaning supplies, table decorations, wages for dishwashers and similar extra help, any other extra expenses that may be necessary in the kitchen you are using. Be exact. Do not estimate that you can hire dishwashers for 75¢ per hour—check by telephone and make certain that you can.

Now add these expenses together; food, plus the extra expenses which will be incurred. Add an extra 5 per cent for the unavoidable extra costs which everyone encounters. To this total add the amount you are trying to earn for your church, club, or whatever group you are serving.

This is your total cost; divide it by the number you will serve (the paying guests, that is), and you will have the price to be charged per plate. It is really much simpler than it sounds; any high school sophomore will figure it for you, if figures are one of your weak points. If this price per plate is higher than you feel your guests will want to pay, either reduce the amount of profit you figured on, or make adjustments in the menu to reduce the cost of the food.

Above all, build good will in your community for your church, your group, and your project, by making the food good; it is only in this way that your success will be a continuing thing.

Women's Luncheons

Chicken Hebron
Salad Marah
Herodias Pie
Beverage

Chicken Hebron
Baked Chicken Salad

4 12-ounce cans boned chicken	¼ cup flour
2 6-ounce cans sliced mush- rooms	1 cup mayonnaise (this must be real mayonnaise)
1 7-ounce can pimento, chopped	milk ½ teaspoon salt
1 cup finely minced onion	⅛ teaspoon pepper
⅛ teaspoon garlic salt	

In a very large mixing bowl, place the chicken cut in pieces, sliced mushrooms (be sure to save the liquid), pimento, and onion. Stir the flour into the mayonnaise. Place the mushroom liquid in a measuring cup and add enough milk to make 1½ cups liquid. Stir this into the mayonnaise, together with the seasonings. Add to the chicken and toss lightly but thoroughly. Pour into a large, ungreased baking pan or casserole, cover, and bake at 375° for 40 to 45 minutes. If you use a roasting pan for the cooking, use aluminum foil for a cover. This is delicious served with toast points, canned French fried onion rings, or crisp chow mein noodles. Makes 2½ quarts, to serve about 25 people.

> *Charm is deceitful, and beauty is vain,*
> *but a woman who fears the* Lord
> *is to be praised.*—*Proverbs 31:30*

Salad Marah
Grapefruit and Orange Salad

Combine two 8-ounce bottles French dressing and ⅔ cup orange juice. Chill. Slice 10 peeled oranges and cut 5 grapefruit into sections. Arrange on endive and spoon dressing over salad. This amount will serve about 25.

Herodias Pie
Coffee Chiffon Pie

Crust

6 cups graham cracker crumbs (about 1¼ pounds crackers)	1 teaspoon salt
⅓ cup sugar	1 cup margarine
1½ teaspoons instant coffee	1 egg
	1 tablespoon water

Mix the dry ingredients thoroughly; melt margarine and stir into the crumbs. Beat the egg and water together, then add to the crumb mixture and blend again. Divide this into thirds and press into the bottoms and sides of three 9-inch pie pans. Bake at 400° for 10 minutes. Cool.

Filling

2 tablespoons unflavored gelatin	¾ teaspoon salt
½ cup cold water	3 tablespoons instant coffee
2½ cups milk	2 cups sugar
2 cups water	6 eggs, separated
2 teaspoons vanilla	

Soften the gelatin in the cold water. Combine milk, water, salt, coffee, and 1½ cups sugar in a large saucepan. Cook over direct heat, stirring until mixture begins to boil. Stir in the softened gelatin; stir until dissolved. Now pour about 1 cup of the hot mixture into the beaten egg yolks; stir, then add egg-yolk mixture to the remaining hot liquid. Return to the heat and cook over very low heat for two minutes, stirring constantly. Remove from the heat and cool. When the mixture has thickened and begun to set, fold in the egg whites which have been beaten stiff with ½ cup sugar added gradually. Fold until the whites disappear. DO NOT STIR. Spoon the mixture into the crumb shells and refrigerate until firm. Be sure the mixture is quite thick before filling the shells; it may be necessary to refrigerate it for a bit. This makes 3 pies; serves 24-25.

Esau Plate
Beets Phoenicia
Eutychus Bread
Aeneas Sweet

Esau Plate
Tuna Lemon Mold

4 packages lemon-flavored gelatin
1 quart hot water
2 cups cold water
½ cup lemon juice
1 pint mayonnaise

1 teaspoon salt
4 7-ounce cans tuna fish
3 cups chopped cucumber or celery
1 cup sliced, stuffed olives
½ cup chopped pimento

2 teaspoons grated onion

Dissolve the gelatin in hot water. Add cold water, lemon juice, mayonnaise, and salt. Blend well with a rotary beater. Chill until slightly thickened (quickest way is to set the bowl in a pan of crushed ice) and then beat in the electric mixer until light and fluffy. Fold in remaining ingredients. Pour into 4 one-quart molds or 25 individual molds. Chill until firm.

Beets Phoenicia
Pickled Beets

6 No. 2 cans tiny whole beets	¾ cup vinegar
2 cups juice from beets	¾ teaspoon salt
⅓ cup mustard with horse-	⅛ teaspoon pepper
radish	4 teaspoons sugar

2 tablespoons grated onion

Drain the beets, reserving 2 cups juice. Combine juice with remaining ingredients and simmer 5 minutes. Pour over beets in a large jar or enamel pan and allow to stand several hours or overnight in the refrigerator. Makes 2½ quarts—serves 25. Both this dish and the salad may be made the day before.

Eutychus Bread
Cheese Squares

4 cups sifted flour	1 stick margarine
5 teaspoons baking powder	2 cups milk
1½ teaspoons salt	2 eggs
¼ cup sugar	paprika

2 cups (½ pound) grated American cheese

Sift the dry ingredients into a bowl; stir in the grated cheese. Melt the margarine in a large saucepan, cool, then add milk and eggs and beat with a rotary beater until well blended. Add all at once to the dry ingredients and stir very gently only until the flour is all absorbed. Pour into a large greased baking pan. Bake at 400° 25 to 30 minutes. Cut into 24-25 squares.

Pleasant words are like a honeycomb,
*   sweetness to the soul and health to the body.*
*   —Proverbs 16:24*

Aeneas Sweet
Fruited Cake

½ cup canned crushed pineapple, undrained
1 cup Baker's Angel Flake
  cocoanut
2 cups sifted flour
1 teaspoon baking powder
¼ teaspoon salt
½ teaspoon baking soda

½ cup shortening
¾ cup sugar
¼ teaspoon ginger
2 eggs
¾ cup canned crushed pineapple, undrained
1 6-ounce package semisweet
  chocolate bits

First, make the topping by combining the pineapple and cocoanut. For the cake, grease and flour a 15 × 10 × 1-inch pan.
Sift together flour, baking powder, salt, and baking soda. Measure the shortening, sugar, and ginger into a large bowl and
cream until light and fluffy. Beat the eggs in one at a time, then
add the flour alternately with the ¾ cup pineapple. Last of all,
stir in the chocolate bits. Spread the dough in the pan. Sprinkle
the topping evenly over the cake. Bake at 375° for 25 minutes,
or until the cake tests done. Makes 25 3 × 2-inch pieces. Notice
that this is a very inexpensive cake, very simple to put together.
It is very rich and sweet, too, and will prove a favorite with all
of your "project" guests.

Every-Member Dinner

Sharon Cup
Sheba Plate
Golden Bits
Cyrus Shreds
Rye Bread   Butter
Eliakim Sweet
Beverage

Sharon Cup
Spiced Plum Cup

You will get about 25 servings of 2 to 3 plums each, from a No. 10 can. Served in a sherbet glass, you really should have 3 plums per serving, so you may have to purchase an additional small can. Drain the syrup from the fruit; add ½ cup vinegar, three 3-inch sticks cinnamon and 10 or 12 whole cloves. Taste to be sure it isn't too tart. Bring the spiced juice to a boil, then reduce the heat and allow to simmer for about 10 minutes. Remove from the heat, add the plums, and set aside to cool. Refrigerate overnight before serving; serve in sherbet glasses with a spoonful of juice over the fruit and a garnish of two or three mint leaves.

Sheba Plate
Hungarian Pork Chops

25 4-ounce pork chops	2 tablespoons salt
1 pint sliced onion	1 teaspoon pepper
1 cup flour	2 teaspoons caraway seed
2 quarts water	1 quart dairy sour cream
1½ pounds egg noodles	

Brown the pork chops quickly in the smallest possible amount of fat, then salt and pepper lightly and set aside to keep warm.

Heat about 3 tablespoons fat in a large skillet, add the onions and cook until they are tender but not brown. Add the flour (you may have to add a few tablespoons of fat first) and blend into the fat completely, then gradually stir in the water and cook, stirring, until the gravy is smooth and thickened. Blend in the next four ingredients. If the gravy is very light, add 1 tablespoon Kitchen Bouquet to get a good color. Arrange the browned pork chops in a baking pan, pour the gravy over, and finish cooking, uncovered, at 325° in the oven, for 1 hour. Cook and drain the noodles and serve with the pork chop on a plate, spooning the gravy over the noodles. Serves 25.

Golden Bits
Parsleyed Carrots

5 quarts pared carrots	1⅓ cups brown sugar, packed
2 quarts water	1 teaspoon salt
1½ tablespoons salt	½ teaspoon Accent
1 teaspoon Accent	7 tablespoons hot water
½ cup butter	

Quarter the carrots lengthwise, then cook in the water with the salt and Accent for about 15 minutes, or until barely tender. Drain and arrange in buttered roasting pan. Add sugar, salt, and Accent to the 7 tablespoons hot water, and cook about 3 minutes, or until a thin syrup is formed. Add butter and, when the butter is melted, pour over the carrots. Bake at 400° for about 30 minutes, basting frequently. Have ready 2 cups finely chopped parsley, and arrange each serving topped with a heaping tablespoon of the parsley. Serves 25.

Do not neglect to show hospitality to strangers, for thereby some have entertained angels unawares.—Hebrews 13:2

Cyrus Shreds
Cole Slaw

3¾ pounds green cabbage
1¼ cups mayonnaise
2 tablespoons vinegar
2 tablespoons water
1 tablespoon sugar

1½ teaspoons salt
¼ teaspoon pepper
1 tablespoon minced onion
1 pound carrots cut into thin
 strips

Wash, core, and shred the cabbage. Place in refrigerator to crisp. Combine mayonnaise, vinegar, water, sugar, and seasonings. Pour over the cabbage at least one hour before serving time, and toss lightly until mixed. Garnish with the carrot strips, which have been crisping in ice water. Serves about 25.

Eliakim Sweet
Chocolate Nut Pudding

¾ pound flour, sifted
2 tablespoons baking powder
1 tablespoon salt
2¼ cups (1 pound) sugar
9 tablespoons cocoa
1½ cups milk

6 tablespoons melted shortening
1 tablespoon vanilla
1½ cups chopped nuts
1 pound 2 ounces brown sugar
1 cup cocoa

4½ cups boiling water

Sift together flour, baking powder, salt, granulated sugar, and the first amount of cocoa. Add the milk, shortening, and vanilla to the dry ingredients; mix only until smooth. Add the nut meats, mix gently, then turn into buttered pudding pans to a depth of ½ inch.

Now, combine the brown sugar and remaining cocoa, and sprinkle over the batter in the pans. Pour boiling water over the top of the batter, dividing it equally among the pans. This makes a rich chocolate sauce on the bottom of the pans after the pudding is baked. Bake at 350° for 35 minutes, then cut in squares and serve warm, topped with sauce from the bottom of the pan. This is delicious; it makes 25 half-cup portions.

A Father-Son Dinner

Elisha's Pottage
Samarian Shortcake with
Edom Sauce
Huldah Bowl
Shebna Pastry

Elisha's Pottage
Mulligatawny Soup

1 cup fat	2¼ cups tart apples, peeled
2 cups flour	and diced
2 tablespoons curry powder	1 cup Baker's Angel Flake
1 gallon chicken or veal stock	cocoanut
1½ cups diced onion	½ teaspoon ground mace
1 cup diced celery	4½ tablespoons salt
1 cup diced carrots	1 tablespoon Accent

1½ quarts milk

Melt the fat in a large soup kettle—at least a 2-gallon size. Stir in the flour and blend over low heat until smooth. Add the curry powder and cook again, stirring. Now add the stock slowly, stirring all the while; cook and stir until the sauce is thickened and smooth. Add onions, celery, and carrots; simmer about 40 minutes or until vegetables are very tender. Add apples, cocoanut, and seasonings and simmer 20 minutes longer. Last of all, add the milk, blend well, and keep hot over low heat. The soup must not boil after the milk is added. This is a real man's dish and very reasonable to make. This amount will serve about 35; with this group, you must allow for second helpings.

Samarian Shortcake
Onion Shortcake

2 pounds onions
1 pound flour
7 teaspoons baking powder
½ tablespoon salt
¾ cup shortening

2 eggs
2 cups milk
1 tablespoon salt
¼ cup shortening
1 cup sour cream

1 egg

Peel the onions and slice carefully; try to keep the slices in pretty rings. Sift flour, baking powder, and the ½ tablespoon of salt together, then cut in the ¾ cup shortening until the mixture resembles coarse meal. Beat the 2 eggs slightly, combine with the milk, and add all at once to the flour mixture. Blend only until the flour is moistened, then spread evenly in eight 9-inch pie pans.

For the topping, sprinkle the onion rings with the tablespoon of salt. Melt the ¼ cup shortening in a large pan and sauté the onions until just tender, not brown. Cover the shortcakes with the sautéed onions. Beat the egg lightly with the cup of sour cream, and drizzle this over the onions. Bake at 425° for 25 minutes, or until the shortcake is done. If this is not to be served at once, bake in two 12 × 18-inch pans and when baked, set over another pan containing a small amount of water to keep the cake fresh and hot.

Edom Sauce
Meat Sauce

½ cup cooking oil
1 cup chopped celery
½ cup chopped onions
2 pounds lean ground beef
1½ tablespoons salt

1½ cups tomato paste
4 cups tomato juice
2 cups water
½ teaspoon pepper

Heat the cooking oil in a large pan; add celery and onions and sauté until tender but not brown. Add the ground beef and salt and cook, turning the meat occasionally with a fork, so that it browns evenly. Add tomato paste, tomato juice, water, and pepper to taste, and simmer about 30 minutes or until the sauce is nice and thick. This may be made ahead of time. This will make 24-25 servings of a 3-ounce piece of shortcake and ⅓ cup sauce.

Since the onion shortcake may be served with a variety of other sauces—creamed chicken or turkey, cheese sauce with tuna, etc.—you will find this a valuable recipe for many occasions. Young married groups will enjoy it, club groups meeting for brunch, and many others.

Huldah Bowl
Mixed Green Salad

1 quart coarsely shredded cabbage	½ cup diced green pepper
3½ quarts coarsely shredded greens	1 cup thinly sliced celery
	6 hard-cooked eggs, chopped
	4 tomatoes, cut in wedges
1½ cups French dressing	

Combine cabbage, greens, pepper, and celery and mix thoroughly. Just before serving, add eggs, tomato wedges, and French dressing. Toss lightly. This will serve 25. For a hearty salad that might be used for a main dish, add ¾ pound ham, salami, bologna, or cheese, cut in thin strips just before serving.

*A cheerful heart is a good medicine,
but a downcast spirit dries up the bones.*
—*Proverbs 17:22*

Shebna Pastry
Fresh Cherry Cobbler

¾ pound corn meal	½ cup shortening
½ pound cake flour	2 teaspoons salt
2 tablespoons baking powder	2½ cups milk

Do not sift corn meal; simply measure the cake flour by weight, sift, then add corn meal and baking powder and stir together. Add shortening and salt and cut until the mixture resembles coarse crumbs. Add the milk and mix with a fork. Roll gently on a floured board or cloth to fit a 12 × 10-inch pan.

6 cups fruit juice	2½ pounds sugar
3 ounces cornstarch	1½ teaspoons salt
1 cup water	5 pounds canned fruit

Cherries, berries, peaches, apricots, apples, or other fruit may be used in this recipe. Heat the fruit juice. While it is heating, blend the cornstarch with the water until very smooth. Then stir into the juice and cook, stirring, until the mixture cooks clear and is smooth and thick. Add sugar and salt and cook, stirring, until the sauce reaches the boiling point. Then turn in the drained fruit and mix carefully. Turn into a 12 × 10-inch pan and cool to room temperature. Cover with the corn meal crust above and bake at 425° until the crust is brown. Makes about 25 four-ounce servings.

and they shall beat their swords into plowshares,
and their spears into pruning hooks;
nation shall not lift up sword against nation,
neither shall they learn war any more.

—Micah 4:3

Young People's Fellowship
Perez Sandwich
Carrot Sticks   Olives
Pound Cake with
Elimelech Sauce
Beverage

Perez Sandwich
Turkey King Sandwich

3 pounds cooked turkey, cubed
½ cup butter or margarine
2 cups chopped onions
4 garlic cloves, minced
½ pound canned mushroom
   pieces
3 large bay leaves
3½ cups canned tomatoes

4 cups water and mushroom
   liquid
⅓ cup lemon juice
¾ cup chopped green pepper
1 teaspoon Worcestershire sauce
1½ tablespoons orégano
1½ tablespoons salt
¾ teaspoon pepper

1 6-ounce can tomato paste

Melt the butter or margarine; cook onion, garlic, and mushrooms slowly until the onion is transparent, stirring occasionally. Add all the remaining ingredients except the turkey and simmer together for 30 minutes, stirring frequently. If the mixture is not the desired consistency, thicken with ¼ cup flour stirred smooth in a little water; add to the hot mixture and cook until thickened, stirring constantly. Remove bay leaves and add turkey. Heat gently. Serve this on half a toasted sandwich bun; put the other half of the bun, toasted and buttered, beside it on the plate. Serves 25, allowing a half cup per serving.

You will find this sauce an invaluable aid in planning menus; it is easily doubled, and is equally delicious with any cooked meat, tuna fish, or even bologna cut into cubes. Young people love it.

Elimelech Sauce
Butterscotch Sauce

¾ cup margarine	3 cups boiling water
1½ cups brown sugar	1½ teaspoons vanilla
½ cup flour	or molasses
⅛ teaspoon salt	½ cup chopped nuts

Melt the margarine in a saucepan; stir in the brown sugar. Add flour and salt and mix to a smooth paste. Add the boiling water gradually, stirring constantly, and cook, stirring, until the mixture comes to a boil. Place pan containing sauce over hot water and cook, covered, 15 minutes. Add vanilla or molasses and nuts. Serve over pound or any plain cake. Serves 25, allowing about 3 tablespoons per serving.

Bazaar Supper

Assorted Relishes with
Spiced Tomato Juice
Chebar Steak
Potatoes Tammuz
Hamonah Corn
Hot Rolls　　　　　Butter
Asher Pastry

For the relishes prepare ahead of time carrot strips, celery curls, and radish roses, and have them crisping in ice water in the refrigerator. Plan on 4 or 5 carrot strips, 2 celery curls, 1 radish rose, and 1 ripe olive per serving. For the spiced tomato juice, you will need 1½ quarts tomato juice. Bring to a boil with 4 ounces chopped onion, 2 bay leaves, 6 cloves, 1½ teaspoons dry mustard, 3 celery stalks, chopped, and a tablespoon salt. Boil together about 5 minutes, then strain and add 1½ quarts canned consommé. Serve either hot or cold. Serves 25.

Chebar Steak
Potted Steak

6½ pounds bottom round steak, not over ½ inch thick	flour
3 tablespoons salt	1 cup chopped onion
½ teaspoon pepper	1 pound celery, coarsely cut
1½ teaspoons Accent	1 cup flour
	4 cups hot water

½ No. 2½ can tomatoes

If shoulder or arm roast is less expensive than bottom round, use it. Simply ask your butcher to slice it ½ inch thick for you. Divide the steaks neatly into 4-ounce portions. Stir salt, pepper, and Accent together; sprinkle half over the steaks. Now, using flour as needed, cover the steaks and pound in the flour with light cleaver strokes. Do this thoroughly so that the flour is worked well into the meat.

You should have about a pound of suet trimmed from your meat; if you do not have this much, ask the butcher for enough to make a pound. Cut this into neat bits. Set aside 1 cup. Place the remainder in a large pan or skillet and render it out slowly; remove all the crisp bits. Brown the steaks well in the hot fat and place in a roasting pan.

In the same skillet or pan, render out the remaining cup of suet; add onions and celery and sauté lightly. Blend in the flour and stir until smooth and brown. Add the water gradually, stirring constantly to insure smoothness. Add the salt and pepper mixture which was reserved and the tomatoes. Bring to a boil and pour over the steaks. Bake at 450° for 15 minutes; reduce heat to 350° and bake 1 hour longer, or until tender. Serves 25. Recipe may be doubled.

Potatoes Tammuz
Rosin-Baked Potatoes

Select the proper number of potatoes; if ordered from a restaurant supply house or large grocery, they may be ordered of a uniform 8-ounce size. This is the best serving size. You will be able to buy powdered rosin from a chemical or pharmaceutical supply house; one pound will be ample for 25 potatoes. Cut heavy weight, aluminum foil into squares large enough to go around the potatoes, make a double fold on top, and fold over ½ inch on each end.

Scrub the potatoes thoroughly—all this preparation can be done hours ahead of time. While the potatoes are still wet, roll them in the powdered rosin so that they are completely coated. Wrap in the aluminum foil, making a double fold on top and on each end. An 8-ounce potato prepared in this fashion will cook in exactly one hour at 375° and may be held in a very low oven (under 325°) for another hour. They are truly delicious.

Hamonah Corn
Curried Corn

6 tablespoons margarine	2½ teaspoons Accent
3 cups fine dry crumbs	6 No. 2 cans whole-kernel corn
2 teaspoons salt	1 cup chopped green pepper
¾ teaspoon pepper	½ teaspoon curry powder

Melt the margarine; add crumbs, salt, pepper, and Accent and mix thoroughly. Add corn, green pepper, and curry powder; blend again, then turn into 17 × 26-inch roasting pans and bake at 325° for 45-50 minutes.

You will notice that no salad is mentioned with this meal; because of the appetizer it isn't necessary, but if your costs will permit, a nice mixed-green salad would be a good addition.

Asher Pastry
Pumpkin Chiffon Pie

6 cups canned pumpkin	8 eggs, separated
1½ cups milk	1 envelope unflavored gelatin
1 teaspoon salt	½ cup cold water
1¼ pound brown sugar	grated rind 1 lemon
½ teaspoon ginger	2 tablespoons lemon juice
2 teaspoons nutmeg	4 extra egg whites
2 teaspoons cinnamon	⅔ cup granulated sugar
½ teaspoon allspice	4 8-inch baked pie shells

whipped cream for garnish

Mix together in a saucepan the first 8 ingredients. Bring to the boiling point over moderate heat. Beat the egg yolks, add about a cup of the hot pumpkin mixture to the eggs, mix well, then stir the egg mixture into the cooked mixture. Cook over low heat, stirring, until the mixture thickens. Soak the gelatin in the cold water for about 5 minutes, then stir into the hot pumpkin mixture. Stir until the gelatin is completely dissolved. Add lemon rind and juice and chill until the filling starts to set. Whip the 12 egg whites until stiff, then fold sugar in gradually to form a meringue. Fold this into the pumpkin filling, folding gently but thoroughly until the mixture is completely blended. Pour into pie shells and chill. Serve with a garnish of whipped cream or nuts, or both. Makes 4 pies.

Trust in the LORD *with all your heart,*
and do not rely on your own insight.
—*Proverbs 3:5*

Married Couples' Supper

Assorted Olives   Celery Sticks   Cucumber Spears
Drumsticks Judah with Panned Polenta
Salad Jael
Bread Sticks
Midian Pudding
Beverage

Drumsticks Judah
Barbecued Drumsticks

50 chicken drumsticks, cooked   1½ teaspoons salt
1 cup butter, melted   ½ teaspoon Accent
¾ cup catsup   dash of cayenne
¼ cup paprika   2 teaspoons chili powder

If you want to cut down on expense, the "city chicken legs" which butchers fix up do very nicely for this dish. Oven fry them or the chicken drumsticks early in the morning of the dinner. Arrange cooked drumsticks on the bottom of a drippings pan. Combine butter and seasonings and spread carefully over the drumsticks. Bake at 375° for 15 minutes, covered. (Use aluminum foil if your pan doesn't have a cover.) Then uncover, baste with remaining sauce, and bake 10 minutes longer.

Panned Polenta

2 quarts boiling water   ½ teaspoon Accent
3 teaspoons salt   3 cups corn meal
                 3 cups cold water

Bring the 2 quarts water to a boil with the salt and Accent in it. Mix the corn meal to a smooth paste with the 3 cups cold water, then add to the boiling water, stirring all the while. Place over boiling water and cook 30 minutes, or over very low direct heat 7 to 10 minutes, stirring constantly to prevent lumps. Pour into 2 loaf pans 8½ × 4 × 3 inches. Chill until firm. This can all be done the day before; to prepare for serving, simply unmold and slice, dip slices in corn meal, and brown in hot fat. Or heat the slices in a greased pan in a hot oven. Makes 25 servings of 2 drumsticks and 1 slice fried polenta each.

Salad Jael
Waldorf Salad

10 cups diced apples, unpeeled	1 cup mayonnaise or cooked
5 cups diced celery	salad dressing
2½ cups broken walnut meats	¼ cup heavy cream

As you must have suspected, this is just that old favorite, Waldorf Salad. It will be equally delicious made with fresh pears. Combine apples and celery and sprinkle with lemon juice to prevent discoloration. Just before serving, add the nuts and mix with the salad dressing thinned with the cream. Garnish with a maraschino cherry if desired. This serves 25.

Barak Dressing
Cooked Salad Dressing

½ cup sifted flour	⅛ teaspoon paprika
½ cup sugar	1 cup water
2 teaspoons salt	¾ cup mild vinegar
½ teaspoon Accent	2 whole eggs, beaten
2 teaspoons dry mustard	½ cup cream

Mix together the flour, sugar, and seasonings, then stir in the water gradually. Mix until smooth and blended. Stir in the vinegar. Bring to a boil over low heat, stirring constantly; then boil 1 minute, still stirring, until the dressing thickens. Remove from the heat. Beat the eggs, beat in a little of the hot sauce, then stir the egg mixture into the dressing. Stir in the cream, then chill. Makes about 3 cups, or enough to serve 2 tablespoons each to 25.

Midian Pudding
Fruited Bread Pudding

2 quarts soft bread cubes
2 quarts milk
1⅓ cups sugar
16 eggs, beaten
2 teaspoons salt

1½ tablespoons vanilla
1 quart pitted dates, chopped
2 cups chopped walnuts
½ cup melted butter or margarine

The bread cubes should be about ½ inch square. Combine bread, milk, sugar, beaten eggs, salt, vanilla, dates, walnuts, and melted butter and pour into a greased pan 9 × 14 × 2 inches. Bake at 350° for 1 hour. Serve with whipped cream. This will serve 24 or 25, but you should count on second helpings; it is a delicious dessert.

Women's Fellowship Lunch
Adam Plate
Hot Biscuits   Marmalade
Clement Pudding with
Sauce Rephaim

Adam Plate
Apple Salad Plate

1 pound head lettuce	¼ teaspoon Accent
25 red-skinned apples	20 ounces cream cheese
2 cups grapefruit juice	a little milk
5 cups grated carrots	½ teaspoon salt
1 cup chopped celery	¼ teaspoon pepper
2½ cups seedless raisins	¼ teaspoon Accent
1 cup salad dressing	50 slices bologna or salami
½ teaspoon salt	100 small stuffed olives

Wash the lettuce and drain; you should have 2 or 3 leaves for each plate to be served. Wash the apples, core, and mark the skin into 12 parts. Pare alternate parts, then cut apples into sections, petal-fashion, not quite through the bottom. Brush with grapefruit juice (orange juice will do quite as well). Spread the sections apart very gently—don't force them, or the apple will break apart. Now, combine carrots, celery, raisins, mayonnaise or salad dressing, salt, and Accent. Blend well. With a No. 20 dipper or scoop, fill the apple with the carrot-celery-raisin mixture.

Moisten the cream cheese with a little milk until it spreads easily, season with salt, pepper, and Accent, and spread on the bologna or salami slices. Roll up, secure with wooden toothpicks, and stick an olive on each end of the pick. To serve, arrange 2 filled meat slices on the platter with 1 stuffed apple and 2 hot biscuits. Serves 25.

Clement Pudding
Bavarian Cream

8 egg yolks, slightly beaten
1 cup sugar
½ teaspoon salt
1 quart scalded milk
4 tablespoons unflavored gelatin soaked in 1 cup cold water

8 egg whites, beaten stiff
1 quart heavy cream, beaten stiff
¾ cup powdered sugar
1 tablespoon vanilla

Mix the egg yolks with the sugar and salt. Gradually stir in the scalded milk. Cook over hot water, stirring constantly, until the mixture thickens slightly. Remove from the heat, add the soaked gelatin, then stir until the gelatin is completely dissolved. Cool to room temperature. Fold in the stiffly beaten egg whites, then set the bowl in a pan of ice water and stir, scraping from the bottom and sides of the pan, until the mixture begins to thicken. Add the cream, beaten stiff, the powdered sugar, and the vanilla, folding in carefully. Turn into 25 individual molds which have been lined with strips of sponge cake or lady fingers; garnish or flavor as you prefer. It is a good idea to make this dessert a day ahead, so that it has plenty of time to set.

Sauce Rephaim
Berry Sauce

2 quarts berry juice (boysen-berry has the best flavor)
6½ tablespoons cornstarch
1 cup sugar
¼ teaspoon salt

Bring the berry juice to a boil. Combine the cornstarch, sugar, and salt, blending thoroughly. Add to the hot berry juice and cook, stirring, until thickened and clear. Remove from the heat and cool thoroughly. To serve, place ⅓ cup cooled sauce in a serving dish, place unmolded pudding on the sauce, then top with whipped cream, a teaspoonful of sauce, and a berry. Serves 25.

Quantities Needed to Serve Fifty

	Serving	Amount to Buy
Bread (1½ pound loaf)	3 half slices	3 loaves
Butter	½ ounce	1½ pounds
Cake	1 slice	4 large cakes
Coffee	5-6 ounces	1 pound for 1 cup per person
Instant Coffee	1 cup	2 2-ounce jars
Coffee Cream	2 tablespoons	1½ quarts
Whipping Cream	1 tablespoon	1 quart
Sugar for Coffee	1½ teaspoons	1 pound
Cubed Sugar	1 large or 2 small	1 pound large or ½ pound small
Mixed Fruits for Fruit Cup or Fruit Salad	⅓ to ½ cup	4 to 6 quarts
Ice Cream, bulk	8 servings per quart	6½ quarts
Ice Cream, brick	6 servings per brick	8½ quarts
Meat: Beef Pot Roast	3 ounces cooked	18-20 pounds
Standing Rib	3-3½ ounces cooked	20-25 pounds
Chicken for cut-up		17-20 pounds, dressed
Boned Chicken	1½ ounces cooked	13-17 pounds, drawn
Roast Chicken	2-3 ounces	25-35 pounds, drawn 35-50 pounds, dressed
Ground Meat Balls	⅕ pound	12 pounds
Roast Leg Lamb	2½-3 ounces	25-35 pounds
Turkey	2-3 ounces	20-25 pounds, drawn 25-35 pounds, dressed
Pie (9-inch)	⅛ pie	9 pies

	Serving	Amount to Buy
Punch, fruit	¾ cup	2½ gallons
Salad: fish, chicken, etc.	½ cup	6½ quarts
Salad Dressing, garnish	1 tablespoon	1 quart
Salad Garnish: lettuce	1 large leaf	8 heads
Vegetables:		
Canned	½ cup	3 No. 10 cans
Fresh Asparagus	4-5 stalks	12-16 pounds
Green Beans	½ cup	10-12 pounds
Cabbage	½ cup	16 pounds
Carrots	½ cup	16 pounds
Cauliflower	½ cup	25 pounds
Peas	½ cup	25 pounds
Potatoes	⅔ cup	15 pounds
Spinach	½ cup	17 pounds
Tomatoes	slices	10 pounds
Frozen Asparagus	3 ounces	13 boxes
Green Beans	3 ounces	13 boxes
Peas	3 ounces	13 boxes
Lima Beans	3 ounces	13 boxes
Gravy	2 tablespoons	2 quarts
Chili con Carne	1 cup	12½ quarts
Lemonade, Iced Tea, etc.	8-ounce glass	3 gallons
Tomato Juice	½ cup	2 No. 10 cans
Spaghetti	6 ounces	6 pounds
Rice	6 ounces	5 pounds
Rolls: Hard	1-1½	4½-6½ dozen
Pan	1½-2	6-8½ dozen

"You shall not have in your bag two kinds of weights, a large and a small."—Deuteronomy 25:13

CHAPTER SEVENTEEN

WEIGHTS, MEASURES, DEFINITIONS

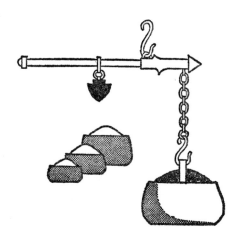

The standard of Hebrew weights and measures was kept in the sanctuary, and a copy of this standard was kept in the home.

Jesus summed up all hospitality when he said, "I was hungry and you gave me food, I was thirsty and you gave me drink, I was a stranger and you welcomed me."
—*Matthew 25:35*

THE WEIGHTS of various foods, the measure of containers, the servings contained in each, are important indeed to the home-maker who is faced with shelf after shelf of packaged foods marked at different prices, for how is she to be certain that she has shopped intelligently unless she knows exactly what and how much she is buying?

In considering biblical weights and measures, we must take into consideration the great period of time covered in the Bible, embracing many nations and many epochs.

With the Jews the most ordinary unit of weight was the shekel. The average weight of the Hebrew shekel amounted to 176.29 grains. The principal larger weight was the maneh, equal to 50 shekels.

The word "maneh" or "mana" passed from the Phoenicians to the Greeks, who called it "mna" or "mina."

Weights and measures had to be of the correct standard. They were stamped with the name of the controller who passed them for use just as the scales in the corner market are stamped, for your information, as having been checked and approved. Thus, we find in the museum at Jerusalem a lead weight inscribed: "while Agathocles was Controller of weights and measures."

So it goes, from "beginnings" to "sweets," but over and over again we are reminded that, while we may be in a bit more of a hurry, while life may be a bit more complicated than in Jesus' time, basically the lesson contained in the Bible still applies because life itself is fundamentally the same.

Ten Commandments for Cookery Measurements

1. Always use standard measuring utensils; investing in them will repay you over and over again in better finished dishes.

2. Never shake a measure level; level off with a spatula or the straight edge of a knife.

3. Measure liquids with the measuring cup at eye level; there may be a full tablespoon difference in 3/4 cup at eye level and 3/4 cup when you are looking down on it.

4. To measure shortening, simply fill the cup with cold water to the 1 cup line, pour out as much water as the amount of shortening needed, then add shortening to bring the level of the water to the 1 cup mark again.   Then pour off water.

5. If you have neglected to supply yourself with spoonful and part-spoonful measures, then use a regular spoon and divide lengthwise.

6. Cook dishes in utensils of proper size; don't try to squeeze a 4-cup recipe into a one-quart casserole, or dry out a 4-cup recipe by spreading it thin on the bottom of a two-quart pan.

7. Measure fine flours after they have been sifted once; simply stir coarse flours, corn meal, or bran with a fork before measuring; never sift these.

8. Make one measuring cup do for all the ingredients of a recipe by measuring dry ingredients first.   Measure liquids after dry ingredients, fats after liquids, and syrups after fats.

9. Save time by memorizing the table of measurements on page 330; you will be using it so often that it should come to you as easily as does your favorite prayer.

10. Be accurate; the most important thing a good cook can learn is that a recipe is like a formula: if you will measure accurately, it will be equally good every time you make it.

A Guide to Container Sizes

Size	Weight	Contents	Servings	Uses
--------	8 ounces	1 cup	2	Fruits and vegetables
No. 1 Picnic	10½ ounces	1¼ cups	2	Soups
Vacuum	12 ounces	1¼ cups	2	Corn, etc.
No. 300	14½ ounces	1¾ cups	3	Vegetables
No. 1 Tall	1 pound	2 cups	4	Vegetables
No. 303	16-17 ounces	2 cups	3-4	Vegetables and fruit
No. 2	1 pound 2 ounces	2½ cups	4-5	Vegetables, fruit, and juices
No. 2½	1 pound 12 ounces	3½ cups	6-7	Fruits and vegetables
No. 3 Cyl.	1 quart 14 ounces	5¾ cups	8-12	Juices. Often called No. 5
No. 10	3 quarts	12 cups	24	Vegetables and fruits

Vegetables packed in glass will be found principally in No. 303 (1 pound) jars, and fruits for the most part in No. 2½ (28 ounce) jars.

READ DESCRIPTIVE LABELS: More and more canners are wording can labels to give a clear picture of what is inside. The can size, amount of food in the can, variety, style, number of servings, kind of syrup, and uses, are among the information supplied. This helps you and me to buy the style of pack we want and the amount we need. The only way to judge flavor is by individual taste; find a brand that satisfies you and remember to ask for it by name.

Always heat canned or glassed vegetables in their own liquor to conserve the food value that dissolves out into the liquor. If the food is to be served cold, save the liquor to use in sauces, gravies, stews, and so forth.

Common Cookery Measurements

60 drops	equals	1 teaspoon
3 teaspoons	equals	1 tablespoon
2 tablespoons	equals	1 fluid ounce
16 tablespoons	equals	1 cup
2 cups	equals	1 pint
4 cups	equals	1 quart

Equivalents for Measuring Everyday Foods

Butter or Margarine _____1 stick equals ½ cup or ¼ lb.

Eggs, large _____½ whole egg equals 2 tablespoons
5 whole eggs equal 1 cup
8 to 9 whites equal 1 cup
12 yolks equal 1 cup

Milk, evaporated _____14½-ounce can holds 1⅔ cups

dry skim _____1 cup weighs 4 ounces
¾ to 1 cup plus 4 cups water
makes about 1 quart skim milk

Hydrogenated shortenings _____1 cup weighs 6⅔ ounces

Lard _____1 cup weighs 8 ounces

Corn meal _____1 cup weighs 3 to 4 ounces

Macaroni _____1 cup measures 2¼ cups cooked

Noodles _____1 cup measures 2¼ cups cooked

Rolled Oats _____1 cup weighs 5 ounces

Spaghetti _____1 cup measures 2⅛ cups cooked

White flour, sifted all-purpose __1 cup weighs 4 ounces

Cake flour _____1 cup weighs 3½ ounces

Whole wheat flour, stirred _____1 cup weighs 4¼ ounces

Brown sugar, packed _____1 cup weighs 7 ounces

Granulated sugar _____1 cup weighs 7 ounces

Confectioner's (powdered) sugar_1 cup weighs 4 ounces

Cocoanut _____5 cups weigh 1 pound

Cooking chocolate (butter) ____1 square weighs 1 ounce

One lemon yields _____2-3 tablespoons juice

One orange yields _____6-8 tablespoons juice

Bread Crumbs, dry _____5 cups equal 1 pound

fresh _____5 cups equal 1 pound

Cheddar cheese, grated _____4 cups equal 1 pound

A Glossary of Cooking Terms

À la king—food served in a rich cream sauce.

Au gratin—served with a browned covering, usually fine crumbs or cheese.

Baste—to moisten while cooking with melted shortening or liquid.

Blanch—to scald; to dip into boiling water to set color or to make skins easier to remove.

Braise—to cook browned foods slowly with a small amount of liquid, as in meats of less tender cuts.

Coat—to cover with a thin film, such as flour on meat or crumbs on food to be fried.

Cream—to work until smooth, light, and fluffy, like cream.

Dredge—to dip, so as to cover lightly, in flour, sugar, etc.

Garnish—to decorate, usually with brightly colored foods such as parsley, pimento, etc.

Glaze—to cover with a glossy covering, using a thin sugar syrup, a thin frosting, or diluted jelly.

Julienne—food cut into narrow lengthwise strips about the size of match sticks.

Lyonnaise—usually applied to potatoes; generally meaning seasoned with onions.

Marinade—an oil and acid mixture such as French dressing in which food is allowed to stand to gain flavor.

Mince—to chop or cut into very fine pieces; chop fine one way, then chop fine across the opposite way.

Poach—to cook under the boiling point in hot liquid to cover.

Purée—to press fruit or vegetables through a sieve, food mill or blender; also a soup made with food so treated.

Render—to melt down, to extract or clarify by heating slowly until the fat can be drained off.

Roux—a base made by blending melted fat and flour, used mainly for thickening sauces or soups.

Sauté—to brown quickly in a very small amount of fat.

Scallop—to bake foods in layers covered with sauce and crumbs in a dish such as a casserole.

Sear—to brown the surface of meat by the quick application of intense heat, usually in a hot pan or oven.

Shred—to cut into very fine slices or strips.

Simmer—to cook just below the boiling point, in liquid.

Stock—the liquid resulting from the cooking of meat, fish or vegetables. Important for making sauces, gravies, and soups.

Steam—to cook slowly in a little liquid, either in an oven or on top the stove.

Try out—usually used in connection with bacon. To heat slowly, as in render, until the fat is liquid.

The LORD bless you and keep you:
The LORD make his face to shine
   upon you, and be gracious to you:
The LORD lift up his countenance
   upon you, and give you peace.

—Numbers 6:24-26

BIBLICAL INDEX

337

340 *The Bible Cookbook*

RECIPE INDEX

346 *The Bible Cookbook*